WEEKEND
PROJECTS *for*
WOODWORKERS

 W9-AMN-950

WEEKEND
PROJECTS *for*
WOODWORKERS

From the Editors of **The Woodworker's Journal**

Madrigal Publishing Company

73381

EAU CLAIRE DISTRICT LIBRARY

We at Madrigal Publishing have tried to make this book as accurate and correct as possible. Plans, illustrations, photographs, and text have been carefully researched by our in-house staff. However, due to the variability of all local conditions, construction materials, personal skills, etc., Madrigal Publishing assumes no responsibility for any injuries suffered or damages or other losses incurred that result from material presented herein. All instructions and plans should be carefully studied and clearly understood before beginning any construction.

For the sake of clarity, it is sometimes necessary for a photo or illustration to show a power tool without the blade guard in place. However, in actual operation, always use blade guards (or other safety devices) on power tools that are equipped with them.

©1991 by Madrigal Publishing Co. All rights reserved. No part of this book may be reproduced in any form without the permission of the publisher.

Printed in the United States of America.

Library of Congress Cataloging-in-Publication Data:

Weekend projects for woodworkers: 52 great projects you can build in a day or two / the editors of the Woodworker's journal.
    p. cm.
 ISBN 0-9617098-9-8.-- ISBN 0-9617098-8-X (pbk.): $14.95
 1. Woodwork. I. Woodworker's journal.
TT180.W345 1991
684'.08--dc20   90-20672
                                             CIP

Madrigal Publishing Company
517 Litchfield Road
P.O. Box 1629
New Milford, CT 06776

Table *of* Contents

(continued on next page)

Introduction

Many readers of our magazine, *The Woodworker's Journal,* tell us they especially enjoy projects that can be built in a day or two. Such projects—we call them weekend projects—don't take a lot of time or money, two rather precious commodities these days.

Weekend Projects For Woodworkers is a collection of the best weekend projects from the 1986 and 1987 issues of *The Woodworker's Journal.* All the projects we selected are easy to make and require only a minimum of materials and expense. They include a country door harp, a colorful whirligig, a folk art whale silhouette, and an old-time coffee mill—plus toys, baskets, wall shelves, boxes, planters, end tables, stools, and more.

Keep in mind, though, that no one will be timing you, so there is no need to rush through a project. Work carefully and, most importantly, work safely. It doesn't matter if a project takes you a weekend or a week or a month, or six months. Work at a pace that is comfortable for you. If you do, you'll be better able to enjoy the many pleasures that come from the craft of working wood.

We would like to extend our thanks to the following individuals whose valuable project contributions helped make it possible to put this book together: **Skip Arthur,** Butterfly Pull Toy, Rabbit Pull Toy, Rocking Horse; **Ellen Brown,** Canada Goose Mobile; **Brent and Gunnar Kallstrom,** Adirondack Chair; **Robert Leung,** Vanity Mirror; **Tony Lydgate,** Jewelry Box, Three Drawer Jewelry Chest; **Clare Maginley,** Firetruck; **John L. McPartland,** Dictionary Stand; **Dennis Preston,** Shaker-Style Step Stool.

In addition, our thanks to **Hancock Shaker Village,** Hancock, Massachusetts, for permission to take measurements of the Shaker Side Table, and **The Wooden Toy,** Canton, Connecticut, for the Riding Biplane. Also, **Tim Lee** for the photo of the Dog/Cat Bed, **Gerard Roy** for the photo of the Toy Wagon, and **John Kane** for the remainder of the project photos and the back cover photos.

The Editors

Rabbit Pull Toy

This friendly cottontail "hops" as it is pulled along the floor, much to the delight of young children. Ours is made from maple, but any wood — even pine — can be used.

The body (A) can be made first. Cut ¾ in. thick stock to a width of 5⅜ in. and a length of 9 in., then refer to the grid pattern shown in the side view and transfer the profile to the stock. At the same time, mark the location of the holes for the eyes and the back wheel dowel.

Use a band or saber saw to cut out the profile, taking care to stay just outside the marked line. Once cut, use a file and sandpaper to smooth the edge exactly to the line. A router table and a ⅜ in. radius bearing-guided round-over bit is used to apply the ⅜ in. round to the edge, however a file and a bit of sanding will also do the job. Next, using a ⅜ in. diameter drill bit, bore the ⅛ in. deep "eye" holes, then use a ⁷⁄₁₆ in. diameter bit to bore through for the back wheel dowel.

You'll need ½ in. thick stock to make the legs (B) and the ears (C). To get the ½ in. thickness, cut a piece of ¾ in. thick stock to 3 in. wide by 8 in. long. With the marking gauge, scribe the desired ½ in. thickness on all four edges, then use a sharp hand plane to plane the stock to the scribed line.

With the ½ in. thick stock in hand, refer to the grid pattern shown in the side view and transfer the profile of the legs and ears to the stock. Cut out and smooth to the marked line, then use a file and sandpaper to round over the edges.

The two back wheels (D) can be turned on a lathe or cut out on the band saw and sanded smooth. If you have one, a disk sander will come in handy here.

In order to give the rabbit its "hop", the back dowel (E) is not centered on the wheel, but rather it is offset ¼ in. (see side view). Mark this offset dowel hole location, then use the drill press and a ⅜ in. diameter drill bit to bore a ½ in. deep hole in each wheel.

The front wheel is made using a 1 in. diameter hole saw and ⅝ in. thick stock. After sanding, round the corners to about a ¹⁄₁₆ in. radius. The ¼ in. diameter hole at the centerpoint will be cut by the hole saw centering bit.

Lay out and mark the location of the ³⁄₁₆ in. diameter holes on the inside face of the two legs, then use the drill press to bore the holes to a depth of ¼ in.

After cutting the back dowel (E) and the front dowel (G) to length, all parts can be given a thorough sanding. Apply a coat of paraffin wax to the ⁷⁄₁₆ in. diameter hole in the body, then glue and assemble the two back wheels to the back dowel (note that the wheels must be in line with each other). The paraffin wax in the hole cuts down on friction, thereby making the dowel turn easier. Be sure, however, to avoid getting any wax on the ends of the back dowel when its inserted through the hole. If you do, the glue won't stick when the dowel is glued to the back wheel.

Apply wax to the hole in the front wheel and insert the front dowel. As with the back dowel, avoid getting wax on the ends.

Temporarily clamp the legs to the body. When satisfied with the location, use a pencil to scribe the outline of the legs on the body. Remove the clamps and add glue to the body and legs in the area profiled by the pencil line. Now, apply glue to the ends of the front dowel and assemble it to the legs, then clamp the legs to the body.

Drill and countersink each ear for a ¾ in. long by no. 8 ovalhead brass wood screw. Assemble as shown making sure each screw is tightened firmly.

If not available locally, the ½ in. diameter ball (H) can be ordered from Woodworks, 4500 Anderson Boulevard, Fort Worth, TX 76117. A ⅛ in. diameter hole bored through the knob will accept the cord (I). Make sure the cord is knotted firmly to prevent the ball from coming off. A small hole bored ⅜ in. deep at the front of the rabbit will enable the cord to be glued in place.

Any finish that's used should be non-toxic. We generally do not apply a finish to toys likely to be chewed on by young children.

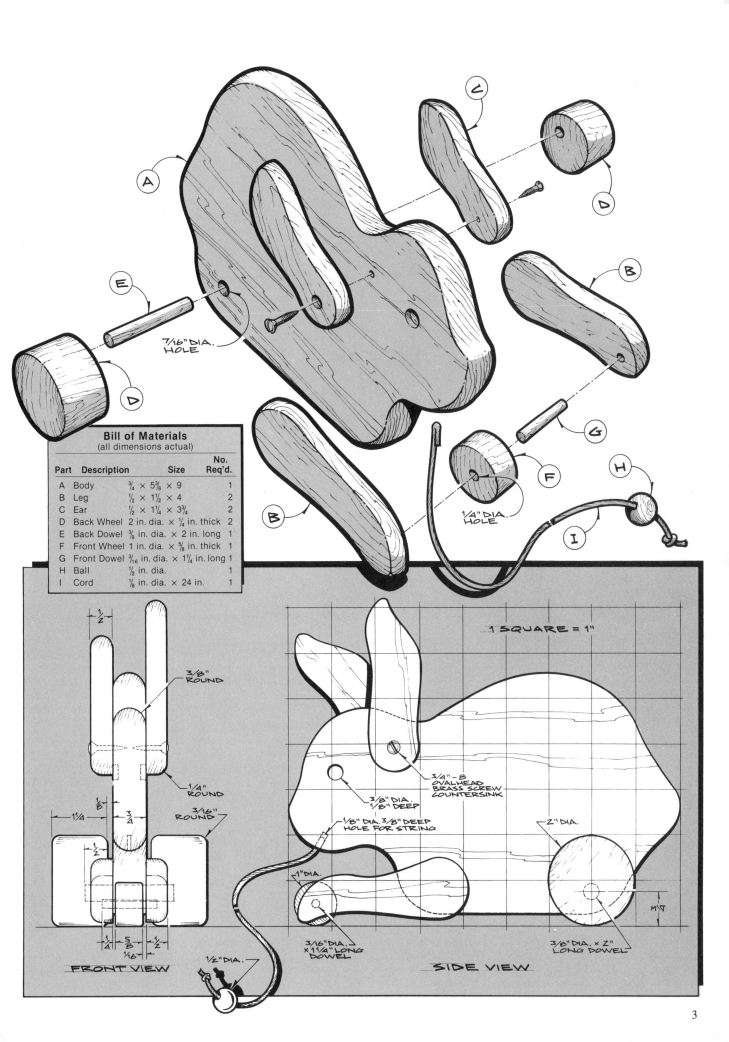

A

C

D

B

E

7/16" DIA.
HOLE

D

Bill of Materials
(all dimensions actual)

Part	Description	Size	No. Req'd.
A	Body	3/4 × 5 3/8 × 9	1
B	Leg	1/2 × 1 1/2 × 4	2
C	Ear	1/2 × 1 1/4 × 3 3/4	2
D	Back Wheel	2 in. dia. × 1/4 in. thick	2
E	Back Dowel	3/8 in. dia. × 2 in. long	1
F	Front Wheel	1 in. dia. × 5/8 in. thick	1
G	Front Dowel	3/16 in. dia. × 1 1/4 in. long	1
H	Ball	1/2 in. dia.	1
I	Cord	1/8 in. dia. × 24 in.	1

B

G

F

H

I

1/4" DIA.
HOLE

1/2

3/8"
ROUND

1/4"
ROUND

3/16"
ROUND

1 1/4

3/4

1/8

1/2

1/4   5/8   1/2
1/16

FRONT VIEW

1/2" DIA.

1 SQUARE = 1"

3/4" – 8
OVALHEAD
BRASS SCREW
COUNTERSINK

3/8" DIA.
1/8" DEEP

1/8" DIA. 3/8" DEEP
HOLE FOR STRING

1" DIA.

3/16" DIA.
× 1 1/4" LONG
DOWEL

2" DIA.

1/4"

3/8" DIA. × 2"
LONG DOWEL

SIDE VIEW

Display Pedestal

T his attractive display pedestal combines a handsome central turned post with a unique hexagonal shape. As you might note from the top view of the drawing, this hexagonal theme is reflected in the shape of the post, cleat, and top. While we built the model shown in mahogany, some other hardwood or pine could also be used.

Start with the post (A). After cutting a rectangular 3¼ in. by 3¾ in. by 23¼ in. long blank, lay out a hexagon on the end of the stock. Incline the table saw blade 30 degrees, adjust the fence so the cut will fall on the waste side of the lines demarking the hexagon, and make the four cuts establishing the hexagonal post. Now move to the router table, and use a ⅜ in. diameter straight bit and the setup shown to rout the 3 in. long by ⅝ in. deep spline grooves in the bottom end of the post. Note that if you intend to leave a little extra length for mounting the post in the lathe, the 3 in. spline grooves would have to be slightly longer; the extra length will be trimmed later.

Bill of Materials
(all dimensions actual)

Part	Description	Size	No. Req'd.
A	Post	3¼ × 3¾ × 23¼	1
B	Leg	1 × 3½ × 11*	3
C	Spline	⅜ × 1¼ × 3	3
D	Cleat	see top view	1
E	Top	see top view	1

*Size of leg blank before shaping.

Now transfer the post to the lathe, refer to the various diameters and lengths shown in the elevation, and turn as illustrated. Note the 1½ in. diameter by ¾ in. long tenon turned on the top end of the post. Next make the three legs (B). Start with 1 in. by 3½ in. by 11 in. long stock, then use the table saw to miter one end at 40 degrees. Now cut a 40-degree stop, locate this stop 3 in. from the edge of the ⅜ in. diameter straight bit set for a ⅝ in. deep cut, and cut the spline grooves in the three leg blanks (see detail). After these spline grooves are cut, a ⅜ in. thick filler block is glued into the open end of the spline groove as shown to create a 3 in. long mortise. Lay out and then band saw the leg profile.

The best way to lay out the hexagonal cleat (D) and top (E) is to draw two circles, 5¾ in. diameter for the cleat, and 13⅞ in. diameter for the top, and use a compass to establish the points of the hexagons. The table saw and miter gauge are used to cut the hexagon sides. Drill and countersink the cleat for screws as shown, and use a ½ in. radius cove cutter to establish the cove detail on the top. Use a band clamp to apply mild pressure as you mount the legs to the post with the splines as shown. Then screw the cleat to the top end of the post, and mount the top to the cleat. Keep the grain in the same direction for both parts. After final sanding, we applied several coats of penetrating oil, followed by paste wax which was lightly buffed to a soft gloss.

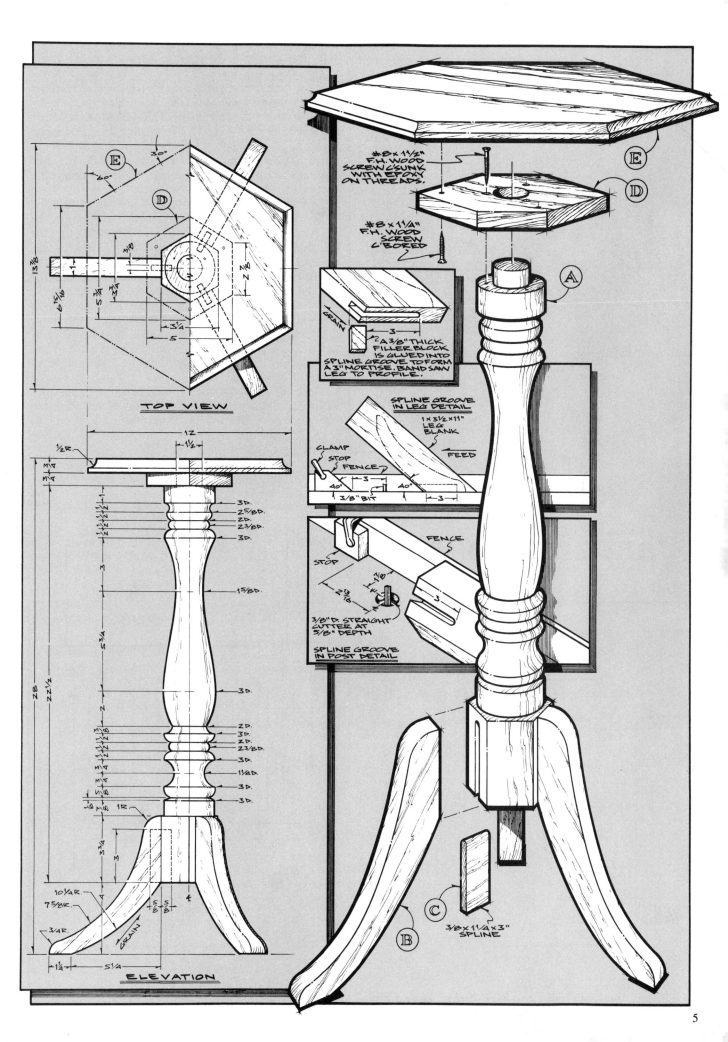

Even though much of the commercial cranberry crop is harvested by machine, the old-fashioned cranberry rake is still used to some extent. This miniature version of the cranberry rake is ideal for displaying dried flowers or for storing some small odds and ends. A small hole bored through the back enables it to be hung on a wall. The tines are made from birch dowel stock, while the remaining parts are made from pine.

To make the two sides (A) you'll need to hand plane thicker stock in order to get the ⅜ in. thickness. Next, cut the stock to a width of 3 in. and a length of 5⅝ in., then transfer the grid pattern from the drawing to the stock. Cut out on the band or jig saw, staying just outside the marked line, then sand exactly to the line. The front (B) and the bottom (D) are also made from ⅜ in. thick stock.

To make the back (C), cut ½ in. thick stock to length and width, then lay out and mark the location of the ¼ in. diameter by ⅜ in. deep holes to accept the tines (E). Cut the tines to a length of 3½ in. before gluing in place. When dry, clamp the back in a vise, then use a belt sander to bevel the end of each tine.

Make the handle as shown, then attach it to the front with glue and a pair of finishing nails driven from the back side. Now assemble the front, back, sides, and bottom with glue and countersunk finishing nails. Fill the countersunk holes and sand smooth.

Final sand all parts before staining. Allow the stain to dry thoroughly, then apply two coats of a penetrating oil.

Cranberry Rake

Bill of Materials
(all dimensions actual)

Part	Description	Size	No. Req'd.
A	Side	⅜ × 3 × 5⅝	2
B	Front	⅜ × 2⅛ × 6⅛	1
C	Back	½ × 2½ × 5⅜	1
D	Bottom	⅜ × 3⅜ × 6⅛	1
E	Tine	¼ diameter × 3½ long	8
F	Handle	½ × ¾ × 5½	1

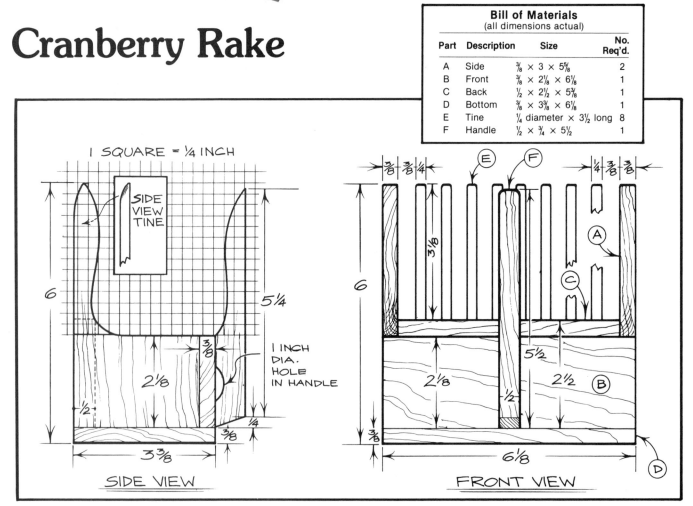

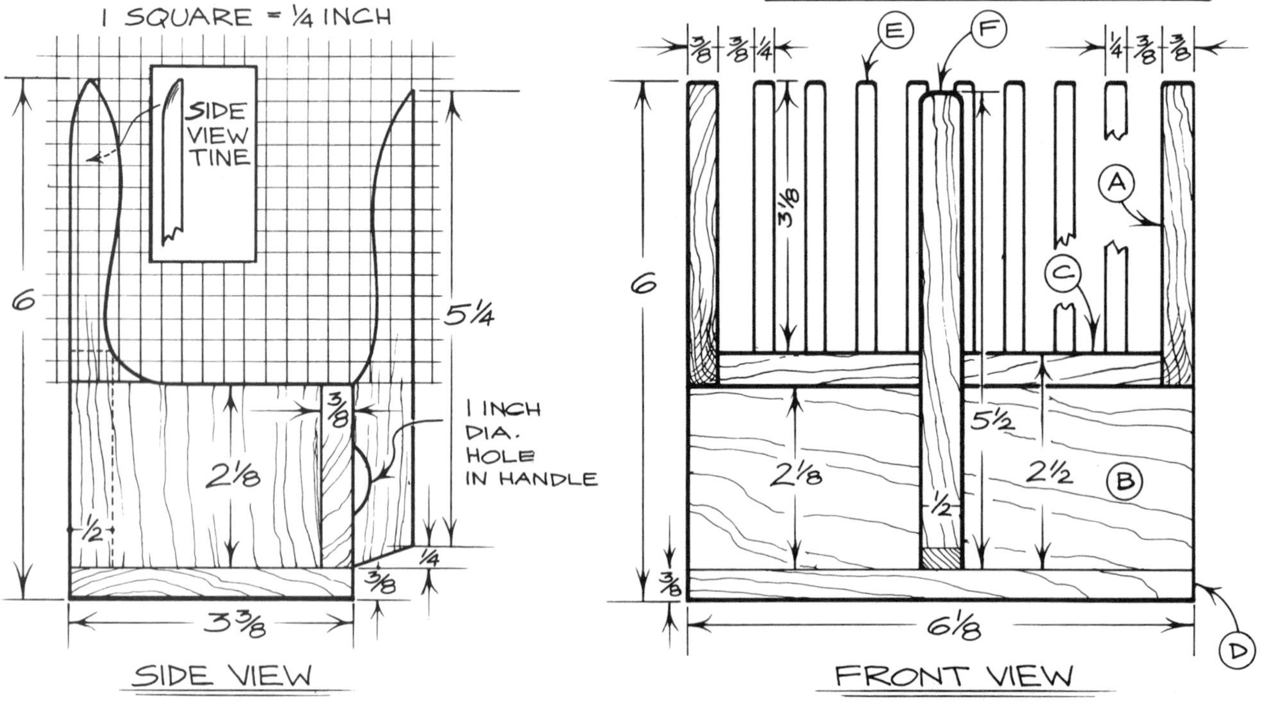
1 SQUARE = ¼ INCH
SIDE VIEW TINE
6
5¼
2⅛
½
⅜
¼
⅜
3⅜
1 INCH DIA. HOLE IN HANDLE
SIDE VIEW
⅜ ⅜ ¼
E
F
¼ ⅜ ⅜
3⅛
A
C
6
5½
2⅛
2½
B
½
⅜
6⅛
D
FRONT VIEW

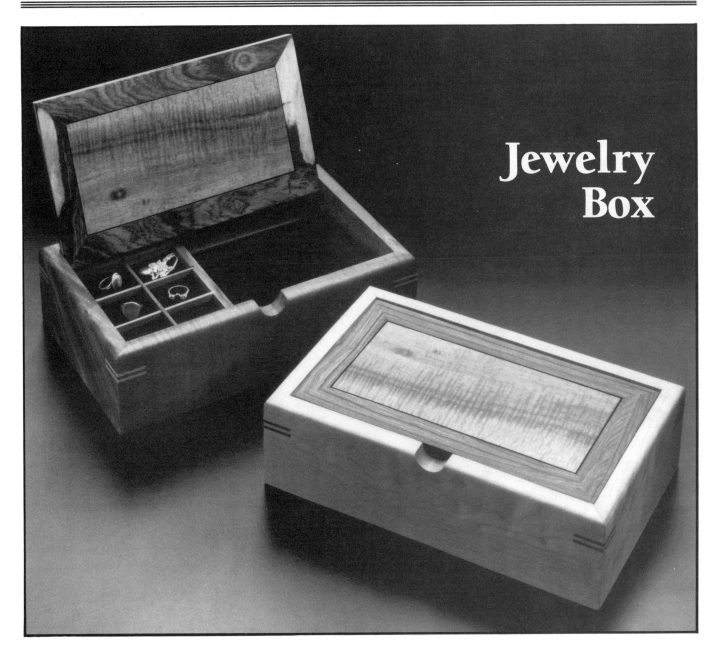

Jewelry Box

N ew designs are truly as scarce as the proverbial "hen's tooth". As one sage aptly pointed out, "Everything has been done before." Even the most accomplished designer/craftsmen generally agree that genuinely new and innovative designs are rare. The best work is usually a skilled adaptation, careful refinement, or creative presentation of some previous form.

Nowhere is this more valid than in the case of jewelry boxes. We've seen all types of boxes — crude, simple, sophisticated, and complex — in practically every design imaginable.

Still, when these jewelry boxes by California master craftsman Tony Lydgate, caught our eye at the A.C.C. Craft fair in West Springfield, Massachussetts, we were impressed.

Although they are one of the simplest designs possible, judicious selection of stock and the incorporation of subtle details combine for a striking effect. Mr. Lydgate, who is nationally recognized as one of the top designer/craftsmen, noted that traditionally these jewelry boxes have been one of his best-selling items. He points out that their success is proof positive that good designs need not be elaborate or unusual.

The boxes shown are crafted in figured maple and Hawaiian koa respectively. Both box lids feature cocobola frames accented with koa panels. While the boxes would look rather boring in a plain wood such as pine, any number of different woods can be combined with great success. A

combination of walnut, figured maple and cherry would be lovely, for instance. Select an especially dramatic section of board in order to highlight the lid panel, and be sure to use contrasting splines to accent the box and lid construction. For those who haven't worked much in exotic woods, the box is an opportunity to discover how the dramatic color and grain of such woods as padauk, bubinga, zebrawood, purpleheart, cocobola and others can be used to transform the plain into the extraordinary. If you don't have a local supplier, a good mail order source for exotic woods is the Berea Hardwoods Company, 125 Jacqueline Drive, Berea, Ohio 44017.

One of the best aspects of making

miter the lid frame front, back and ends. Cut the ⅛ in. wide by ¼ in. deep panel groove in these parts, and establish the ⅛ in. by ¼ in. tongue on all four sides of the panel. *Note:* Depending on the season, you may wish to allow a little space across the width of the panel to permit expansion (see cross-section). Now glue and clamp the frame with the panel in place.

The jig shown in the spline cutting detail is used to cut the spline grooves in both the box and the lid. The blade height setting for both operations is ¹¹⁄₁₆ in. After the spline grooves have been cut, make the splines (F and L). Although the spline detail shows the approximate final spline size, it is best to start with the splines slightly over-size, and then flush them with the box and lid respectively after they have been glued in place. As indicated in the spline detail, cut the splines so the grain will run diagonally across the joints, providing maximum strength.

Hand sand or use a ¼ in. radius round-over bit with the router to apply the rounded edge to the top perimeter of the box. The finger recess in the box front is rough shaped by hand, then smoothed by using a 1⅛ in. diameter drum sander mounted either in the drill press or a hand drill. The finger slot in the lid can be drilled out and cleaned by hand or cut with the router.

Glue the tray supports and lid stop in place, and after rounding over the top back edge of the lid (see cross-section), mount the lid with brass pins (T) as shown.

The tray front and back (M) and sides (N) are cut from ⅜ in. by ¾ in. stock. Use the dado head to rabbet the ends of the sides, then cut the ⅛ in. by ⅛ in. bottom groove and divider slots in these parts. After cutting the tray bottom (O) to size from ⅛ in. thick plywood, and making short and long divider parts from ⅛ in. by ¼ in. stock, assemble the tray front, back and sides around the bottom.

Now make the box and tray liners, consisting of velvet (E and Q) wrapped over cardboard (D and P).

After final sanding, all wood surfaces are treated with a generous application of penetrating oil. Let dry, rub out with 0000 steel wool, wipe on a final application of penetrating oil, and complete with a light protective coat of paste wax buffed to a soft satin sheen.

Bill of Materials
(all dimensions actual)

Part	Description	Size	No. Req'd.
A	Front/Back	⅝ × 3¼ × 12	2
B	End	⅝ × 3¼ × 7½	2
C	Bottom	⅛ × 6⅞ × 11⅛	1
D	Bottom Cardboard	6¼ × 10¾	1
E	Bottom Liner (velvet)	8¼ × 12¾	1
F	Box Spline	³⁄₃₂ × 1 × 1*	8
G	Tray Support	⅛ × ½ × 10¾	2
H	Lid Stop	⅛ × ⅜ × 10¾	1
I	Lid Front/Back	½ × 1 × 10¾	2
J	Lid End	½ × 1 × 6¼	2
K	Lid Panel	½ × 4¾ × 9¼	1
L	Lid Spline	³⁄₃₂ × 1 × 1*	4
M	Tray Front/Back	⅜ × ¾ × 4⅞	2
N	Tray Sides	⅜ × ¾ × 6	2
O	Tray Bottom	⅛ × 4¼ × 5½	1
P	Tray Cardboard	4 × 5¼	1
Q	Tray Liner (velvet)	6 × 7¼	1
R	Short Divider	⅛ × ¼ × 4¼	2
S	Long Divider	⅛ × ¼ × 5½	1
T	Pin	¹⁄₁₆ dia. × 1 in. long	2

*Final size.

this box is the fact that except for the finger lift recess and slot, the entire box construction is a table saw operation. As indicated in the bill of materials, you will need ⅝ in. stock for the box carcase (parts A & B). If you don't have a thickness planer, hand plane ¾ in. stock down to ⅝ in. thickness. Incline the table saw blade to 45 degrees, and miter the ends of parts A and B. Next, with the fence in the same setting and the blade set for ³⁄₁₆ in. height, cut the ⅛ in. by ³⁄₁₆ in. groove in the front, back and ends to accept the bottom (C). Leave the blade at the ³⁄₁₆ in. height, reset the fence, and cut the groove in the front and back for the tray supports (G). Once more, reset the fence and cut the groove in the front for the lid stop (H). After cutting the bottom to size from ⅛ in. thick plywood, glue and assemble the front, back and sides around the bottom; clamp and set aside to dry.

Next, get out stock for the lid (I, J, and K). Again, if you don't have ½ in. stock, resaw and plane ¾ stock to get the ½ in. thick material you will need. Set the miter gauge at 45 degrees and

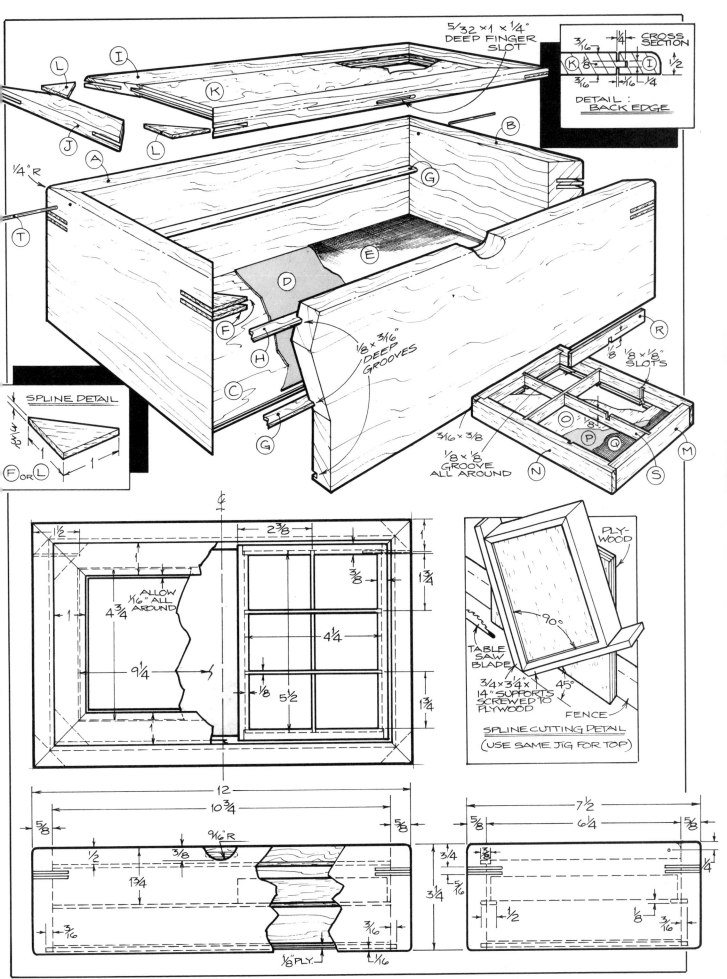

5/32 ×1 × 1/4"
DEEP FINGER
SLOT

CROSS SECTION

3/16
K 8
3/16
I
1/2
1/16 1/4

DETAIL:
BACK EDGE

L
I
K
B
J
A
G
1/4" R
T
E
D
F
H
1/8 × 3/16"
DEEP
GROOVES
C
G
R
1/8
1/8 × 1/8"
SLOTS
O 1/8
P Q
M
3/16 × 3/8
1/8 × 1/8
GROOVE
ALL AROUND
N
S

SPLINE DETAIL
3/4 1/2
F or L
1 1

2 3/8
3/8
1 3/4
ALLOW
1/16" ALL
AROUND
4 3/4
4 1/4
1 3/4
1
9 1/4
1/8 5 1/2
1 1/2

PLY-WOOD
90°
TABLE
SAW
BLADE
3/4 × 3/4 ×
14" SUPPORTS
SCREWED TO
PLYWOOD
45°
FENCE
SPLINE CUTTING DETAIL
(USE SAME JIG FOR TOP)

12
10 3/4
5/8
5/8
1/2
3/8
9/16" R
1 3/4
3/16
3/16
1/8 PLY.
1/16

7 1/2
6 1/4
5/8
5/8
3/4
3/8
5/16
3 1/4
1/2
1/8
3/16
1/4

9

Country Bucket Bench

Early Americans didn't have the luxury of simply turning a tap when water was needed. To get it, one had to hike to the well or, if a well did not exist, to a nearby stream or lake. As might be expected, it was a chore often assigned to one of the youngsters in the family, and it meant hauling the water back to the house in several buckets. The bucket bench, or water bench as it was sometimes called, was found in many of those early houses and provided a convenient means of storing those buckets of precious water. Ours is based on a design that dates back to the 18th century and, like many early bucket benches, it is made of pine.

Begin by edge-gluing enough 1 by 8 pine stock (which will actually measure $\frac{3}{4}$ in. thick by $7\frac{1}{4}$ in. wide) to make the two sides (A) and the two shelves (B). It's a good idea to allow a little extra on the length so that later, after the glue has dried, the stock can be trimmed to the exact length dimensions. At the same time the stock can be ripped to 14 in. wide.

Next, lay out and mark the location of the two $\frac{3}{4}$ in. wide by $\frac{3}{8}$ in. deep dadoes cut in each side to accept the shelves. Equip the table saw with a $\frac{3}{4}$ in. wide dado cutter set to make a $\frac{3}{8}$ in. deep cut, then using the miter gauge, pass the stock over the cutter to make the dadoes as shown. Take care to hold the stock down firmly and be sure to keep hands away from the cutter.

Since the $\frac{3}{4}$ in. dado cutter is set to make a $\frac{3}{8}$ in. deep cut, this is a good time to cut the $\frac{3}{4}$ in. wide by $\frac{3}{8}$ in. deep rabbet on the back edge of each shelf. You'll need to attach an auxiliary wood fence to the regular rip fence for this operation, because the dado cutter must just touch the rip fence in order to make a $\frac{3}{4}$ in. wide cut.

To accept the two backs (D), a $\frac{3}{4}$ in. wide by $\frac{1}{2}$ in. deep by $8\frac{3}{4}$ in. long rabbet is cut in the back edge of each side. We used a router equipped with an edge-guide and a $\frac{1}{2}$ in. diameter router bit to make these cuts. You'll need to make several passes to complete the rabbet. Square the rounded corners with a sharp chisel.

To complete work on the sides, transfer the grid pattern (shown in the side view) to the stock, then use a band or saber saw to cut just outside the marked line. Use a file and sandpaper to smooth exactly to the line.

The top (C) can now be cut to length and width as shown. Use the edge-guided router to cut the $\frac{3}{4}$ in. wide by $\frac{3}{8}$ in. deep grooves to accept the top ends of the sides. Once again, use the

chisel to square the rounded corners.

At this point the sides, shelves, and top can be assembled. Final sand all parts, starting with 80 grit, then follow with 120, 150, and 220. However, if the surface is reasonably smooth before you start, you'll probably be able to skip the 80 grit step. Once sanded, apply glue to the mating surfaces, then assemble with flathead wood screws, counterbored and plugged as shown. Counterbore the holes so that the plugs sit just above the surface, then sand each one flush.

The two backs can now be made. Cut to length and width before using a

$\frac{1}{4}$ in. dado cutter to create the tongue and groove edges. Final sand each board before assembly. Note that the back boards are secured to the rabbeted back edge of the sides with a single flathead wood screw driven through the centerpoint of each end. The single screw on each end allows the board to expand and contract with seasonal changes in humidity.

For a final finish we used two coats of Minwax's Early American Wood Finish. When thoroughly dry, two coats of Deft Clear Wood Finish were added to complete the project.

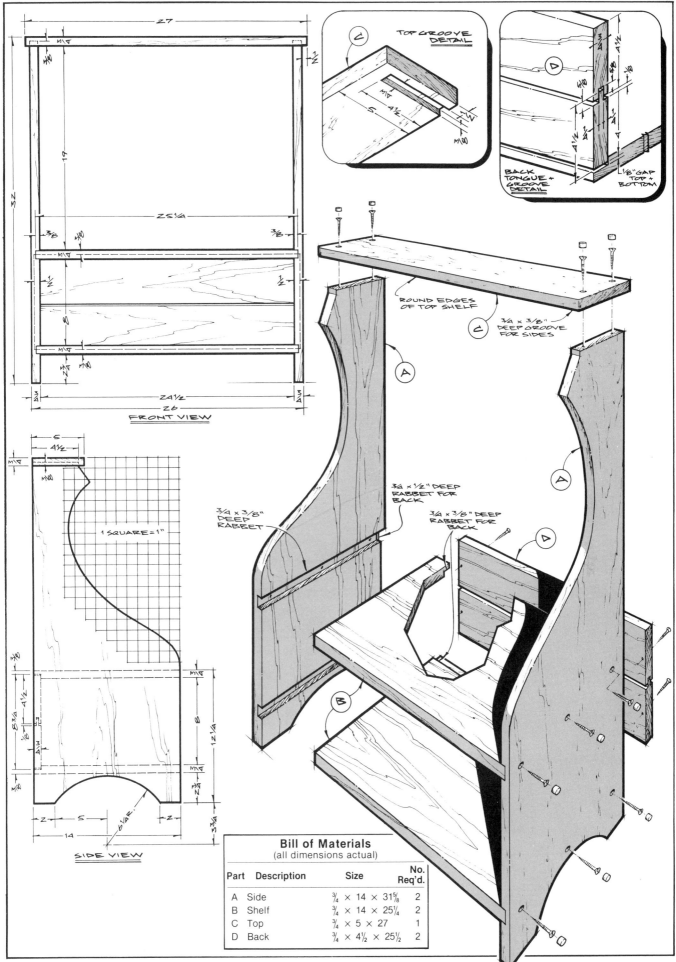

TOP GROOVE DETAIL

BACK TONGUE & GROOVE DETAIL

1/8" GAP TOP + BOTTOM

FRONT VIEW

SIDE VIEW

1 SQUARE = 1"

ROUND EDGES OF TOP SHELF

3/4 × 3/8" DEEP GROOVE FOR SIDES

3/4 × 1/2" DEEP RABBET FOR BACK

3/4 × 3/8" DEEP RABBET FOR BACK

3/4 × 3/8" DEEP RABBET

Bill of Materials (all dimensions actual)			
Part	Description	Size	No. Req'd.
A	Side	$\frac{3}{4} \times 14 \times 31\frac{5}{8}$	2
B	Shelf	$\frac{3}{4} \times 14 \times 25\frac{1}{4}$	2
C	Top	$\frac{3}{4} \times 5 \times 27$	1
D	Back	$\frac{3}{4} \times 4\frac{1}{2} \times 25\frac{1}{2}$	2

11

In order to please the eye, a woodworking project need not necessarily require a month of work or a week's paycheck. In fact, some of the most appealing projects we've ever come across have been remarkably simple in design and inexpensive to build.

To make the turning blank for the disk (A), cut two pieces of ¾ in. thick stock to 10 in. square, then face glue (make sure the grain runs in the same direction) and clamp the two parts to create a block that measures 1½ in. thick by 10 in. square. When dry, use a compass to scribe a 9¾ in. diameter (4⅞ in. radius) circle and, with a band or saber saw, cut out the circle, staying slightly on the waste side of the line.

The best surface of the blank should face the front, so at this point, examine both sides to determine the front and back of the clock. Now, on the back of the clock, again use the compass, this time to scribe a 2 in. radius (4 in. diameter) circle. Later on, this circle will serve as a guide when the faceplate's waste circle is attached. Now, on the clock's front side, scribe the 3⁹⁄₁₆ in. radius (7⅛ in. diameter) for the small markers (C) and the 3⅞ in. radius (7¾ in. diameter) for the large markers (B).

Next, at the centerpoint of the circle, bore a ⅜ in. diameter hole completely through the stock, taking care to make sure the hole is square. Now, on the back side, lay out and mark the location of the 2½ in. square mortise. Use a sharp chisel to cut the mortise to a depth of ¾ in. Our mortise was sized to accept a quartz movement sold by Mason and Sullivan, 586 Higgins Crowell Road, West Yarmouth, MA

02673 (part number 3609X-34). However, if you plan to use another movement, you may need to revise the mortise dimensions we've given.

Lay out the location of the large and small markers on their respective radii, then bore holes as shown in the front view. Turn the four large markers (B) to a 1 in. diameter, and the eight small

markers to a ⅜ in. diameter before cutting them to ⅞ in. lengths. Use glue to assemble each one in place, allowing ⅛ in. to protrude. To make the waste circle, scribe a 4¼ in. diameter circle on a piece of ¾ in. thick stock and cut out with the band or saber saw. Attach the faceplate to the waste circle, then attach the faceplate to your lathe and turn the circle to a 4 in. diameter.

Remove the faceplate from the lathe before gluing the waste circle to the back of the disk blank. Note that a piece of paper (brown grocery bag type works well) is sandwiched in between. The paper will make it easy to remove the waste circle later on. The 4 in. diameter circle previously scribed on the back of the disk blank will come in handy to help center the waste circle.

When the glue has thoroughly dried, mount the faceplate to the lathe. Using a roundnose cutter, turn the blank to the profile shown in the full-sized sectional view. Note that the profile is designed so that the glue line can't be seen from the front.

Sand thoroughly while still on the lathe, smoothing to 220 grit. For a final finish we applied three coats of Deft's Semi-Gloss Clear Wood Finish, rubbing down the final coat with 0000 steel wool.

The movement is assembled as shown. We used Mason and Sullivan's Universal hour and minute hands (part number 4880X) and second hand (part number 4892X). These hands are longer than needed, so you'll have to clip each one to length. The hanger (supplied with the movement) permits the clock to be hung on the wall.

Disk Clock

Bill of Materials
(all dimensions actual)

Part	Description	Size	No. Req'd.
A	Disk	9¾ dia. × 1½ thick*	1
B	Large Marker	1 dia. × ¾ thick*	4
C	Small Marker	⅜ dia. × ¾ thick*	8
D	Quartz Movement		1
E	Hour/Minute Hand		1 pair
F	Second Hand		1

*Thickness dimension before turning.

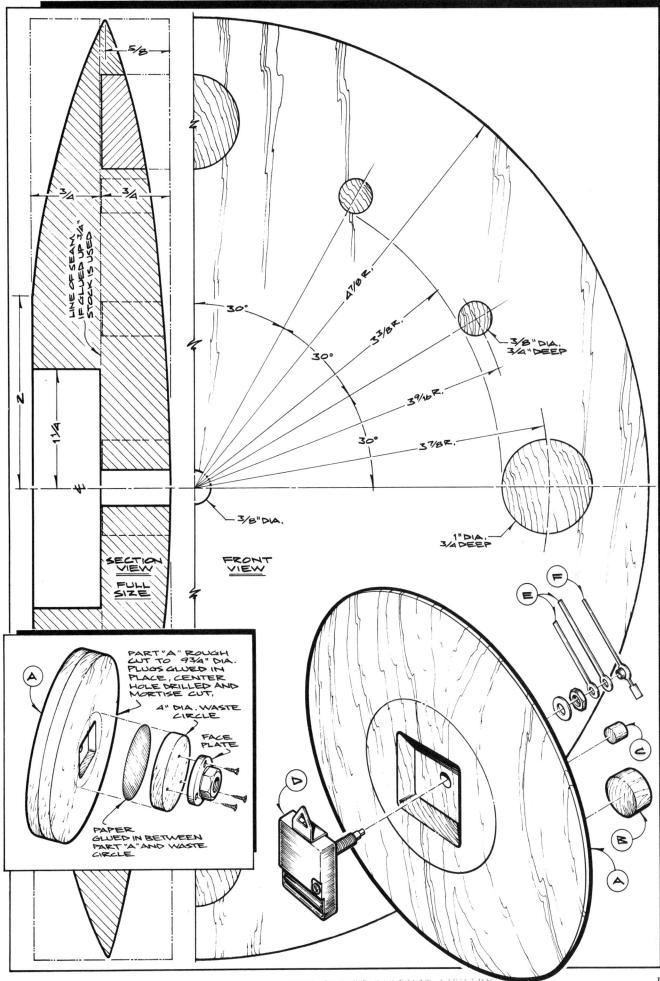

5/8

3/4 3/4

LINE OF SEAM, IF GLUED UP 3/4" STOCK IS USED

2

1 1/4

SECTION
VIEW

FULL
SIZE

FRONT
VIEW

30°

30°

30°

4 7/8 R.

3 3/8 R.

3 9/16 R.

3 7/8 R.

3/8" DIA.
3/4" DEEP

1" DIA.
3/4 DEEP

3/8" DIA.

A

PART "A" ROUGH
CUT TO 9 3/4" DIA.
PLUGS GLUED IN
PLACE, CENTER
HOLE DRILLED AND
MORTISE CUT.

4" DIA. WASTE
CIRCLE

FACE
PLATE

PAPER
GLUED IN BETWEEN
PART "A" AND WASTE
CIRCLE

D

E

F

C

B

A

EAU CLAIRE DISTRICT LIBRARY

Rocking Horse

This cute version of a traditional rocking horse makes a delightful gift for a child. A toy like this must be plenty sturdy though, so it should be made from maple or birch.

To start, you'll first need a piece of tracing paper that measures at least 14 in. square. If necessary, tape two smaller pieces together to get the needed size. With a pencil and ruler, divide the tracing paper into 1 in. squares. Now, referring to the grid pattern of the head (A), transfer the profiles to the tracing paper. You'll need to transfer all the profiles including the eyes, ears, nose, mouth, and mane.

Next, from ¾ in. thick stock, cut stock for the head to 11¼ in. wide by 18 in. long. Final sand both sides of the board, then tape a piece of carbon paper, carbon surface down, to one side of the board, making sure that all the surface is covered. Two pieces may be needed for complete coverage.

Note, as shown on the drawing, how the grain of the wood runs in relation to the profile of the head. Place the tracing paper on the carbon so that the grain is properly orientated before securing it with a few pieces of tape.

Carefully trace all the lines (including the notched bottom edge) on the tracing paper, taking care to bear hard enough with your pencil so the lines will transfer from the carbon paper to the stock. Once all the lines have been traced, remove the carbon and tracing papers and set them aside.

The band saw or jigsaw is now used to cut out the outside profile of the head. Make the cut just outside the marked line, then sand the edge.

Now place the carbon and tracing paper on the unmarked face of the stock, taking care to align the outside profile on the paper with the outside

profile of the stock. When aligned, tape both papers in place and trace all the lines.

Except for the bottom notch, all edges on the head are rounded-over. This can be done by hand using a file and sandpaper, but you can also use a router with a ¼ in. bearing-guided round-over bit. Use 220 grit sandpaper to final sand the rounded edges. Also, at this time, mark the location of the handle hole and bore it out.

Artist's acrylic paint (available at art supply stores) is used to paint the head. Refer to the grid pattern and the color key for the location of the colors. Note that the tongue is painted red while the eyes and teeth are white. The burnt umber, raw sienna, and burnt sienna are thinned a bit with water.

Allow the paint to dry thoroughly, then apply a wash coat of shellac to all surfaces. When dry, trace over all the

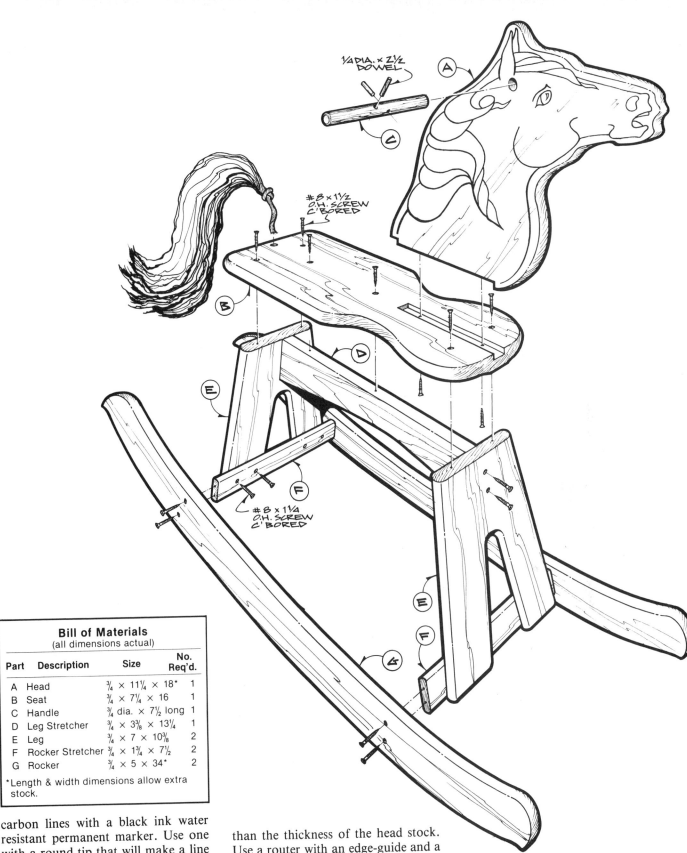

¼ DIA. × 2½ DOWEL

#8 × 1½ O.H. SCREW C'BORED

#8 × 1¼ O.H. SCREW C'BORED

Bill of Materials
(all dimensions actual)

Part	Description	Size	No. Req'd.
A	Head	¾ × 11¼ × 18*	1
B	Seat	¾ × 7¼ × 16	1
C	Handle	¾ dia. × 7½ long	1
D	Leg Stretcher	¾ × 3⅜ × 13¼	1
E	Leg	¾ × 7 × 10⅜	2
F	Rocker Stretcher	¾ × 1¾ × 7½	2
G	Rocker	¾ × 5 × 34*	2

*Length & width dimensions allow extra stock.

carbon lines with a black ink water resistant permanent marker. Use one with a round tip that will make a line about ⅛ in. wide. The wash coat of shellac serves to keep the marker ink from bleeding into the wood fibers, which results in a fuzzy line.

Now, cut the seat (B) to length and width from ¾ in. stock. Lay out and mark the location of the ⅜ in. deep by 5¼ in. long groove that accepts the head. For a proper fit, the groove width should be about ¹⁄₆₄ in. wider

than the thickness of the head stock. Use a router with an edge-guide and a ⅜ in. diameter straight bit to cut the groove.

Transfer the profile of the seat from the grid pattern to the stock. Cut out with the band or jigsaw and smooth the edges. Next, use the router and a ¼ in. bearing-guided round-over bit to round all the edges, both top and bottom. On the top, though, stop the bit just short of the groove.

Bore the ⅜ in. diameter tail hole, then final sand all surfaces of the seat to 220 grit. The head can now be joined to the seat with glue and a pair of countersunk no. 8 by 1½ in. long ovalhead wood screws.

Next, cut out the leg stretcher (D), the legs (E), the rocker stretcher (F) and the rockers (G). Refer to the draw-

15

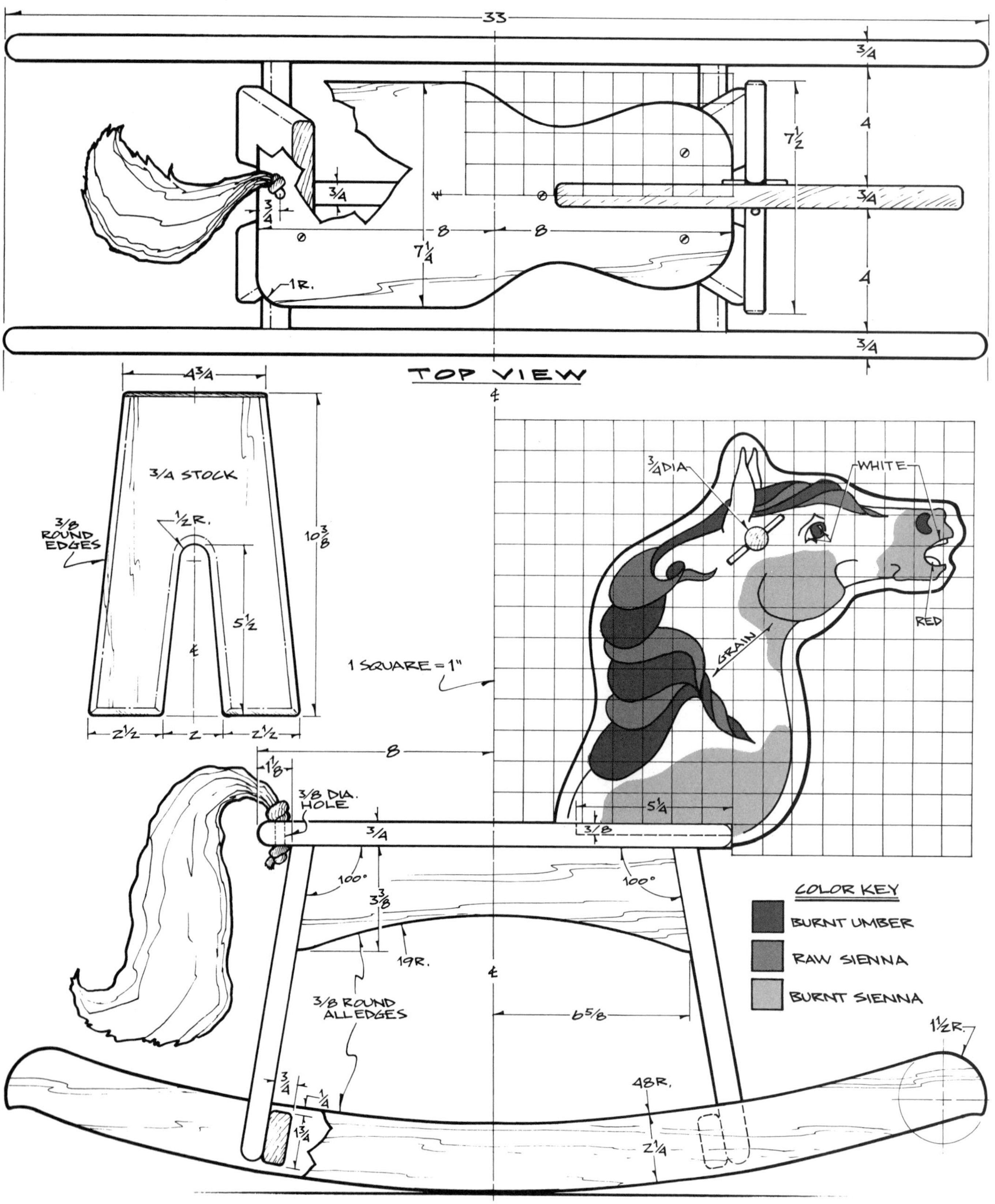

33
3/4
4
7 1/2
3/4
4
3/4
3/4
3/4
8
8
7 1/4
1R.
TOP VIEW
4 3/4
3/4 STOCK
3/8 ROUND EDGES
1/2R.
10 3/8
5 1/2
2 1/2
2
2 1/2
3/4 DIA
WHITE
RED
GRAIN
1 SQUARE = 1"
8
1 1/8
3/8 DIA. HOLE
3/4
5 1/4
3/8
100°
100°
3 3/8
19R.
COLOR KEY
BURNT UMBER
RAW SIENNA
BURNT SIENNA
3/8 ROUND ALL EDGES
6 5/8
1 1/2R.
3/4
1/4
1 3/4
48R.
2 1/4

ing for all the various dimensions. Note that the top edge of each leg is beveled at 10 degrees. You'll need a homemade compass to scribe the rocker radii. To make the compass, rip a 5 foot length of ¾ in. stock to about ¼ in. wide. Bore a hole in one end to accept a pencil point, then measure the needed radius and drive a brad for the pivot point.

After parts D, E, F, and G are cut out, use your router and the ¼ in. bearing-guided round-over bit to round the edges that will be exposed after the project is assembled. Once rounded, sand smooth with 220 grit.

Use glue and screws to assemble parts E to F. When dry add part D, making sure the top edges of both parts are flush. Join parts G, then complete the assembly by adding the seat and head unit. The handle (C) is held in place with ¼ in. by 2½ in. long dowels.

For a durable final finish, apply two coats of polyurethane to the entire project. The tail, made from hemp rope, completes the project.

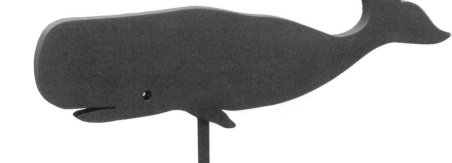

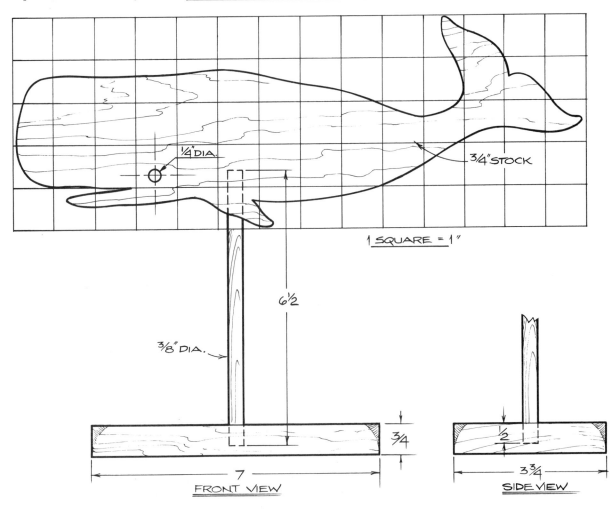

Wooden silhouettes are a recognized form of American folk art. It is believed that these silhouettes evolved from shapes commonly found on weathervanes, and so they are sometimes referred to as "weathervane silhouettes."

To make the whale, transfer the profile from the grid pattern to a piece of ¾ in. thick pine stock that measures at least 5 in. wide and 14 in. long. Use a band or saber saw to cut just outside of the waste side of the marked line, then sand exactly to the line. Bore a ⅜ in. diameter hole to a depth of about 1¼ in. to accept a ⅜ in. diameter by 6½ in.

long dowel rod. Next, locate the centerpoint of the whale's ¼ in. diameter eye and bore the hole completely through the stock.

Make the base from a piece of ¾ in. thick stock that measures 3¾ in. wide by 7 in. long. Use a file or rasp to round the top edges before sanding smooth. Bore a ⅜ in. diameter by ½ in. deep hole at the centerpoint, then glue the dowel rod in place.

Final sand all parts before painting or staining. We finished our whale with two coats of flat gray paint, but any color paint or stain will be acceptable.

Whale
Folk Art Silhouette

1 SQUARE = 1"

¼"DIA.

¾"STOCK

⅜"DIA.

6½

3/8"DIA.

7

¾

FRONT VIEW

½

3¾

SIDE VIEW

Shaker Style
Step Stool

While not an exact duplicate of an original Shaker design, this interpretation is very close to their classic step stool both in appearance and construction. To soften the rectilinear appearance of the stool, a gentle radius has been added to the aprons.

The stool as shown is constructed of cherry, however any hardwood or pine could also be used. For maximum strength be sure to avoid stock with any knots or defects. All parts are ¾ in. thick, making this an ideal project for those who do not have access to a thickness planer and must purchase their stock in standard dimensions, surfaced both sides. As shown in the cutting diagram, all the parts can easily be cut from a 1 × 12 × 64 in. long board.

Begin by cutting all stock to length and width. The lengths on the ends into which the dovetails will be cut should be about ¹⁄₃₂ in. oversize so the dovetails can be trimmed or sanded flush after assembly.

This project offers the novice, or the experienced woodworker who has never attempted hand cutting dovetails, the opportunity to practice this technique. A good dovetail saw and a sharp chisel are an absolute necessity.

While hand-cut dovetails are not a particularly difficult technique to master, they do require proper instruction, patience, and practice. Be sure to make a few practice dovetail joints first on some scrap stock before committing your project stock.

Begin by laying out the dovetails on the ends of parts B, referring to the drawings for all dimensions. Ideally, the length of the tail should be equal to the thickness of part A, plus about ¹⁄₃₂ in. Later, when the joint is assembled, the tails will stick out ¹⁄₃₂ in., allowing them to be sanded perfectly flush with the side. As you lay out the dovetail locations, work accurately, and use a hard sharp pencil.

Once the tails have been laid out, mark the waste material between dovetails with an "x" to avoid confusion. Scribe the tail location not only on the face surface of the board, but also on the end grain. Secure the step (B) in a vise and use a fine-tooth dovetail saw to make the angled cuts. Work carefully, cutting on the waste side of the line, just grazing but not removing it.

Bring the cuts almost — but not quite — to the scribed bottom line. A coping saw can now be used to cut across the grain, removing the waste. Remove the workpiece from the vise and clamp it flat on the bench over a scrap board, then use the chisel to dress the sides and bottom of the cutouts.

The pins on the sides (parts A) can best be laid out and scribed by using the finished dovetails as a template. To do this, clamp part A in the vise, end up. Lay the dovetailed steps (B) in their proper position on parts A and trace the dovetails with a sharp knife or pencil. Use a square to carry the scribed lines to the face of the board. For reasons mentioned earlier, this distance should be equal to the thickness of B plus ¹⁄₃₂ in.

Once again, mark the waste portions with an "x," then cut out in the manner used to cut the dovetails. A well fitted joint should go together with only light tapping from a mallet and scrap block. If needed, trim further with the chisel. When the fit is good, apply glue to all surfaces and clamp securely. Don't forget to lay out for and cut the dovetails for the aprons and stretchers.

As for final fit, remember that while a loose, sloppily cut dovetail is neither strong nor attractive, a dovetail that requires hammering to assemble is also unacceptable. When dry-fit, the dovetail joint should mate easily with only the slightest resistance. Any tighter than this and you will soon discover that with the application of glue the joint will be impossible to assemble. Although clamps are not usually required with the properly fitted through dovetail joint, you will need to use clamps when mounting the two apron parts. *Tip:* While a conventional compass is used to lay out the 3¾ in. radius on both sides, you will need a string and a pencil to scribe the 36¼ in. radius on the apron parts. Mark the center point on the aprons and scribe a line through it, then use a T-square to check that the aprons are perpendicular to the string at this center line before scribing the radius.

After final sanding, this piece was finished with several coats of a good quality penetrating oil.

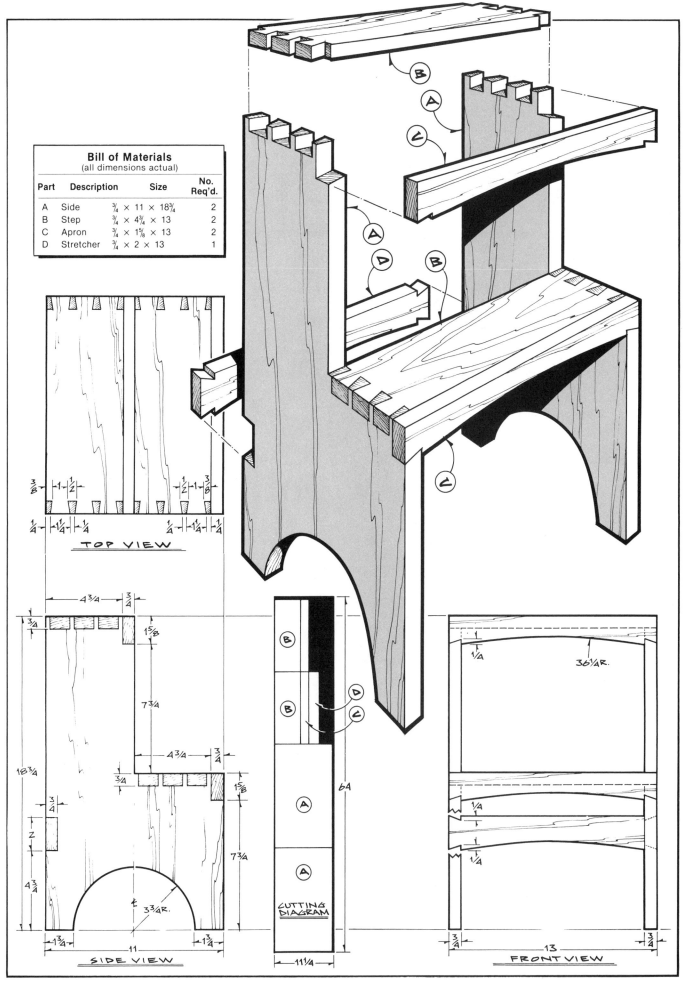

Bill of Materials
(all dimensions actual)

Part	Description	Size	No. Req'd.
A	Side	$\frac{3}{4} \times 11 \times 18\frac{3}{4}$	2
B	Step	$\frac{3}{4} \times 4\frac{3}{4} \times 13$	2
C	Apron	$\frac{3}{4} \times 1\frac{5}{8} \times 13$	2
D	Stretcher	$\frac{3}{4} \times 2 \times 13$	1

TOP VIEW

SIDE VIEW

CUTTING DIAGRAM

FRONT VIEW

Cassette Tape Holder

Bill of Materials
(all dimensions actual)

Part	Description	Size	No. Req'd.
A	Back	$\frac{1}{2} \times 4\frac{11}{16} \times 13\frac{5}{16}$	4
B	End	$\frac{1}{2} \times 2\frac{3}{4} \times 13\frac{5}{16}$	4
C	Spline	$\frac{1}{8} \times \frac{1}{2} \times 13\frac{5}{16}$	4
D	Spacer	$\frac{3}{16} \times \frac{1}{4} \times 13\frac{5}{16}$	8
E	Top/Bottom	$\frac{3}{4} \times 9 \times 9$	2
F	Base	$\frac{3}{4} \times 9 \times 9$	1
G	Threaded Rod	$\frac{1}{4} \times 14\frac{1}{2}$ in. long	1
H	Threaded Insert	$\frac{1}{4}$ - 20 $\times \frac{1}{2}$ in. long	2
I	Lazy Susan Bearing*	3 in. square	1

* Available from, Trend-Lines, 375 Beacham St., Chelsea, MA 02150. Order part no. LS3C.

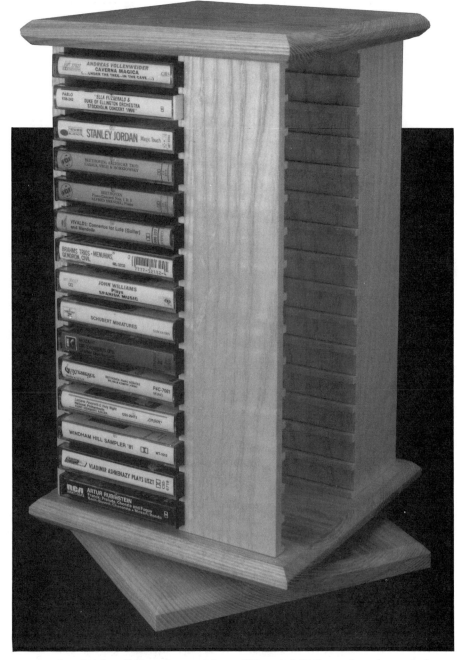

A s those of you who enjoy cassette tapes know well, storage of the tapes is vital. Without some means of organization, the tapes are forever getting lost or misplaced. This revolving cassette holder will keep up to sixty tapes at your fingertips. Our holder is made from ash, but most any hardwood or softwood could be used as well.

If you are a novice woodworker, this project is a great opportunity to get acquainted with the dado head and practice making dado cuts. Start by getting out stock for the backs (A) and ends (B). Note that while one side of each of parts A serves as a back, the opposite side is dadoed to hold the cassettes. You will need $\frac{1}{2}$ in. thick stock for parts A and B. If you have a thickness planer, this is no problem. The $\frac{1}{2}$ in. material can also be resawed from $\frac{5}{4}$ in. stock, if necessary.

The two most critical elements when making this project are the location of the dadoes and the length of parts A and B. In order to insure that all parts A and B have identical length, use a stopblock with the miter gauge when crosscutting to length. Now, mark what will be the top end of these pieces. Set the dado head to cut an $\frac{11}{16}$ in. wide slot, and raise the dado head for a $\frac{3}{16}$ in. depth of cut. Set up a stopblock with the miter gauge and make the first dado cut at the *top* end of all parts A and B. Reset the stopblock for the next dado, make the same cut in all the pieces, and continue with this pattern until the 15 dado slots have been cut in each part A and B. By cutting each

consecutive slot in all the pieces with the same stopblock settings, the slots will remain parallel in spite of slight variations in the actual setups. Another method of accomplishing this is by ripping the facing parts A and B from a wider board *after* cutting the dadoes.

Next, cut the spline grooves to accept the $\frac{1}{8}$ in. by $\frac{1}{2}$ in. splines (C) and rabbet parts B as shown to accept the $\frac{3}{16}$ in. by $\frac{1}{4}$ in. spacer (D). The $\frac{3}{4}$ in. wide by $\frac{3}{16}$ in. deep grooves in parts A that will accept both the retainer and the interlocking perpendicular parts A are also cut using the dado head. Glue up and assemble parts A through D.

Now cut the top and bottom (E) to size. Apply the 45-degree chamfer with the router and a chamfering bit, drill the top to accept the threaded insert

(H) and drill through and counterbore the bottom as shown for the threaded rod (G) and locking nut.

Make the base (F) and assemble the tape holder. Because end grain joints have little or no strength, the top and bottom are not glued to the ends of parts A and B. Instead, the threaded rod is used to secure the two parts. This system not only creates a strong assembly, it also allows the top and bottom to move freely with seasonal changes in humidity. Note the screw access hole drilled through the base so the mounting screws can be accessed. The lazy susan bearing (I) is *first* screwed to the base and then, through the access hole, into the bottom of the upper assembly. All sanding and finishing should be complete before final assembly.

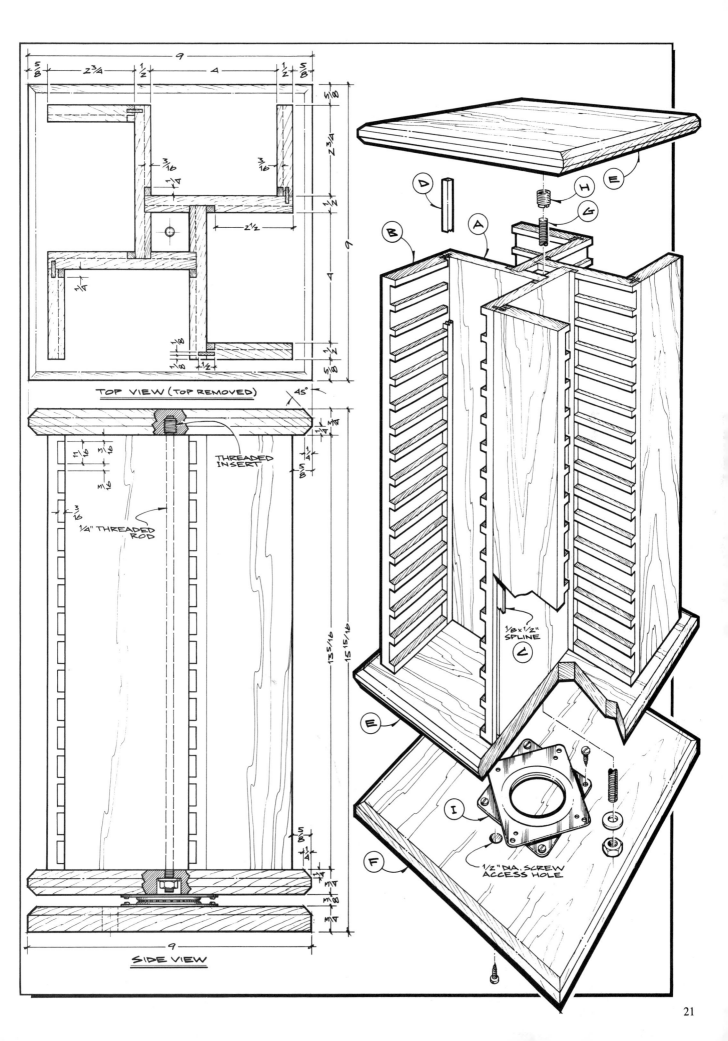

TOP VIEW (TOP REMOVED)

9

⅝   2¾   ½   A   ½   ⅝

3/16   ¼   3/16

2½

¼

¼

⅝   ½   2¾   9   A

½

⅛   ½   ⅝

45°

THREADED INSERT

¼   3/16
1 1/16   3/16
3/16
1 3/16
¼" THREADED ROD

13 5/16   15 15/16

⅝   ¼

⅝   ¼   ¾   3/8   ¾

9

SIDE VIEW

D

A

B

H   E

G

C   ⅛ x ½" SPLINE

E

I

F   ½" DIA. SCREW ACCESS HOLE

21

Adirondack Chair

When we first saw this rustic Adirondack pine chair we were intrigued with the idea, but we also had some doubts. With the steeply angled back and long curved seat both slatted, how comfortable could the chair be? Well, much to our surprise, it is very comfortable. As a lawn or patio chair, it is something like a chaise lounge, allowing you to stretch out and relax. The wide arms are ideal for that paper plate picnic lunch and a tall glass of lemonade.

Best of all, the chair is easy to make.

Except for the back slats (I), which are cut from wider stock on the table saw using a tapering jig, all the remaining parts are made from $\frac{3}{4}$ in. thick common pine boards, and should therefore require no ripping.

Start with the two seat frame members (A). After applying the 18 degree taper to the back bottom, transfer the grid pattern illustrated in the auxiliary side view, and band or saber saw the seat curve. Notch for the lower back frame (G) and radius the back corner as shown. Cut the front

legs (B) to length, and then the back legs (C), using the table saw to establish the 57 degree miter on the top end of the back legs. Cut the two stretchers (D and E) to length, and make the eleven seat slats (F).

Now make the back frames (G and H), as shown in the auxiliary top view. Use a pencil tied to a string anchored by a nail to mark the respective radii. For part G, the length of the string between the pencil and nail will be $15\frac{1}{2}$ in., while for part H the string length will be 23 in.

The seven back slats (I) are all cut on the table saw, using a tapering jig. All should be cut to the same initial dimensions ($2\frac{3}{4}$ in. wide tapering to 2 in. and 32 in. long). Then butt the back slats together and scribe a 21 in. radius across the top. Secure the slats with clamps and a cleat (to prevent chattering) and cut the 21 in. radius with a saber saw.

Make the arms (J), laying out their shape from the top view grid pattern, and cut to shape with the band or saber saw. Notch the arms to accept the back legs, and lay out and shape the two arm braces (K) as illustrated in the front view grid pattern.

The chair is assembled with plastic resin glue (white or yellow glue won't stand up to regular exposure to water), 2 in. galvanized deck screws, and plated carriage bolts as shown in the exploded view. When laying out the back slats, note that their spacing is about $\frac{3}{8}$ in. at the top, tapering to less than $\frac{1}{8}$ in. at the bottom. Chamfer any sharp edges, and sand corners and ends as needed to prevent splintering.

We finished our chair with Cuprinol brand wood preservative. Cuprinol will help the wood retain its natural rustic look, while preventing rot and decay. A reapplication of the Cuprinol once a year will insure years of trouble-free outdoor use from this chair.

Bill of Materials
(all dimensions actual)

Part	Description	Size	No. Req'd.
A	Seat Frame	$\frac{3}{4} \times 5\frac{1}{2} \times 38\frac{1}{2}$	2
B	Front Leg	$\frac{3}{4} \times 5\frac{1}{2} \times 20$	2
C	Back Leg	$\frac{3}{4} \times 3\frac{1}{2} \times 25\frac{1}{2}$	2
D	Back Stretcher	$\frac{3}{4} \times 3\frac{1}{2} \times 18\frac{1}{2}$	1
E	Front Stretcher	$\frac{3}{4} \times 3\frac{1}{2} \times 20$	1
F	Seat Slat	$\frac{3}{4} \times 1\frac{1}{2} \times 20$	11
G	Back Frame (lower)	$\frac{3}{4} \times 3\frac{1}{2} \times 20$	1
H	Back Frame (upper)	$\frac{3}{4} \times 4\frac{1}{2} \times 22$	1
I	Back Slat	as shown	7
J	Arm	$\frac{3}{4} \times 7\frac{1}{4} \times 31$	2
K	Brace	$\frac{3}{4} \times 3\frac{1}{2} \times 7\frac{1}{2}$	2

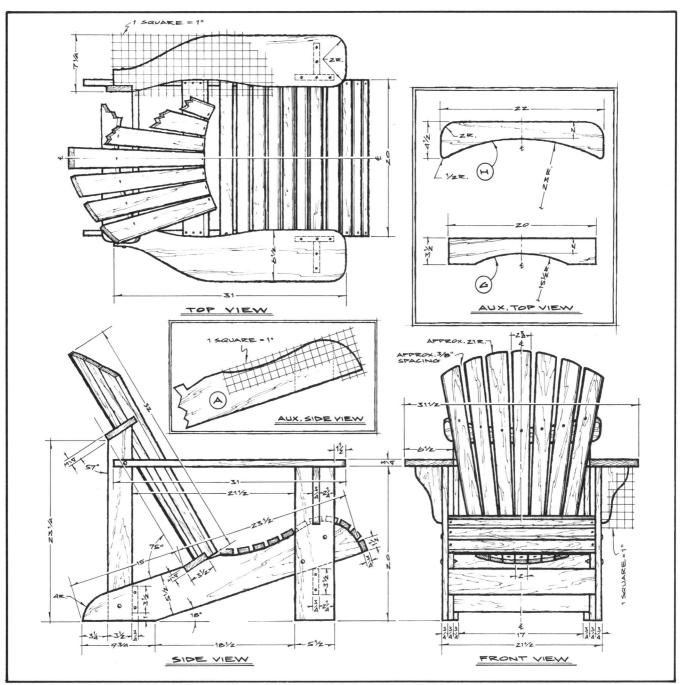

TOP VIEW

AUX. TOP VIEW

AUX. SIDE VIEW

SIDE VIEW

FRONT VIEW

(continued on next page) 23

I

J

U

J

H

J

¼ x 3½" LONG CARRIAGE BOLT

C

C

D

A

K

A

G

F

B

K

E

B

¼ x 2" LONG CARRIAGE BOLT

2" GALVANIZED DECK SCREWS

24

Canada Goose Basket

Small wooden baskets seem to be popular lately, especially those in the shapes of various kinds of animals. This one, in the profile of a Canada goose, is shown used as a bread server, but it also can be used to display a dried flower arrangement, or to hold paper napkins, or simply as a place to store odds and ends.

We used clear pine for ours, although a few small knots are acceptable. To make the sides (A), you'll need two pieces of stock, each measuring $9\frac{1}{2}$ in. wide by 10 in. long. If you don't have access to a thickness planer and you can't get $\frac{1}{2}$ in. thick stock locally, your best bet is to hand plane $\frac{3}{4}$ in. material.

Next, transfer the full-size pattern shown on page 27 to the stock. Note that the grain runs diagonally to give the board maximum strength after it is cut out. Had we run the grain horizontally, short grain across the neck of the goose would have presented a potential weak point—one that might have broken if the basket were dropped.

After transferring the pattern, use a band or saber saw to cut out the profile. As you make the cut, stay slightly on the waste side of the line; then after the cut is complete, sand the stock exactly to the line. Start with 80 grit sandpaper, then follow with 100 and 150. Next, bore the $\frac{3}{8}$ in. diameter by $\frac{1}{4}$ in. deep hole for the handle in each side as shown.

The twelve slats (B) are cut next. You'll need to resaw thicker stock to get the $\frac{1}{4}$ in. thickness, so in Fig. 1 we've shown how to do it. Start with a piece of $\frac{3}{4}$ in. thick stock that measures $2\frac{1}{4}$ in. wide by 40 in. long. Raise the table saw blade to a height of 1 in., then locate the rip fence to establish a $\frac{1}{4}$ in. wide cut. Using a push stick to keep hands clear of the fence, make the first cut (Step 1). Flip the stock and repeat the cut on the other edge (Step 2). Following this, take the stock to the band saw and make the last cut to separate the stock (Step 3). The lip that remains is removed with a hand plane. Now, using the table saw, the stock can be ripped to 1 in. before crosscutting to 6 in. lengths.

The slats are joined to the sides with glue and $\frac{1}{2}$ in. by no. 4 flathead wood screws, each one countersunk $\frac{1}{8}$ in., then covered with wood filler and sanded smooth. The handle (C) is also glued in place at this time.

To paint the project you'll need black, brown, and white enamel paints. A small container (about two fluid ounces) of each will be more than enough. Using the brown, begin by painting the inside and edge surfaces of each side, then do the slats and the handle. We found that a primer coat was not necessary, so the paint was applied directly to the pine.

The goose is painted as shown in the full size pattern. Use a narrow brush and work carefully. Some of the colors (light brown, medium brown, and grey) require mixing. The mixing ratios are given in the pattern. Allow to dry thoroughly after painting.

(continued on next page)

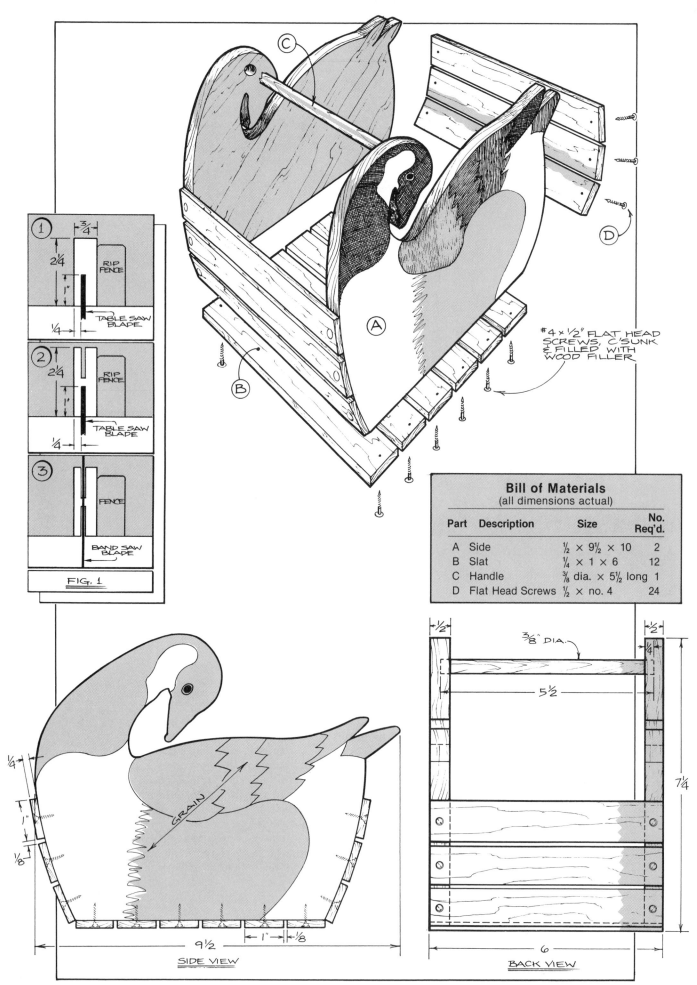

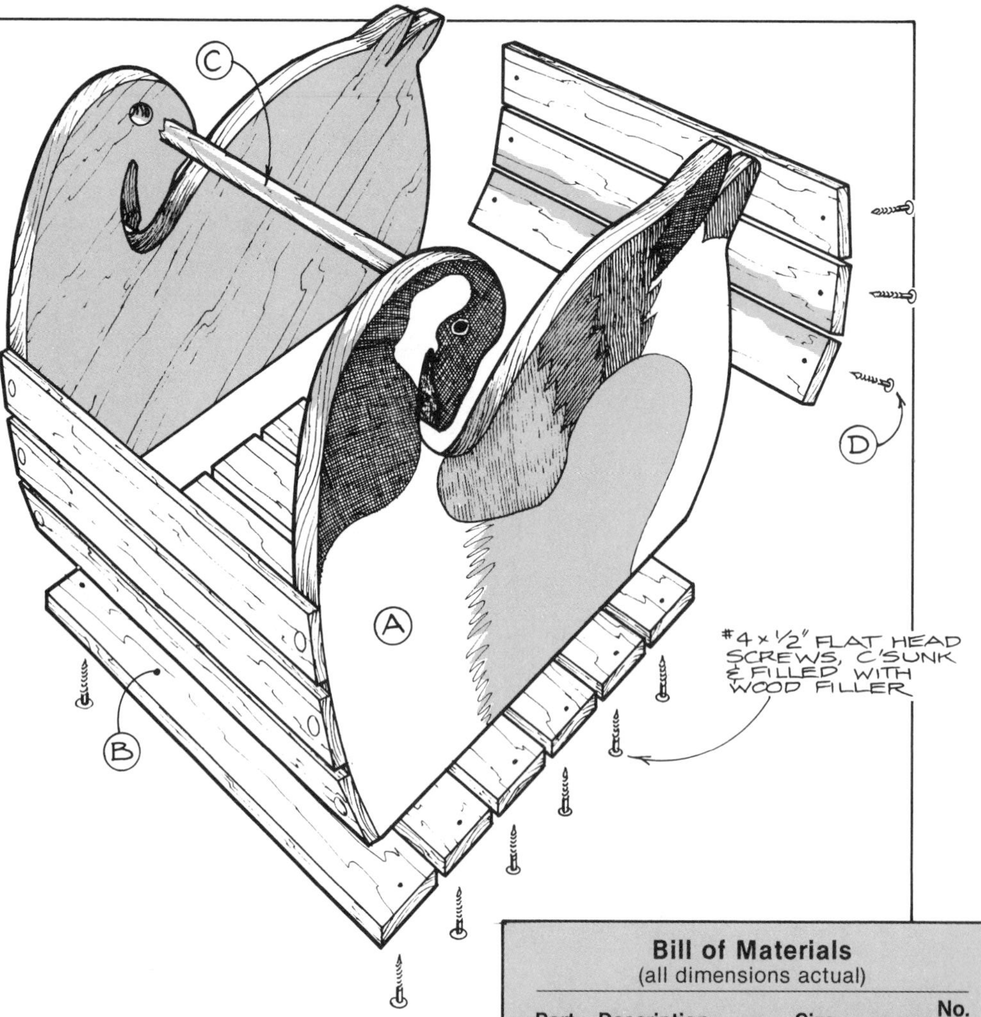
C
D
A
B
#4 × 1/2" FLAT HEAD SCREWS, C'SUNK & FILLED WITH WOOD FILLER

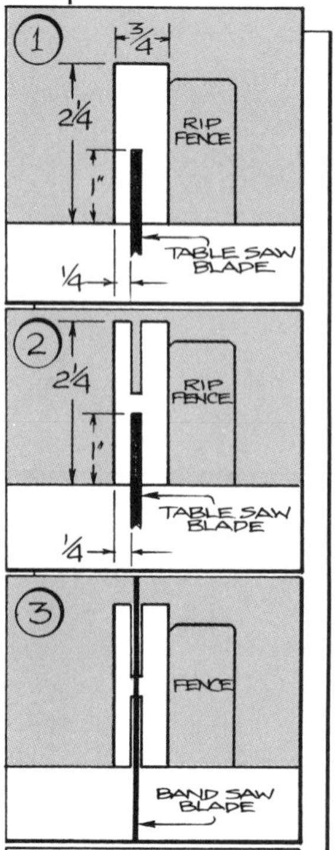
1
3/4
2 1/4
RIP FENCE
1"
TABLE SAW BLADE
1/4
2
2 1/4
RIP FENCE
1"
TABLE SAW BLADE
1/4
3
FENCE
BAND SAW BLADE

FIG. 1

Bill of Materials
(all dimensions actual)

Part	Description	Size	No. Req'd.
A	Side	1/2 × 9 1/2 × 10	2
B	Slat	1/4 × 1 × 6	12
C	Handle	3/8 dia. × 5 1/2 long	1
D	Flat Head Screws	1/2 × no. 4	24

1/4
1"
1/8
GRAIN
9 1/2
1"
1/8

SIDE VIEW

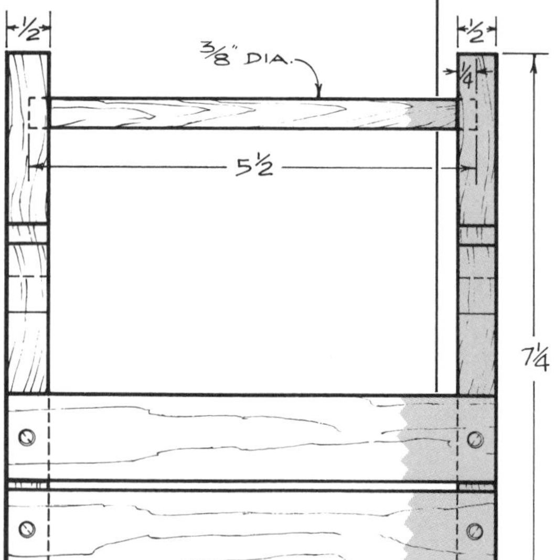
1/2
1/2
3/8" DIA.
1/4
5 1/2
7 1/4
6

BACK VIEW

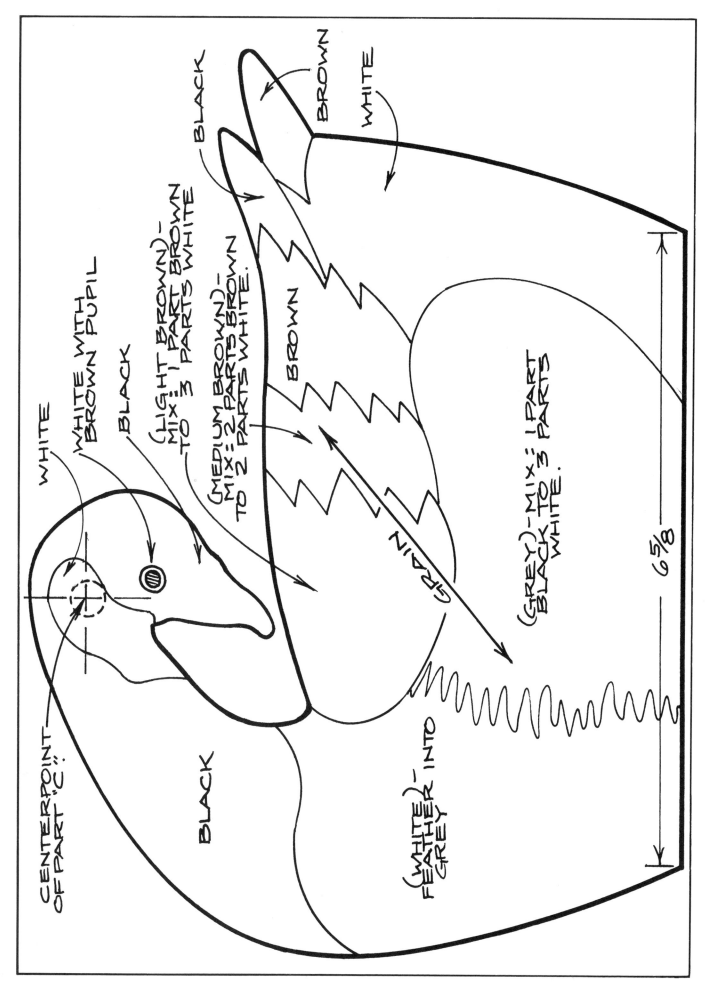

CENTERPOINT OF PART "C".

WHITE

WHITE WITH BROWN PUPIL

BLACK

(LIGHT BROWN)— MIX: 1 PART BROWN TO 3 PARTS WHITE

(MEDIUM BROWN)— MIX: 2 PARTS BROWN TO 2 PARTS WHITE.

BLACK

BROWN

WHITE

BROWN

GRAIN

(GREY)—MIX: 1 PART BLACK TO 3 PARTS WHITE.

(WHITE)— FEATHER INTO GREY

BLACK

6 5/8

27

Zebrawood Veneered End Table

Now flip the stock over and repeat the procedure on the opposite side. Once both sides are cut, repeat the process on the top and bottom edges to complete the ⅛ in. shoulder all around the tenon. Keep in mind that the tenon thickness is regulated by the height of the cutter or saw blade. It's always a good idea to make some trial cuts in scrap stock to get the tenon thickness just right. Finally, to complete work on the tenon, use the table saw to bevel the end of the tenon to 45 degrees.

The mortise at the midpoint of each apron can be cut next. Carefully lay out the location, then chop out with a sharp chisel.

The two stretchers (parts C) are made in much the same way the aprons are made. After the tenons are cut, lay out and mark the curved cutout along the top edge, then cut it out with a band or saber saw. To cut the half lap notches, set the table saw blade to a depth of 1³⁄₁₆ in., then use the miter gauge to pass the stock, on edge, through the blade. Several passes are needed to complete the cut.

The top (consisting of parts E, F, G, and H) is made next. Cut ¾ in. thick birch plywood to 14½ in. square. Rip the ash edging (F) stock to 1 in. thick and ¾ in. wide and cut it to length. Miter the ends to 45 degrees, then glue and clamp in place as shown in the exploded view. The 1 in. thickness will allow the edging to overhang about ⅛ in. on both the top and bottom. Once dry, remove the clamps and use a router equipped with a laminate trimmer bit to trim the edge flush with the plywood (see edge trimming detail). Once trimmed, apply the veneer on the top and bottom surfaces, then cut the 45-degree chamfers (see cross section top detail) on the table saw or with a chamfering bit on the router.

Final sand all parts, then assemble the legs, aprons, and stretchers. Glue is used on the leg-to-apron joints, but the stretcher-to-apron joints and the lap joints do not require glue. These latter joints are end grain joints, and glue is of no real value. Use bar or pipe clamps to secure the glued joints. The top is joined with two dowel pins (D). Before joining apply a coat of glue along the top edge of both stretchers.

Ours is finished with two coats of Deft clear wood finish. We purchased their aerosol can and sprayed on both coats, resulting in a smooth, low gloss finish that is quite durable.

L ight and delicate seem to be the words that best describe this lovely piece. Part of its appeal probably stems from the fact that the top appears to "float" just above the base.

Birch plywood is used as the core material for the top, with zebrawood veneer on the upper surface and ash veneer below. Solid ash stock is used for the edging and for all other parts of the table.

The four legs (parts A) can be made first. Note that the legs are tapered only on the two outside surfaces (the two inside surfaces are plumb) and that the taper runs the entire length of the leg. If you have one, a tapering jig will come in handy here.

If you don't have a tapering jig, there is another way to make the legs. With a long straightedge and a sharp pencil, scribe the taper on the two outside faces of the leg blank, then use a hand plane to remove the waste stock.

Next, lay out and mark the location of the ¼ in. wide by 1¾ in. long by ¾ in. deep apron mortises on the two untapered surfaces of each leg. Chop each one out with a sharp chisel or, if you prefer, use the drill press and bore a series of ¼ in. diameter by ¾ in. deep holes to remove most of the material. The remaining waste stock can then be cleaned out with a chisel.

The four aprons (parts B) can now be cut to overall length and width from ½ in. thick stock. The tenons on each end are best cut using the table saw equipped with a dado head cutter, although repeated passes with a regular saw blade will also work. Carefully lay out and mark each tenon, then raise the dado head cutter or saw blade to a height of ⅛ in. Next, using the miter gauge, pass the stock over the cutter to establish the ¾ in. tenon length. A second pass with the dado head will clean up the remaining material; several more passes will be needed if a regular saw blade is used.

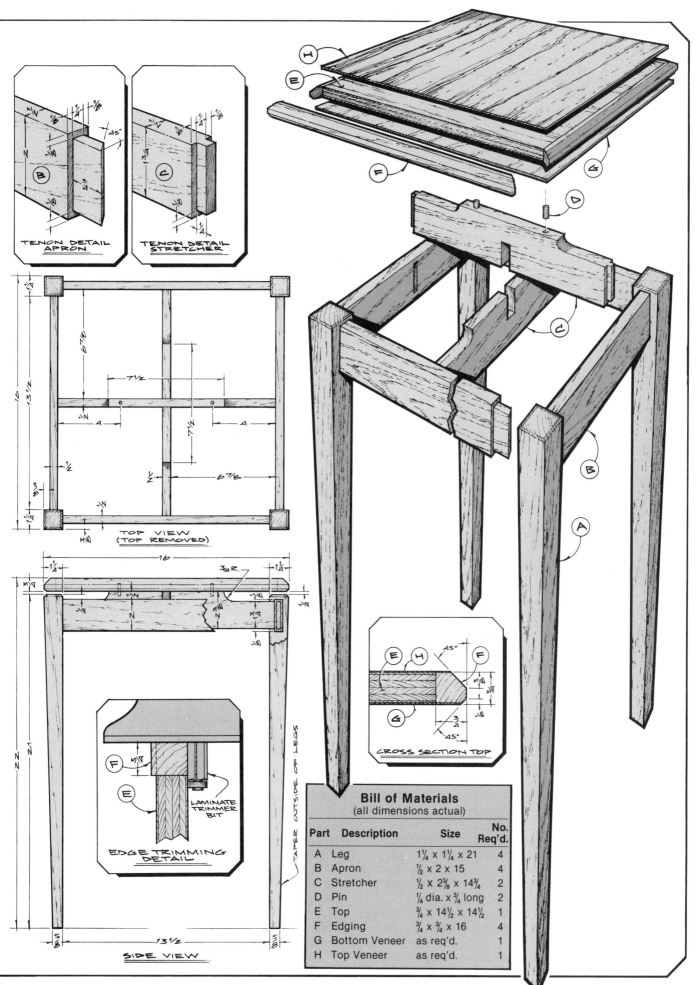

TENON DETAIL
APRON

45°

B

TENON DETAIL
STRETCHER

C

TOP VIEW
(TOP REMOVED)

7½

7½

6⅞

6⅞

13½

16

½

½

½

A

A

SIDE VIEW

16

¾ R.

22

21

⅝

13½

⅝

TAPER OUTSIDE OF LEGS

EDGE TRIMMING
DETAIL

F

E

LAMINATE
TRIMMER
BIT

H

I

E

F

G

D

C

B

A

CROSS SECTION TOP

E

H

F

G

45°

45°

Bill of Materials
(all dimensions actual)

Part	Description	Size	No. Req'd.
A	Leg	1¼ x 1¼ x 21	4
B	Apron	½ x 2 x 15	4
C	Stretcher	½ x 2⅜ x 14¾	2
D	Pin	¼ dia. x ¾ long	2
E	Top	¾ x 14½ x 14½	1
F	Edging	¾ x ¾ x 16	4
G	Bottom Veneer	as req'd.	1
H	Top Veneer	as req'd.	1

Apothecary Chest

This clever adaptation of a traditional Early American apothecary chest is certain to complement any home with a Colonial or country style interior decor. The beauty of the chest is that it is far more functional than the old apothecary chests with only small sized drawers. While this design imitates the multiple "box" drawer look, the middle and lower drawers are in fact oversize and accommodate larger items. As shown in the exploded view, the two middle drawers, and the single full-width lower drawer retain the old box drawer look through the use of inlayed false divider strips. We constructed our chest from pine, the material most accessible to local craftsmen of old.

As we often do with easy pine projects, we have designed this piece so that it can be constructed from commonly available ¾ in. thick pine boards, requiring no edge-gluing. The sides (A), top (B), case dividers (C), and drawer dividers (H) can all be cut from 1 × 12 stock, which measures ¾ in.

thick by 11¼ in. wide dressed. You will need a 1 × 12 × 10 ft. long board for the four case divider parts, and a 1 × 12 × 9 ft. long board for the drawer dividers, two sides and top. The back (D) is cut from ¼ in. thick plywood or hardboard. The base front (F) and base sides (G) are cut from a 1 × 6 × 5 ft. long board, with the waste being used for the filler (E). A 1 × 8 × 7 ft. long board can be crosscut into all the drawer fronts. Note that although we show ½ in. stock being used for the various drawer side and back parts, if you can't obtain ½ in. thick material you might consider utilizing ¾ in. thick stock for the drawer case parts instead. Refer to the cutting diagram for the layout of all the ¾ in. thick parts.

After cutting the sides, top, and case dividers to length and width, use the table saw equipped with a dado head to cut the ¼ in. deep by ¾ in. wide dadoes in the sides for the three lower case dividers, and to rabbet the top end of the sides ¼ in. deep by ¾ in. wide to accept the uppermost case divider.

Next, use the dado head and an auxiliary fence to establish the ¼ in. by ¼ in. rabbet along the inside back edges of the sides to accept the plywood back. Lastly, cut the 2½ in. radius reveal in the bottom end of the sides.

Now, using a router, cut the ¼ in. by ¾ in. by 10 in. stopped dadoes in the three uppermost case dividers to accept the drawer dividers. If you use a ¾ in. diameter straight cutter, each stopped dado can be cut with a single pass, although using two passes and removing ⅛ in. of stock at a time will result in less wear on both the router and the bit. Since the router will leave rounded corners where the dado is stopped, you'll need to use a sharp chisel to cut the corners square. Note that there are three drawer dividers to separate the four top drawers, and a single divider to separate the two middle drawers.

After ripping the drawer divider stock to a 10¾ in. width, and crosscutting the four dividers to their 6½ in. length, notch the upper and lower front edges ¼ in. by ¾ in. as shown. Now, assemble the case using glue, countersunk screws, and plugs. A dry test assembly is recommended to insure an accurate fit of the parts before you final assemble, however. The ¼ in. by 21 in. by 28 in. back (D) will serve to help square up the case if it is cut accurately.

When the case has dried, cut and fit the base front and sides. To make the base parts, first rip the stock to establish the 4 in. width. Then use a ¼ in. radius round-over bit to radius one edge of the stock, and lastly cut the miters to establish the base front and the base sides. Now transfer the profile to the base front using the illustrated grid pattern, lay out the 2 in. radius reveal on the base sides, and cut these parts out using either the band saw or saber saw.

Cut the filler strip (E) to size, and glue and screw it in place before securely gluing and screwing the base front in position. Note that the base front is screwed through the filler strip (see exploded view). Before the base sides are applied, you will need to drill several slotted holes, as illustrated, in the sides. These slotted holes, which are made by drilling side-by-side holes and cleaning out between with a rattail file, will allow the sides to expand and contract relative to the base sides, which are in a cross-grain orientation. Use glue on the base front and sides at the miters. Add the top to complete the case assembly. The top is glued in place (a good long grain-to-long grain glue surface). The dowel pins shown in the exploded view are only for the purpose of properly locating the top.

While we suggest a drawer construction as shown in the exploded view, you will probably want to use the method you prefer or are most familiar with. Keep in mind that the dimensions provided in the bill of materials are for the various drawer parts using our method of construction. Note carefully that all dimensions given are calculated from "point to point." In practice, of course, the drawers must be sized slightly smaller, to fit properly. For example, with the smallest drawers, the measurement of the drawer front (I) will probably be about 5¹⁵⁄₁₆ in. by 6¼ in., or ¹⁄₁₆ in. less in width and length than the bill of materials specifications. Experienced woodworkers recognize that drawers are sized to fit the available opening, whatever that opening might be. The bill of materials dimensions are therefore only a rough guideline to help in calculating material required.

The false drawer front dividers are established by using the dado head to cross-cut a slot as shown to accept an inlaid strip (U). Note that the two middle drawer faces each have one inlay strip, while the bottom drawer face has three. We recommend making these strips slightly thicker than

necessary, and then planing and sanding them flush with the drawer faces after they have been glued in place. These operations must be completed before the drawers are assembled.

A light stain, such as Minwax's Colonial Maple, followed by an application of penetrating oil, completes the project. The porcelain drawer knobs (V), which are available at most hardware stores, lend the piece just the right accent.

Bill of Materials
(all dimensions actual)

Part	Description	Size	No. Req'd.
		Case	
A	Side	¾ × 11 × 25	2
B	Top	¾ × 11¼ × 30	1
C	Case Divider	¾ × 10¾ × 28	4
D	Back	¼ × 21 × 28	1
E	Filler	¾ × 1¼ × 27½	1
F	Base Front	¾ × 4 × 30½	1
G	Base Side	¾ × 4 × 11¾	2
H	Drawer Divider	¾ × 10¾ × 6½	4
		Small Drawer	
I	Front	¾ × 6 × 6⁵⁄₁₆	4
J	Side	½ × 6 × 10½	8
K	Back	½ × 5½ × 5¹³⁄₁₆	4
L	Bottom	¼ × 5¹³⁄₁₆ × 10¼	4
		Medium Drawer	
M	Front	¾ × 6 × 13⅜	2
N	Side	½ × 6 × 10½	4
O	Back	½ × 5½ × 12⅞	2
P	Bottom	¼ × 10¼ × 12⅞	2
		Large Drawer	
Q	Front	¾ × 6 × 27½	1
R	Side	½ × 6 × 10½	2
S	Back	½ × 5½ × 27	1
T	Bottom	¼ × 10¼ × 27	1
U	Inlay Strip	³⁄₁₆ × ¾ × 6	5
V	Knob	1 in. dia. porcelain	12

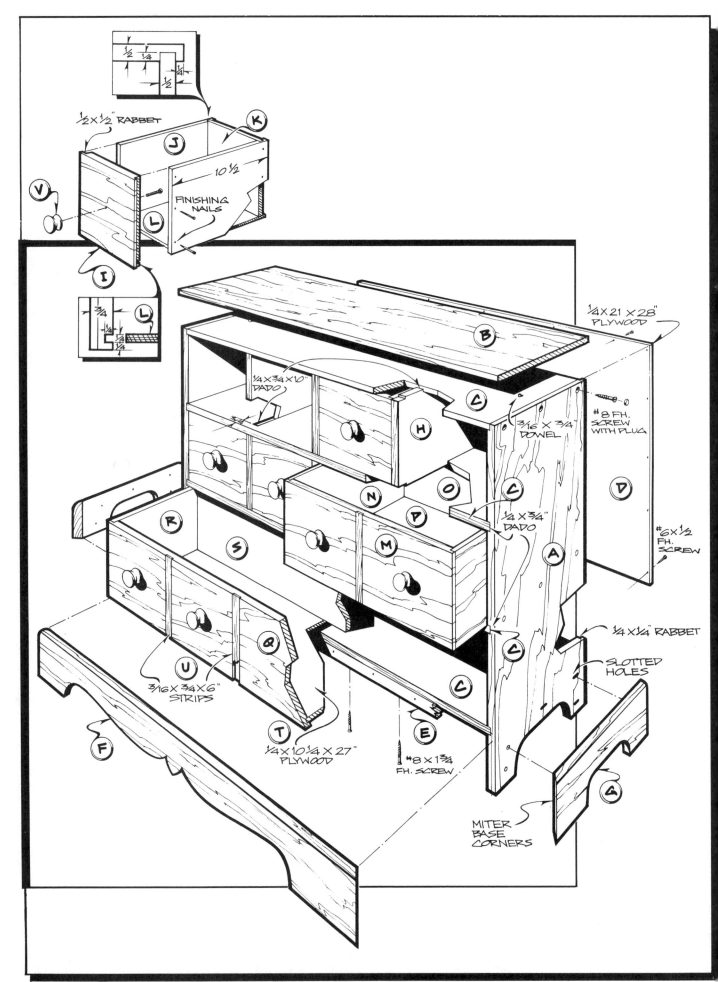

½ × ½" RABBET

½   ¼   ¼   ½

J   K

V

L

I

10 ½

FINISHING NAILS

¾   ¼   ¼

I   L

B

¼ X 21 X 28"
PLYWOOD

¼ X ¾ X 10"
DADO

C

H

#8 F.H.
SCREW
WITH PLUG

3/16 X ¾
DOWEL

D

O

N   P   C

¼ X ¾"
DADO

R

S   M   A

#6 X ½
F.H.
SCREW

U   Q

¼ X ¼ RABBET

SLOTTED
HOLES

3/16 X ¾ X 6"
STRIPS

T

C

E

F   C

G

¼ X 10¼ X 27"
PLYWOOD

#8 X 1¾
F.H. SCREW

MITER
BASE
CORNERS

CUTTING DIAGRAM FOR CASE PARTS AND DRAWER FRONTS

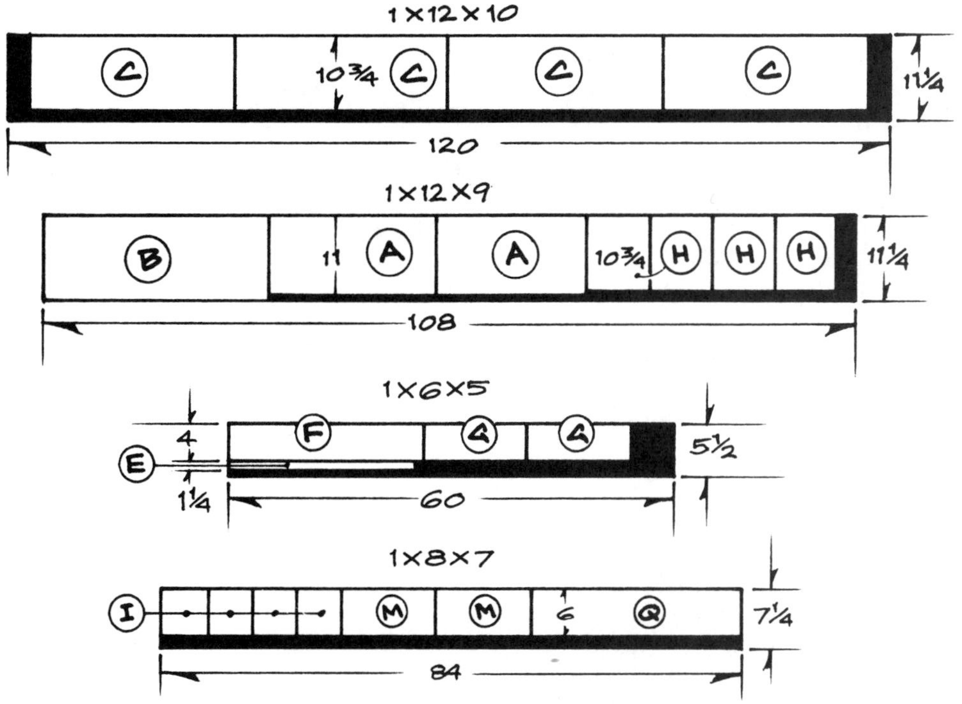
1×12×10
C
10¾
C
C
C
11¼
120
1×12×9
B
11
A
A
10¾
H
H
H
11¼
108
1×6×5
4
F
G
G
5½
E
1¼
60
1×8×7
I
M
M
6
Q
7¼
84

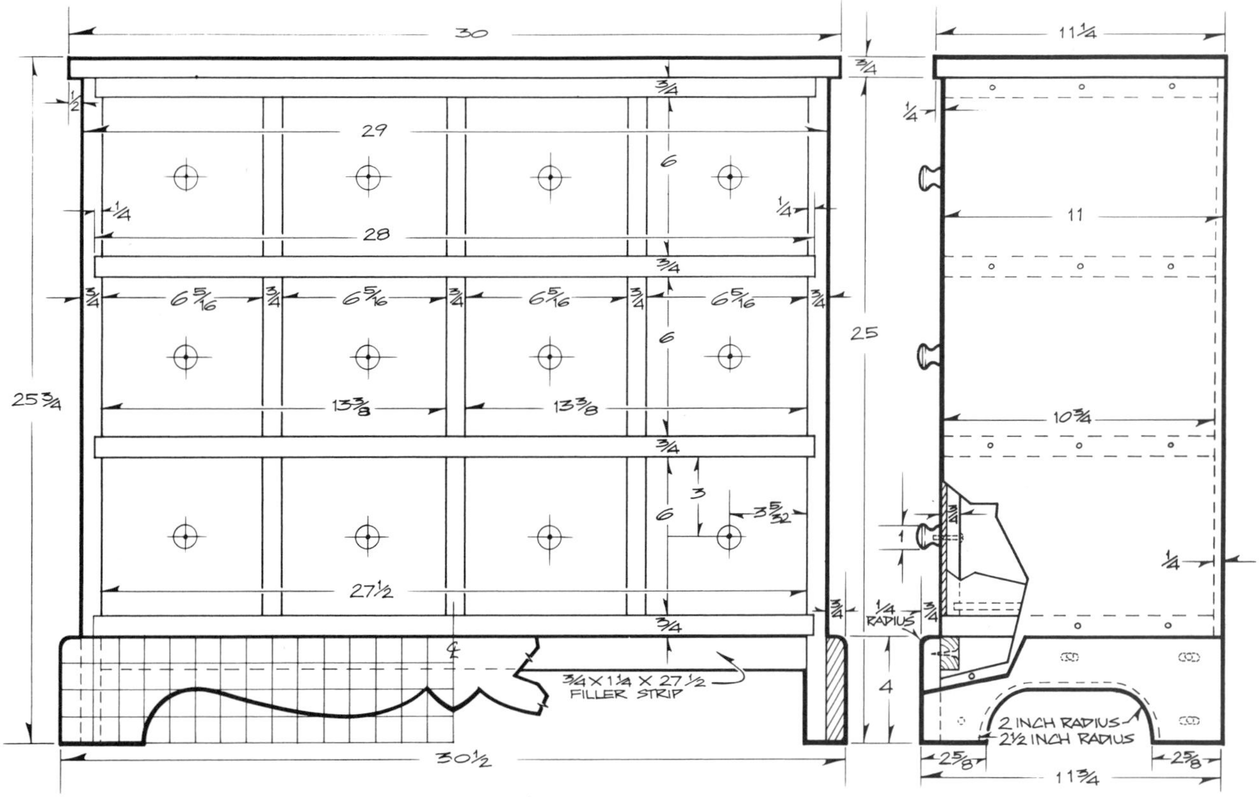
30
¾
½
¾
29
6
¼
¼
28
¾
¾
6 5/16
¾
6 5/16
¾
6 5/16
¾
6 5/16
¾
6
25¾
13⅜
13⅜
25
¾
3
6
3 5/32
27½
¾
¾
¼ RADIUS
¾
¾ × 1¼ × 27½ FILLER STRIP
4
30½
11¼
¼
11
10¾
1
¼
2 INCH RADIUS
2½ INCH RADIUS
2⅝
2⅝
11¾

Toy Firetruck

A well-built toy like this can provide hours of fun for an imaginative child. Such toys take a pretty good beating though, so it's best to use a hardwood. This one is made from maple (except for a cherry bumper) so it will stand up to plenty of wear and tear.

Begin by cutting the undercarriage (A) to length and width from ¾ in. thick stock. At this point it should be given a good final sanding because later on, after other parts are added, it won't be as easy to thoroughly smooth. Do the top, bottom, and all four edges.

The lower cab (B) and the upper cab (C) are cut from 1¾ in. thick and ¾ in. thick stock respectively. Allow a little extra on the length and width when you cut them to size. Apply glue to the mating surfaces of the two parts (see exploded view) and clamp firmly with two or three C-clamps. The upper and lower cab assembly can now be glued to the undercarriage.

Make the two blocks (D) next, cutting them to the dimensions shown before boring ½ in. deep holes to accept the pins (N). These pins can be turned on a lathe (see detail) or ordered from Craftsman Wood Service Co.,

Bill of Materials
(all dimensions actual)

Part	Description	Size	No. Req'd.
A	Undercarriage	¾ × 3 × 12	1
B	Lower Cab	1¾ × 4 × 3	1
C	Upper Cab	¾ × 4 × 3	1
D	Block	1 × 1½ × 3	2
E	Axle Holder	(see detail)	3
F	Main Ladder Base	¾ × 4 × 2½	1
G	Main Ladder Washer	1½ dia. × ¹⁄₁₆ thick	1
H	Main Ladder Wheel	2 dia. × ⁷⁄₁₆ thick	1
I	Main Ladder Block	1 × 1 × 1	1
J	Main Ladder Post	¼ × ⅜ × 15½	2
K	Main Ladder Rung	⅛ dia. × 1¼ long	22
L	Side Ladder Post	¼ × ⅜ × 9	2/ladder
M	Side Ladder Rung	⅛ dia. × 1¼ long	14/ladder
N	Pin	(see detail)	8
O	Headlight	upholstery tack	4
P	Light	(see detail)	1
Q	Axle	¼ dia. steel rod	3
R	Wheel Washer	1½ dia. × ¹⁄₁₆ thick	6
S	Wheel	2 dia. × ⁷⁄₁₆ thick	10
T	Push Nut	¼	6
U	Bumper	⅜ × ¾ × 4½	1
V	Fog Light	(see detail)	2

1735 West Cortland Court, Addison, IL 60101. Glue the blocks to the undercarriage, then add the pins.

Now cut the three axle holders (E) to the dimensions shown in the detail. Use a drill press to bore the ⁵⁄₁₆ in. diameter hole before gluing to the underside of the carriage.

The axles (Q) are made from ¼ in. diameter steel rod. The 2 in. diameter by ⁷⁄₁₆ in. thick wheels (S) can be turned to the dimensions shown or ordered from Craftsman Wood Service. (The same wheel will also be used later on for part H). Note that the wheels are held to the rod with ¼ in. push nuts (T), an item that can be found at most hardware stores. Simply tap the push nuts in place with a hammer. The 1½ in. diameter by ¹⁄₁₆ in. thick washers (R) serve as spacers. If you prefer though, use ¼ in. diameter dowel rod and glue the wheels to the rod.

Make the main ladder base (F) from ¾ in. thick stock cut to 4 in. wide by 2½ in. long. Mark the centerpoint of the underside and bore a ⁵⁄₃₂ in. diameter pilot hole all the way through to accept a 1¼ in. long by no. 8 roundhead wood screw and washer (G). Now use a Forstner bit to counterbore a ¾ in. diameter by ¼ in. deep hole as shown in the main ladder assembly detail.

The 2 in. diameter wheels sold by Craftsman Wood Service have a contoured side and a flat side. Glue and clamp the main ladder block (I) to the flat side of the main ladder wheel (H). For maximum glue strength, keep the grain running in the same direction for both parts. When dry, drill a pilot hole for the wood screw (see main ladder assembly detail) and assemble as shown. To firmly anchor the screw, we added a spot of epoxy glue to the pilot hole before assembly.

The main ladder (parts J and K) and the two side ladders (parts L and M) can now be made. Use ⅛ in. diameter dowel stock for the rungs. The main ladder is joined to part I with a pair of ¾ in. long by no. 10 roundhead wood screws and washers as shown. The side ladders simply hook on the pins.

The light (P) can be turned to the dimensions shown or, as a substitute, use a ⅝ in. diameter by 1¼ in. long dowel pin glued into a ¾ in. deep hole. We used upholstery tacks for the headlights (O), but four ¼ in. diameter by ⅛ in. deep holes will serve just as well. The addition of the bumper (U) and fog light pins (V) completes the assembly. No final finish is needed.

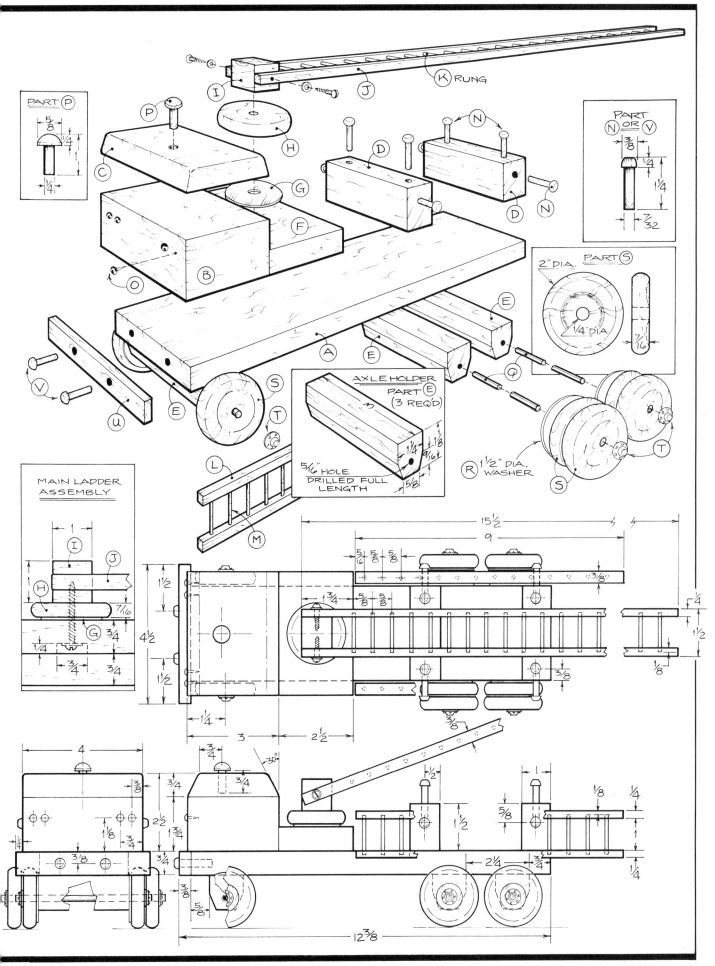

PART (P)

5/8
1/4
1/4

PART (N) OR (V)
3/8
1/4
1 1/4
7/32

PART (S)
2" DIA.
1/4 DIA.
7/16

(K) RUNG
(J)
(I)
(P)
(H)
(C)
(D)
(N)
(G)
(F)
(B)
(O)
(A)
(E)
(E)
(V)
(U)
(E)
(S)
(T)
(L)
(M)

AXLE HOLDER
PART (E)
(3 REQ'D)
3
1/4
1/8
9/16
5/8
5/16" HOLE
DRILLED FULL
LENGTH

(Q)
(R) 1 1/2" DIA. WASHER
(S)
(T)

MAIN LADDER
ASSEMBLY

1
(I)
(J)
(H)
(G)
7/16
3/4
1/4
3/4
3/4
4 1/2
1 1/2
1 1/2
1/4

15 1/2
9
5/16 5/8 5/8
3/4
5/8 5/8
3/8
1/4
1/2
1/8
3/8
3/8
3
2 1/2
3/8

4
3/4
3/4
30°
3/8
3/4
3/4
3/4
2 1/2
3/4
1/8
1/4
1/4
1/8
3/8
3/8
5/8
1/2
1 1/2
5/8
1
2 1/4
3/4
1/4
3/8
5/8
12 3/8

35

Door Harp

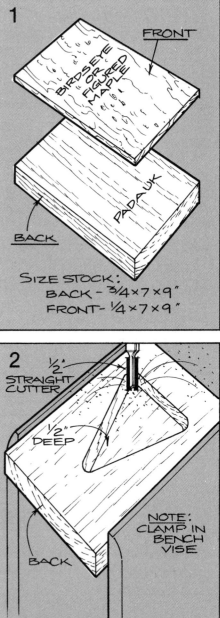

1 BIRDSEYE OR FIGURED MAPLE — FRONT

BACK — PADAUK

SIZE STOCK:
BACK – ¾ × 7 × 9"
FRONT – ¼ × 7 × 9"

2 ½" STRAIGHT CUTTER

½" DEEP

BACK

NOTE: CLAMP IN BENCH VISE

MARK SOUND CHAMBER (SEE PATTERN) & FREE HAND ROUT WITH ROUTER.

H ung on the inside of your front door, this melodious harp will welcome all who enter with a delicate serenade. The motion of the door agitates the clappers against the steel guitar strings, resulting in a brief random tune. Although the door harp is thought to be of Scandinavian origin, this little heart-shaped example will be at home anywhere.

One of the best things about this project is the ease with which it can be made. Simply follow the step-by-step instructions and illustrations. If you don't have padauk and bird's-eye maple, any number of attractive combinations of wood will serve as well. Sections of ⅜ in. diameter dowel stock will work as clappers if you don't have

a plug cutter.

We've seen many different door harp designs, some decorated with exotic woods and intricate inlay work, and others simply painted or stained. Door harps make great gifts, and are an opportunity for even the beginner to create something that not only looks good, but also sounds good.

All the hardware needed for this project, including two guitar strings and the six chrome plated zither tuning pins are available in kit form from Folkcraft Instruments, Box 807W, Winsted, CT 06098. Order kit no. 11001. The two guitar strings allow for extra length should the door harp strings ever need replacing.

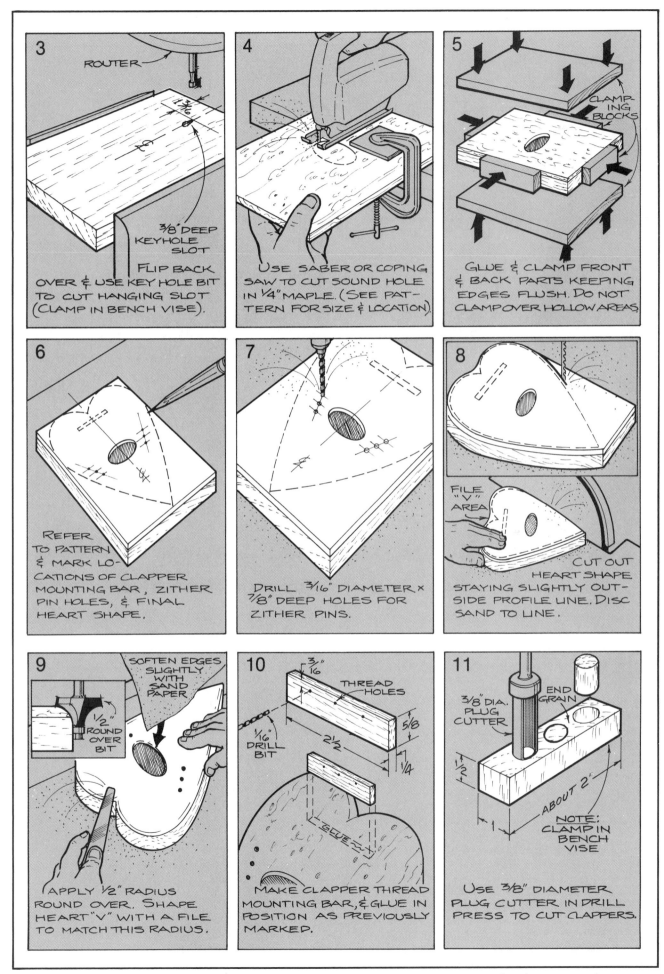

3 ROUTER

3/8" DEEP KEYHOLE SLOT

FLIP BACK OVER & USE KEY HOLE BIT TO CUT HANGING SLOT (CLAMP IN BENCH VISE).

4 USE SABER OR COPING SAW TO CUT SOUND HOLE IN 1/4" MAPLE. (SEE PATTERN FOR SIZE & LOCATION).

5 CLAMPING BLOCKS

GLUE & CLAMP FRONT & BACK PARTS KEEPING EDGES FLUSH. DO NOT CLAMP OVER HOLLOW AREAS.

6 REFER TO PATTERN & MARK LOCATIONS OF CLAPPER MOUNTING BAR, ZITHER PIN HOLES, & FINAL HEART SHAPE.

7 DRILL 3/16" DIAMETER X 7/8" DEEP HOLES FOR ZITHER PINS.

8 FILE "V" AREA

CUT OUT HEART SHAPE STAYING SLIGHTLY OUTSIDE PROFILE LINE. DISC SAND TO LINE.

9 SOFTEN EDGES SLIGHTLY WITH SAND PAPER

1/2" ROUND OVER BIT

APPLY 1/2" RADIUS ROUND OVER. SHAPE HEART "V" WITH A FILE TO MATCH THIS RADIUS.

10 3/16" THREAD HOLES

1/16" DRILL BIT

2 1/2"

5/8"

1/4"

GLUE

MAKE CLAPPER THREAD MOUNTING BAR, & GLUE IN POSITION AS PREVIOUSLY MARKED.

11 3/8" DIA. PLUG CUTTER

END GRAIN

1/2"

ABOUT 2"

1

NOTE: CLAMP IN BENCH VISE

USE 3/8" DIAMETER PLUG CUTTER IN DRILL PRESS TO CUT CLAPPERS.

(continued on next page)

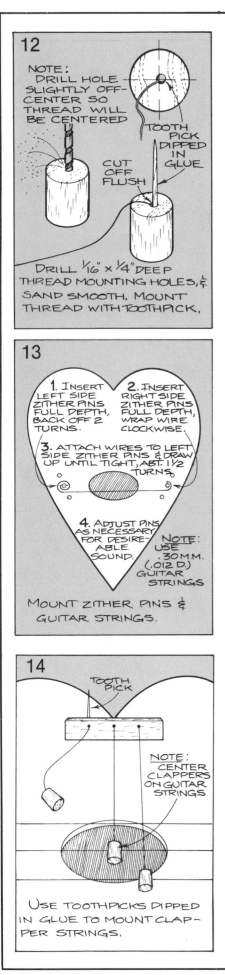

12

NOTE:
DRILL HOLE SLIGHTLY OFF-CENTER SO THREAD WILL BE CENTERED

TOOTH PICK DIPPED IN GLUE

CUT OFF FLUSH

DRILL $1/16" \times 1/4"$ DEEP THREAD MOUNTING HOLES, $\frac{1}{4}$ SAND SMOOTH. MOUNT THREAD WITH TOOTHPICK.

13

1. INSERT LEFT SIDE ZITHER PINS FULL DEPTH, BACK OFF 2 TURNS.

2. INSERT RIGHT SIDE ZITHER PINS FULL DEPTH, WRAP WIRE CLOCKWISE.

3. ATTACH WIRES TO LEFT SIDE ZITHER PINS & DRAW UP UNTIL TIGHT, ABT. 1½ TURNS.

4. ADJUST PINS AS NECESSARY FOR DESIRE-ABLE SOUND.

NOTE: USE .30 M.M. (.012 D.) GUITAR STRINGS

MOUNT ZITHER PINS & GUITAR STRINGS.

14

TOOTH PICK

NOTE: CENTER CLAPPERS ON GUITAR STRINGS

USE TOOTHPICKS DIPPED IN GLUE TO MOUNT CLAP-PER STRINGS.

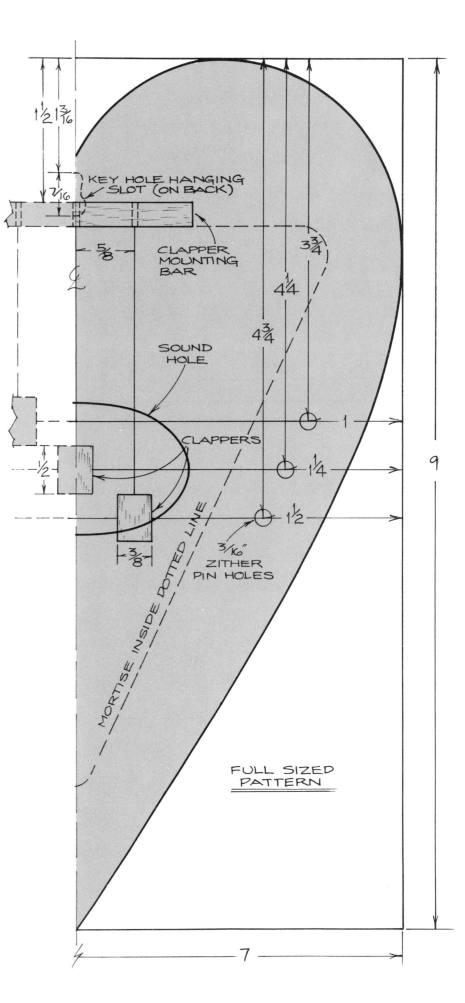

KEY HOLE HANGING SLOT (ON BACK)

$1\frac{1}{2}$ $1\frac{3}{16}$

$7/16$

$5/8$

CLAPPER MOUNTING BAR

$3\frac{3}{4}$

$4\frac{1}{4}$

$4\frac{3}{4}$

SOUND HOLE

CLAPPERS

$\frac{1}{2}$

1

$1\frac{1}{4}$

$1\frac{1}{2}$

$3/8$

$3/16"$ ZITHER PIN HOLES

MORTISE INSIDE DOTTED LINE

9

7

FULL SIZED PATTERN

Mortar and Pestle

A mortar and pestle is an ideal turning project for the woodworker just getting acquainted with the lathe. Ours, which is based on an antique design, is crafted in cherry, though walnut, pine, and maple are good alternate choices. In the kitchen, it will come in handy if you enjoy using freshly ground herbs and spices.

Start by gluing up three pieces of 2 in. thick stock, sufficient to obtain the 5⅜ in. square by 9 in. long turning square required for the mortar. Square one end, dress down the four corners to create an octagon, find the center, and mount on the lathe faceplate. After establishing the outside profile, use the round nose to clean the inside. *Tip:* A Forstner bit can be used to drill out the bulk of the inside waste, cutting down on your turning time.

Make the 2¾ in. square by 12 in. long pestle turning square by gluing up stock, then dress, center, mount and turn to the indicated dimensions. Trim both the mortar and pestle to their final lengths, and finish with a non-toxic finish. Behlen's Salad Bowl Finish, sold by Woodcraft, 210 Wood County Industrial Park, P.O. Box 1686, Parkersburg, WV 26102; tel. 1-800-225-1153, is a good one. Once dry, it is approved by the U.S. Food and Drug Administration for use in contact with food.

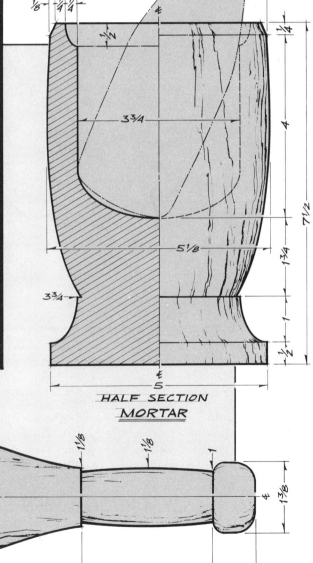

HALF SECTION
MORTAR

PESTLE

Country Vegetable Bin

front. A ½ in. radius is applied to the top edge of the base apron, and the top edge of the front is beveled at 10 degrees to match the bevel on the sides. The tulip may be incised on the front either now or after assembly. To carve the tulip, first refer to the grid pattern and transfer a ½ in. grid and a pencil sketch of the tulip to the front. Our carving was made entirely with an X-Acto brand knife (we used their blade no. 19), but a sharp-pointed pen knife could be used as well. Cuts should be made with the grain to avoid tearing or chipping. Several light cuts pared to the line are usually more effective than attempting to complete the deeper cuts with one pass, especially if you are not familiar with this type of carving. The photo detail shows which areas to incise.

Assemble the bin as shown, using glue and finishing nails. Cut and fit the plywood back (J); add the top (H) and top door (I). All finishing nails should be set and filled. The upper edge of the top door is beveled at 10 degrees; the lower edge is radiused as shown. Mount the top door, drill for the pivot dowels, mount the lower door, and install a magnetic catch (available at hardware stores) to keep it closed.

After sanding, we finished our bin with a cherry stain followed by two coats of penetrating oil.

This handsome vegetable bin is one of the best "easy pine" projects we've seen in a while. The bottom bin is for onions, and the top bin is for potatoes. A heart cutout on either side provides ventilation for the potatoes, and the tulip carving incised on the front lends the piece an authentic country flavor.

The entire piece (except the plywood back) is constructed of ¾ in. thick common pine, which is available at lumber and building supply centers. If you don't want to edge-glue stock to achieve the widths required (see bill of materials), you can purchase pre-edge-glued solid pine material instead.

Start by cutting the sides (A) to overall length and width. Use the dado

head to establish the ¾ in. by ¼ in. deep groove for the bottom (B), and the ½ in. by ½ in. rabbet along the inside back edge to accept the back. The ¾ in. by ¼ in. stopped groove for the shelf (C) can be cut with the router using a straight bit. Bevel the top end of the sides as shown at 10 degrees to provide the top slant, and use a saber saw to cut the 1 in. radius profile at the bottom edge (see side view), and to make the heart cutout (drill a starter hole for the saber saw blade).

Now cut the bottom (B), shelf (C), door stop (D), front (E), lower door (F), and base apron (G) to overall length and width. Note that a ⅜ in. radius is applied to both edges of the door and to the bottom edge of the

Bill of Materials
(all dimensions actual)

Part	Description	Size	No. Req'd.
A	Side	¾ × 14 × 32	2
B	Bottom	¾ × 13½ × 17	1
C	Shelf	¾ × 12¾ × 17	1
D	Door Stop	¾ × 1¾ × 16½	1
E	Front	¾ × 12⅛ × 16½*	1
F	Lower Door	¾ × 12¼ × 16½	1
G	Base Apron	¾ × 5 × 18	1
H	Top	¾ × 2 × 18¾	1
I	Top Door	¾ × 12¾ × 18¾	1
J	Back	½ × 17½ × 32	1
K	Hinge	1½ × 2	1 pair
L	Magnetic Catch	as shown	1

*Allow slight extra width for beveled top edge.

Note: Our bin is sized roughly to counter height. Overall height, width and depth could be scaled down.

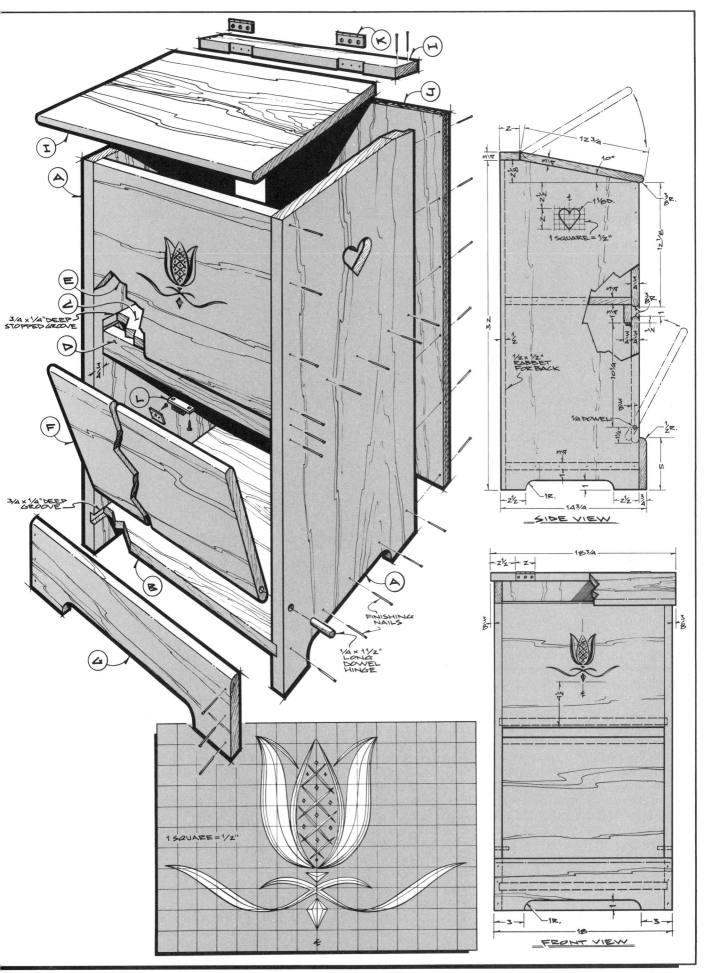

K

H

I

A

E
C
3/4 x 1/4" DEEP
STOPPED GROOVE
D
3/4

L

F

3/4 x 1/4" DEEP
GROOVE

B

G

FINISHING
NAILS

1/4 x 1 1/2"
LONG
DOWEL
HINGE

A

J

SIDE VIEW

2
1 3/4
10°
3 1/4
2 3/8
3 1/4
M 1/4
8 3/4 R.
12 7/8
1 1/8 D.
1 SQUARE = 1/2"
3/4
M 3/4 R.
3/4
3/4
1
3/4
1/2
3 2
1/2
1/2 x 1/2"
RABBET
FOR BACK
10 1/4
8 1/4
1/4 DOWEL
1 1/2
1/2 R.
5
M 3/4
2 1/2
1 R.
2 1/2
3/4
14 3/4

FRONT VIEW

18 3/4
2 1/2 2
3 3/8
3 3/8
4 1/2
3 18 3
1 R.

1 SQUARE = 1/2"

41

Early American Wall Shelf

Easy-to-build wall shelves have traditionally been among our most popular projects. A piece such as this is well within the capability of the novice woodworker, and would even make an ideal first project. Except for the ⅛ in. thick plywood drawer bottoms, the entire piece is crafted from solid pine.

The wall shelf we show is made from ½ in. thick stock. If you don't have a thickness planer or can't find a source for ½ in. material, you may need to have ¾ in. thick stock milled down to ½ in. at your local lumberyard. Although we chose to build this piece from ½ in. thick stock because it lends the project a lighter look, another alternative would be to simply use ¾ in. stock. Take note, however, that various dimensions will change if you opt for the ¾ in. thick material.

Begin by getting out stock for parts A through J. After cutting all parts to overall length and width, refer to the various grid patterns and lay out the profiles of the sides and back. Mark out the shelf dado locations on the sides, set the dado head for a ½ in. wide by ¼ in. deep cut, and establish the shelf dadoes. Using the same dado head setting, cut the ¼ in. deep by ½ in. wide divider dadoes, and establish the rabbets on the ends of the drawer sides and front. The table saw is also used to cut the ⅛ in. wide by ¼ in. deep drawer bottom grooves in the drawer front and sides. The router, a straight cutter, and the edge guide are used to rabbet the shelf sides as shown to accept the back.

Now, use either the band saw or a saber saw to cut out the curved profiles of the sides and back. Sand as necessary to remove the saw marks, and glue and assemble the sides, shelves, divider, and back as shown. We added finishing nails, set and filled, for extra strength.

Assemble the drawers as indicated, using glue and finishing nails. Several finishing nails inserted through the drawer bottom up into the drawer back will anchor the bottoms along the back edge. As you will note from the bill of materials, the drawers are dimensioned full-size for the actual opening, and must be sanded slightly to permit ease of operation. We did allow for an ⅛ in. space at the drawer back, however. The drawer stops, which are mounted next, will keep the drawers flush with the shelf front, while the ⅛ in. space will insure that they do not bump against the wall when being closed.

After a final sanding to soften sharp edges, apply stain if desired, and finish to suit. We prefer penetrating oil, but lacquer or polyurethane will also be fine. The 1 in. diameter porcelain drawer knobs are a common item available at most hardware stores. They provide just the right touch to accent this project.

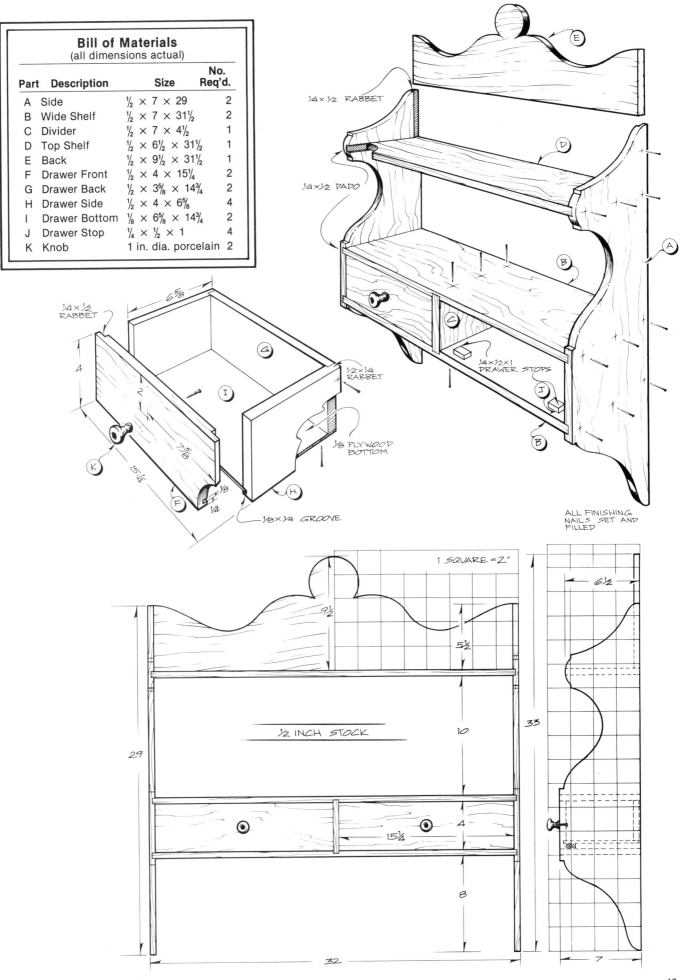

Bill of Materials
(all dimensions actual)

Part	Description	Size	No. Req'd.
A	Side	$\frac{1}{2} \times 7 \times 29$	2
B	Wide Shelf	$\frac{1}{2} \times 7 \times 31\frac{1}{2}$	2
C	Divider	$\frac{1}{2} \times 7 \times 4\frac{1}{2}$	1
D	Top Shelf	$\frac{1}{2} \times 6\frac{1}{2} \times 31\frac{1}{2}$	1
E	Back	$\frac{1}{2} \times 9\frac{1}{2} \times 31\frac{1}{2}$	1
F	Drawer Front	$\frac{1}{2} \times 4 \times 15\frac{1}{4}$	2
G	Drawer Back	$\frac{1}{2} \times 3\frac{5}{8} \times 14\frac{3}{4}$	2
H	Drawer Side	$\frac{1}{2} \times 4 \times 6\frac{5}{8}$	4
I	Drawer Bottom	$\frac{1}{8} \times 6\frac{5}{8} \times 14\frac{3}{4}$	2
J	Drawer Stop	$\frac{1}{4} \times \frac{1}{2} \times 1$	4
K	Knob	1 in. dia. porcelain	2

$\frac{1}{4} \times \frac{1}{2}$ RABBET

$\frac{1}{4} \times \frac{1}{2}$ DADO

$\frac{1}{4} \times \frac{1}{2} \times 1$ DRAWER STOPS

ALL FINISHING NAILS SET AND FILLED

$6\frac{5}{8}$

$\frac{1}{4} \times \frac{1}{2}$ RABBET

$\frac{1}{2} \times \frac{1}{4}$ RABBET

4

2

$7\frac{5}{8}$

$15\frac{1}{4}$

$\frac{1}{8}$ PLYWOOD BOTTOM

$\frac{1}{8} \times \frac{1}{4}$ GROOVE

$\frac{1}{4}$

1 SQUARE = 2"

$9\frac{1}{2}$

$5\frac{1}{2}$

$6\frac{1}{2}$

$\frac{1}{2}$ INCH STOCK

10

33

29

$15\frac{1}{4}$

4

8

32

7

43

Vanity Mirror

with Drawer

Bill of Materials
(all dimensions actual)

Part	Description	Size	No. Req'd.
A	Body	as shown	1
B	Body	as shown	1
C	Body	as shown	1
D	Drawer	as shown	1
E	Drawer Front	½ × 1 × 6	1
F	Knob	see Step 10	1
G	Drawer Bottom	as shown	1
H	Felt	as shown	1
I	Support Arm	½ × ½ × 2⅞	1
J	Arm Mount	⅞ × ⅞ × _____*	1
K	Mirror Frame	¾ × 6 × 6	1
L	Mirror	¼ thick × 5 in. dia. beveled edge**	1
M	Leg	⁵⁄₁₆ × ¾ × 3½	2
N	Foot	⅝ × ¾	1

*Arm mount height as needed to level mirror.

**Available from: Floral Glass & Mirror Co., 895 Motor Parkway, Hauppauge, NY 11788. Telephone: (800) 647-7672.

This vanity mirror, by well-known California woodworker Robert Leung, combines some basic turning work with a simple band saw box technique to create an attractive and functional dresser top vanity. Mr. Leung uses a variety of exotic woods in his work, including rosewood and andamon padauk, to lend the pieces a special look. Any hardwoods will suffice, of course, but keep in mind that a selection of interesting woods that contrast well with each other can dramatically improve the visual impact of the project. Birdseye maple with walnut accents or ash with padauk accents are but two of the combinations that work best. If you can't find them locally, a mail-order source for exotic woods is the Berea Hardwoods Co., 125 Jacqueline Drive, Berea, OH 44017.

The best place to start this project is with the body of the vanity. Take note that while our step-by-step technique shows this particular project, you can utilize the same basic technique to design any number of different band saw boxes. Create your own shapes, and make multiple stacked drawer boxes by starting out with thicker stock and including a band sawn spacer section between each drawer.

As shown in our step-by-step, we started with 1¾ in. thick stock. After band sawing and sanding, this should produce a finished drawer unit about 1½ in. thick. We recommend that you use a narrow blade (¼ in. or less) in the band saw to establish the various cuts with a minimum of waste. The index line scribed in Step 1 is important since it will insure that the grain matches up perfectly when the sections (A, B, and C) are reassembled in Step 6. If done right, the glue lines between the sections should be all but invisible. The ⅛ in. diameter by ¾ in. long dowels shown in Step 10 could be substituted with ⅛ in. brass rod, and a store-bought brass or wood ¾ in. diameter knob could be used instead of the turned knob (F) shown, if you don't have access to a lathe. The ¼ in. by ¼ in. rabbet cut in Step 11 is made with Sears' rabbeting bit no. GT25581, using their arbor set no. GT25601.

In Step 12, the felt (H) is glued onto the plywood bottom (G), then trimmed flush with the edge before the bottom is glued in place. Take care not to use too much glue when securing the felt, lest it soak through and mat the fibers down.

The mirror frame (K) can be turned on the lathe, or you may use the router and a template to cut the mirror recess and to profile an edge detail. To turn the mirror frame, start with ¾ in. by 6 in. by 6 in. stock, and use a faceplate mounting in the lathe to turn the ¼ in. deep mirror recess and edge detail (see cross section). The faceplate mounting requires that the workpiece be glued to an identically sized piece of scrapwood, with a layer of brown Kraft paper in between. This assembly is then screwed to the faceplate. An X scribed across the scrap piece will serve as a guide to center the work on the faceplate. When the turning is complete, carefully separate the scrap stock from the mirror frame stock using a mallet and chisel. The dado head can now be utilized to establish the ⅛ in. by ⅞ in. leg notches on either side, before the top profile is band sawed and disk sanded smooth. You can also use the router and a template to rout the mirror recess, although for the edge detail a simple round-over using a conventional router bit will eliminate the need to hand grind a bit to match the illustrated edge detail. Don't forget to chisel the notches in the mirror frame back before mounting the mirror glass. The 5 in. diameter bevel-edged mirror glass we used was purchased from a mail-order source (see bill of materials). Be sure to use special mirror adhesive, called mirror mastic, which can either be ordered from the

same mail-order source as the mirror, or obtained from your local glass shop. Do not use just any glue or epoxy, since the chemicals present in some adhesives can dissolve the silver on the mirror back. Final sand before mounting the mirror, as sandpaper will scratch the glass surface.

The mirror support arm (I), the arm mount (J), the legs (M), and the foot (N) should be made from the same wood as the knob (F). Make all the parts except the arm mount, then assemble the mirror. Now make the arm mount so that it will serve to hold the mirror level when the mirror is folded flat in the closed position (see side view). Note that ⅛ in. diameter brass pins serve as pivots for the mirror and the support arm. We finished the vanity with several coats of Tung oil.

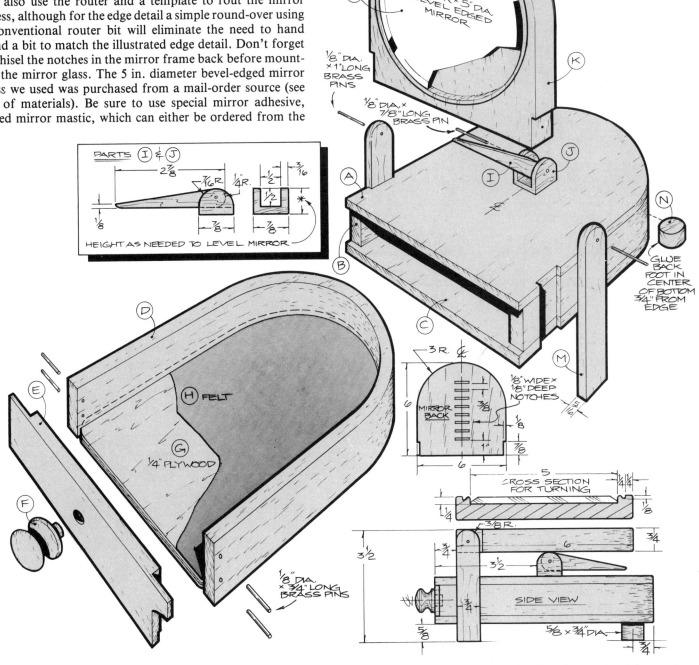

(continued on next page)

MAKING THE DRAWER

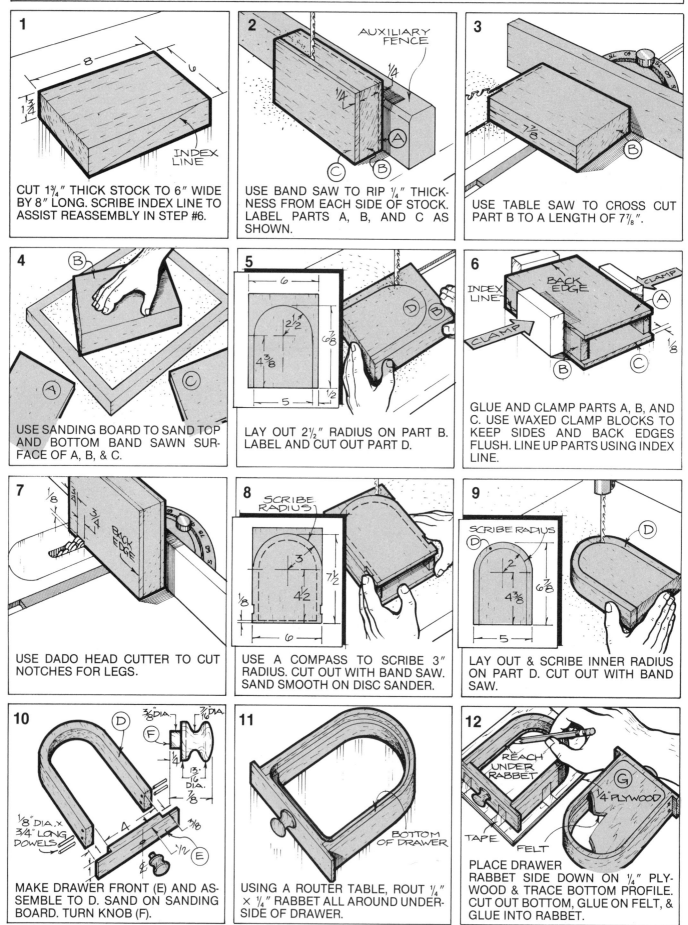

1 CUT 1¾" THICK STOCK TO 6" WIDE BY 8" LONG. SCRIBE INDEX LINE TO ASSIST REASSEMBLY IN STEP #6.

2 USE BAND SAW TO RIP ¼" THICKNESS FROM EACH SIDE OF STOCK. LABEL PARTS A, B, AND C AS SHOWN.

3 USE TABLE SAW TO CROSS CUT PART B TO A LENGTH OF 7⅞".

4 USE SANDING BOARD TO SAND TOP AND BOTTOM BAND SAWN SURFACE OF A, B, & C.

5 LAY OUT 2½" RADIUS ON PART B. LABEL AND CUT OUT PART D.

6 GLUE AND CLAMP PARTS A, B, AND C. USE WAXED CLAMP BLOCKS TO KEEP SIDES AND BACK EDGES FLUSH. LINE UP PARTS USING INDEX LINE.

7 USE DADO HEAD CUTTER TO CUT NOTCHES FOR LEGS.

8 USE A COMPASS TO SCRIBE 3" RADIUS. CUT OUT WITH BAND SAW. SAND SMOOTH ON DISC SANDER.

9 LAY OUT & SCRIBE INNER RADIUS ON PART D. CUT OUT WITH BAND SAW.

10 MAKE DRAWER FRONT (E) AND ASSEMBLE TO D. SAND ON SANDING BOARD. TURN KNOB (F).

11 USING A ROUTER TABLE, ROUT ¼" × ¼" RABBET ALL AROUND UNDERSIDE OF DRAWER.

12 PLACE DRAWER RABBET SIDE DOWN ON ¼" PLYWOOD & TRACE BOTTOM PROFILE. CUT OUT BOTTOM, GLUE ON FELT, & GLUE INTO RABBET.

46

Stacking Wine Rack

There's no better place to store wine than in a wine rack. Not only does it eliminate fumbling around in a dark cabinet to find the right bottle, but it also holds the bottles at the correct angle with the cork end low so the cork remains moist.

The design of our wine rack was intended to create a modular look; hence the stacking feature. While our photo shows three units, as many as six may be safely stacked. Take note that while the units are keyed together with dowels, the base unit should not be drilled out on the bottom edge for dowels, and the top unit should remain clear along the top edge.

We used a router and template method to create a distinctive wine glass motif on the rack ends. You may choose to substitute some other design or even leave the ends plain. Should

you decide to eliminate the routed motif, we suggest a decorative plug using an attractive contrasting wood, such as padauk.

Another aspect of this wine rack that you'll appreciate is the simplicity of its construction. Start by milling ¾ in. thick stock for the ends and stretchers. As shown in the circle cutting detail, you will need two boards measuring 6½ in. by 16¼ in. for the four stretchers in each rack. Note that two stretchers are obtained from each board. Lay out four 3½ in. diameter circles on each board, 3¾ in. on center. As shown in the detail, this layout will leave ¼ in. between the circles and ¾ in. on each end. If you don't have a 3½ in. diameter hole saw, use the fly cutter in the drill press to cut out the circles. The fly cutter will leave a fairly clean cut, but the circles will require sanding with

a drum sander mounted in the drill press.

Next, rip the stretcher board to create the two 2½ in. wide stretcher parts, and tenon the ends.

Now cut the blanks for the ends. We made a simple fixture, as shown in the routing detail, to center each of the end pieces under the template for routing the wine glass detail. The fixture consists of two pieces of ¾ in. by 3 in. stock that are glued or screwed to the underside of the plywood template, with a notched block with slotted screw holes serving as a clamp to hold the end blank tightly. This fixture, with the blank in place, is then clamped to the workbench for routing. Take note that the actual template size (the outside profile of the wine glass) will depend

(continued on next page)

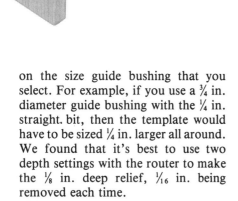

Bill of Materials
(all dimensions actual)

Part	Description	Size	No. Req'd.
A	End	$\frac{3}{4} \times 9 \times 9\frac{7}{8}$	2/Rack
B	Stretcher	$\frac{3}{4} \times 2\frac{1}{2} \times 16\frac{1}{4}$*	4/Rack

*Width after ripping; length includes tenons.

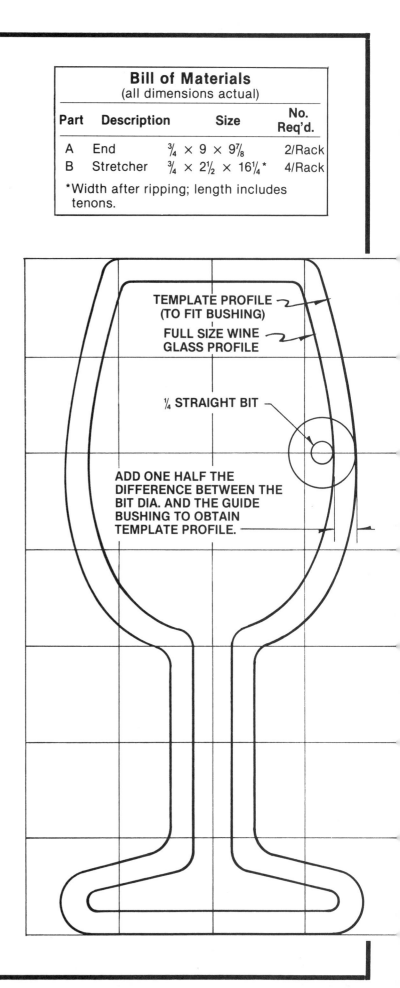

TEMPLATE PROFILE
(TO FIT BUSHING)

FULL SIZE WINE
GLASS PROFILE

¼ STRAIGHT BIT

ADD ONE HALF THE
DIFFERENCE BETWEEN THE
BIT DIA. AND THE GUIDE
BUSHING TO OBTAIN
TEMPLATE PROFILE.

on the size guide bushing that you select. For example, if you use a ¾ in. diameter guide bushing with the ¼ in. straight. bit, then the template would have to be sized ¼ in. larger all around. We found that it's best to use two depth settings with the router to make the ⅛ in. deep relief, ¹⁄₁₆ in. being removed each time.

Cut the mortises to accept the stretcher tenons, nip the end piece corners and apply a ⅛ in. chamfer all around. Also drill the ⅜ in. by ½ in. holes to accept the short lengths of dowel that key the racks together, if you plan to make more than one rack. The wine glass relief was painted using a fine brush and an acrylic paint, and then allowed to dry. Final sand all parts before gluing and assembling. A coat of Deft Spray Lacquer will complete the project.

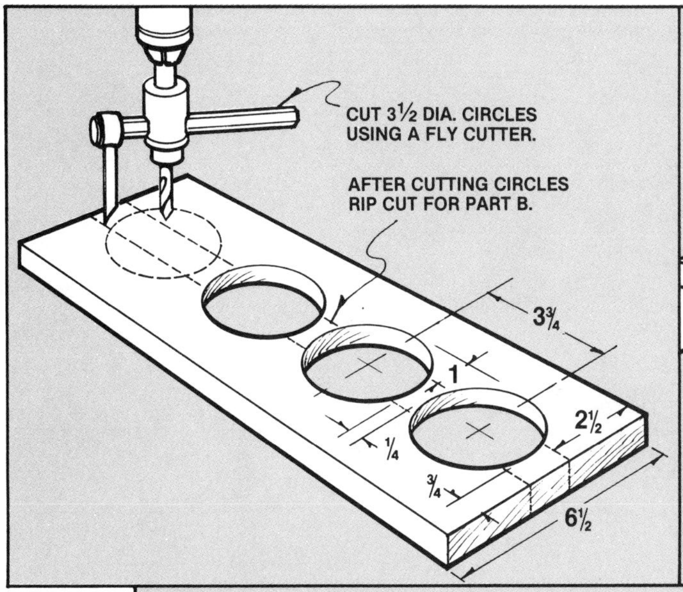
CUT 3½ DIA. CIRCLES
USING A FLY CUTTER.
AFTER CUTTING CIRCLES
RIP CUT FOR PART B.
3¾
1
2½
¼
¾
6½

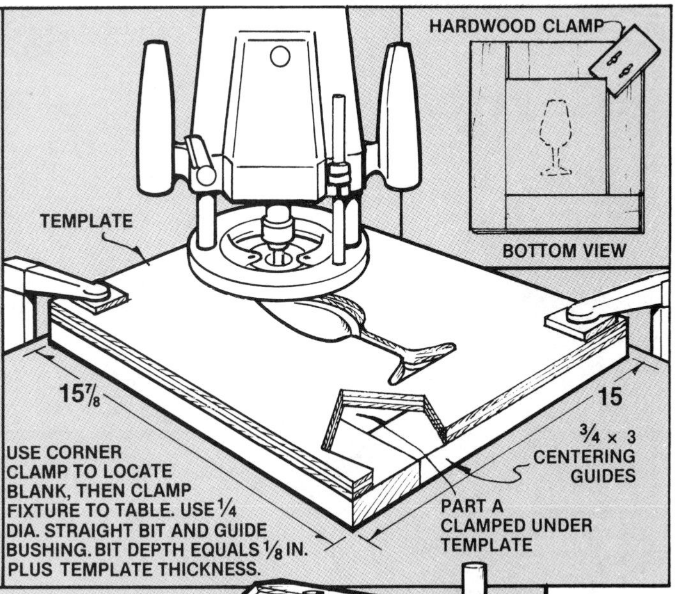
HARDWOOD CLAMP
BOTTOM VIEW
TEMPLATE
15⅞
15
¾ × 3
CENTERING
GUIDES
USE CORNER
CLAMP TO LOCATE
BLANK, THEN CLAMP
FIXTURE TO TABLE. USE ¼
DIA. STRAIGHT BIT AND GUIDE
BUSHING. BIT DEPTH EQUALS ⅛ IN.
PLUS TEMPLATE THICKNESS.
PART A
CLAMPED UNDER
TEMPLATE

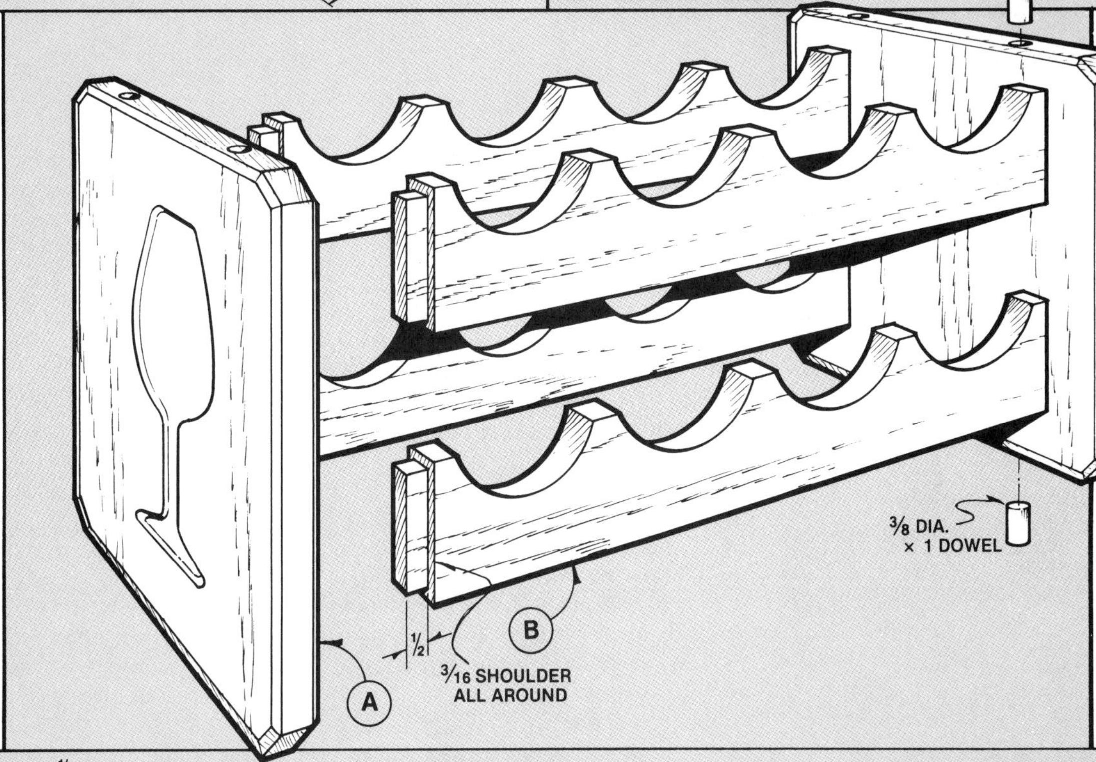
⅜ DIA.
× 1 DOWEL
B
½
3/16 SHOULDER
ALL AROUND
A

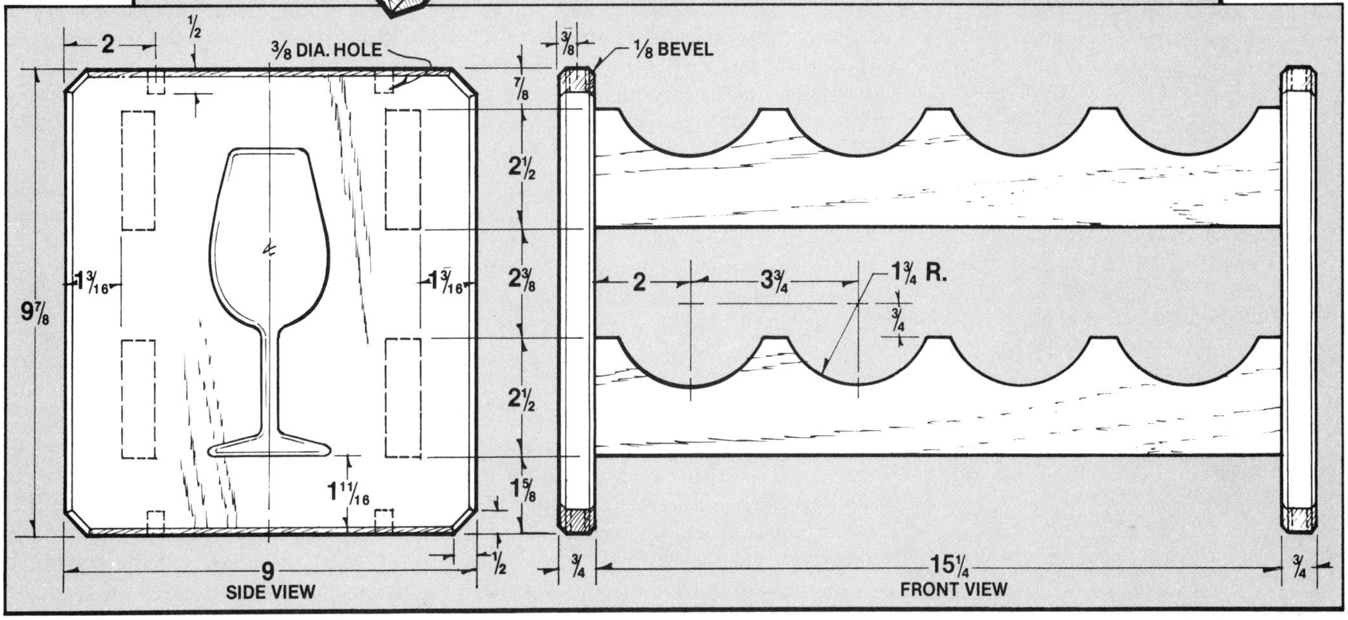
2
½
⅜ DIA. HOLE
⅜
⅛ BEVEL
⅞
2½
1 3/16
1 3/16
2⅜
9⅞
2½
1 11/16
1⅝
9
½
SIDE VIEW
2
3¾
1¾ R.
¾
¾
15¼
¾
FRONT VIEW

Kicking Donkey Whirligig

The kicking donkey is a classic whirligig design. It features a dual movement: the head is bucking while the back legs and hooves are applying an unexpected jolt to the farmer's posterior.

Bill of Materials
(all dimensions actual)

Part	Description	Size	No. Req'd.
A	Spine	¾ × 1½ × 14	1
B	Front Base	½ × 1½ × 9	1
C	Rear Base	½ × 1½ × 3	1
D	Block	5⁄16 × ½ × 1¾	1
E	Donkey Body	see grid	2
F	Donkey Head	see grid	1
G	Donkey Thigh	see grid	1
H	Donkey Leg	see grid	2
I	Farmer	see grid	1
J	Blade Arm	¾ × ¾ × 11	2
K	Blade	⅛ × 3½ × 7	4
L	Drive Shaft	3⁄16 diam. brass rod	1
M	Drive Shaft Sleeve	¼ in. diam. × 10⅞ copper tubing	1
N	Tube Sleeve	¼ in. diam. × ⅞ copper tubing	1
O	Pivot Bushing	¼ in. diam × 1 in. copper tubing	1
P	Rudder	cut from 8½ × 10 aluminum sheet	1
Q	Tail	4 in. long rope	1

Begin by making the spine (A). The ¼ × ¼ in. groove to accept the drive shaft sleeve is cut on the table saw. Next, notch the spine as shown to accept the offset section of the drive shaft rod, and use a hacksaw to kerf the spine end into which the rudder will fit. Also, drill the ¼ × 1 in. deep hole in the bottom to accept the pivot bushing. Make the two base sections (B and C), the donkey mounting block (D), and the blade arms (J). Half lap the blade arms as shown, and cut the ⅛ in. wide by 1 in. deep slots in the arm ends to accept the propeller blades.

Transfer the illustrated grid pattern to ¼ in. thick stock, then lay out and cut the various donkey parts (E, F, G, H) and the man's profile (I). The four propeller blades are cut out of ⅛ in. thick material. Since all wood parts for this project will be painted, the type of wood you select is not critical.

Now assemble the whirligig. Epoxy the blade arms together, and glue the four blades into their slots. Use either epoxy or plastic resin glue throughout the whirligig construction to insure that it will not be affected by weather. Next, drill the screw holes in the donkey (see grid for hole locations), mortise for the screw heads and nuts so they will fit flush and assemble the donkey parts. Use washers on either side of parts G and F to reduce friction and serve as spacers.

To make the drive mechanism, first offset the drive shaft (L) end with two 90 degree bends. Drill a hole as shown to accept a small cotter pin, and cut the lengths of ¼ in. copper tubing needed for parts M, N, and O. Mount the tube sleeve (N), add a washer, and insert the cotter pin to hold the washer and sleeve in place. Slide the long sleeve (M) over the drive shaft, epoxy the sleeve into the ¼ × ¼ in. spine groove, and add the front and rear bases. Mount the man to the front base with ⅛ in. dowel pins and glue, then glue the donkey to the mounting block, and the mounting block to the rear base.

Insert the screw eyes in parts F and G, add the short link wire, and then the longer connecting wire, which is fastened around the tube sleeve. It may be necessary to adjust the connecting and/or link wire length to fine tune the donkey motion. Drill through the propeller center, and epoxy the propeller onto the drive shaft end, using a washer to reduce friction between the center and drive shaft sleeve.

Cut out the sheet metal rudder, folding the top edge over to stiffen it. Epoxy the rudder and pivot bushing in place, add the rope tail (Q) on the donkey, and then paint the whirligig, following the color scheme suggested on the grid pattern.

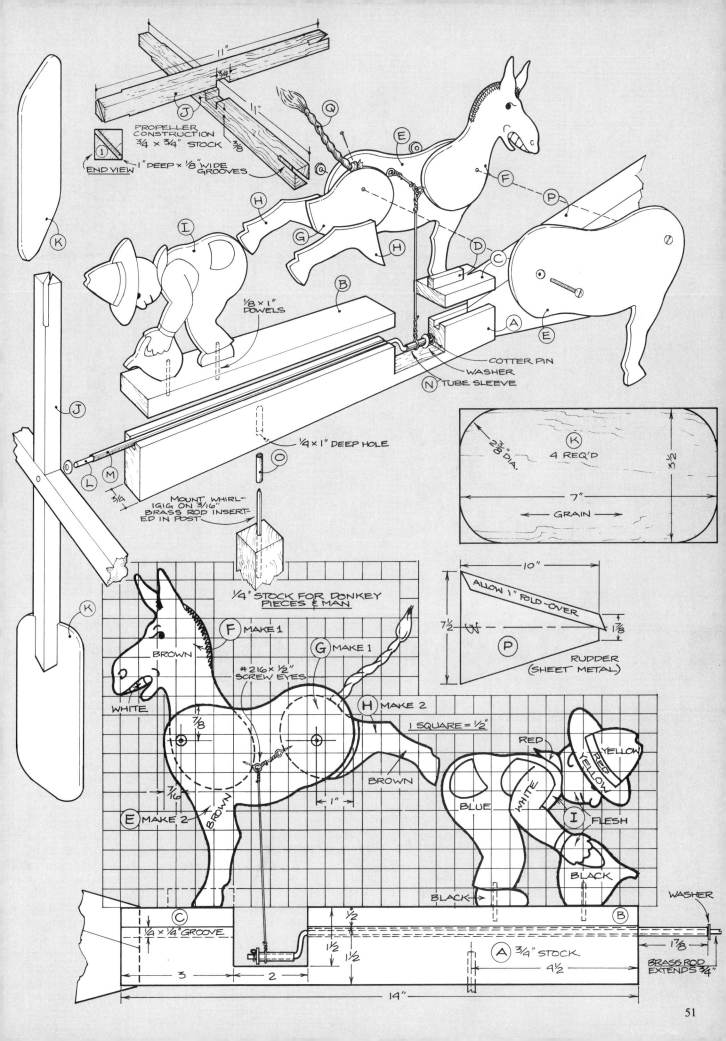

PROPELLER
CONSTRUCTION
3/4 × 3/4" STOCK   3/8

ⓙ

Ⓠ

1"

11"

3/4

11"

END VIEW   1" DEEP × 1/8" WIDE GROOVES

①

Ⓚ

Ⓔ

Ⓕ

Ⓟ

Ⓗ

①

Ⓖ

Ⓗ

Ⓓ

Ⓒ

Ⓐ

Ⓔ

Ⓑ

1/8 × 1"
DOWELS

COTTER PIN
WASHER
Ⓝ TUBE SLEEVE

ⓙ

1/4 × 1" DEEP HOLE

Ⓛ Ⓜ

3/4

Ⓞ

MOUNT WHIRL-
IGIG ON 3/16"
BRASS ROD INSERT-
ED IN POST

Ⓚ
2 3/8" DIA.   4 REQ'D   3 1/2
7"
← GRAIN →

10"
ALLOW 1" FOLD-OVER
7 1/2   1 7/8
Ⓟ   RUDDER
(SHEET METAL)

Ⓚ

1/4" STOCK FOR DONKEY
PIECES & MAN

BROWN

Ⓕ MAKE 1

Ⓖ MAKE 1

7/8

#216 × 1/2"
SCREW EYES

Ⓗ MAKE 2

1 SQUARE = 1/2"

WHITE

BROWN

RED

YELLOW
RED
YELLOW

7/16

BROWN

1"

Ⓔ MAKE 2

BLUE

WHITE

Ⓘ FLESH

BLACK

BLACK

WASHER

Ⓒ
1/4 × 1/4" GROOVE

3

2

1/2

1 1/2   1 1/2

Ⓐ 3/4" STOCK

4 1/2

Ⓑ

1 7/8

BRASS ROD
EXTENDS 3/4"

14"

51

Early American Pine Bookcase

This classic Early American style bookcase will be a handsome addition to most any room. While we used pine for a traditional look, cherry, maple or walnut would also be excellent choices.

Where possible we try to present project designs that can be constructed from commonly available board stock with a minimum of waste. In the case of this bookcase, all the parts except for the plywood back are obtained from ¾ in. thick common pine boards. The two sides (A) and the bottom shelf (B) are cut from a single ¾ in. by 9¼ in. by 10 ft. long board (1 × 10 × 10), the two middle shelves (C) are cut from a ¾ in. by 9¼ in. by 6 ft. long board (1 × 10 × 6), the top shelf and top (D and E) are cut from a ¾ in. by 7¼ in. by 6 ft. long board (1 × 8 × 6), and the

base parts (F and G) are cut from a ¾ in. by 5½ in. by 6 ft. long board (1 × 6 × 6). A ¾ in. by 3½ in. by 4 ft. long board (1 × 4 × 4) will provide sufficient stock for the base molding (H) and cleat (I). The router equipped with a ¼ in. radius Roman ogee bit can be used to create the base molding, but if you don't have the necessary ogee profile bit, a similar ¾ in. molding can be purchased at your local lumberyard.

The two-step illustration indicates the procedure for cutting the ogee molding. Start by mounting the ogee bit in the router table, setting the bit height as shown so the ball bearing guide will gauge off the stock. Now take the 3½ in. wide (1 ×4) pine board and establish the ogee on either side. One side will provide the front section of ogee molding, while the other side

will provide the two side sections. As with all router cuts where you are removing a substantial amount of stock, you will need to make the cut in several passes. If you attempt to establish the full depth in a single pass, the router will bog down and the cut will be rough. Additionally, you will probably burn or ruin the bit.

Next, move the stock to the table saw, set the fence for a ⅝ in. distance, and pass the stock through using a push stick. Use an extra wide push stick, and bear tight against the fence. The saw blade will cut through the end of the push stick. Note that the blade height is about ⅞ in.

The stopped dadoes in the sides to accept parts C and D, the through dado to accept part B, and the rabbet along the back inside edge of the sides

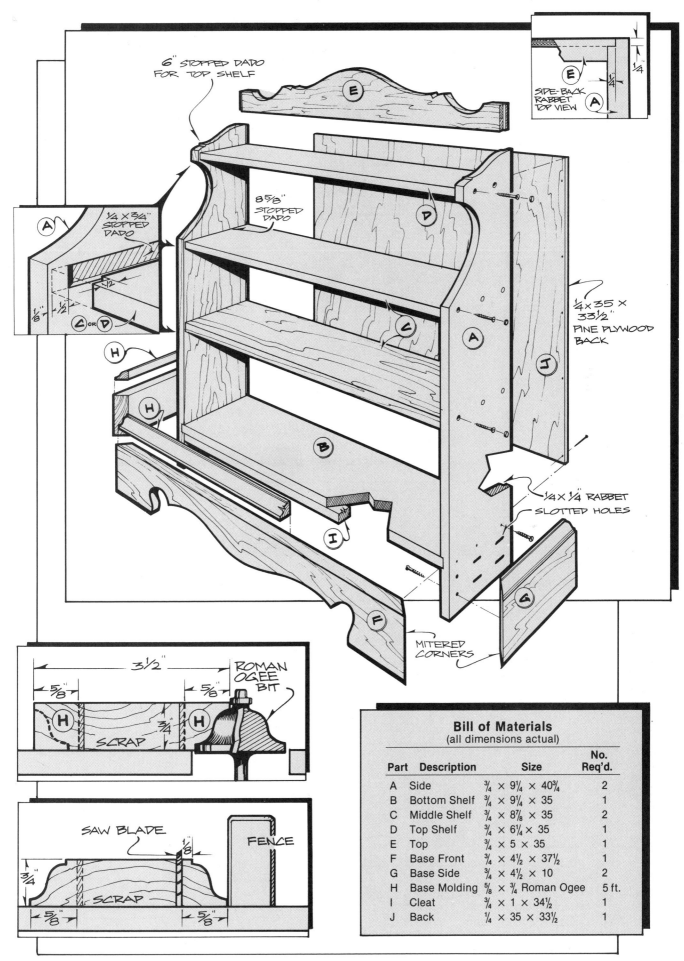

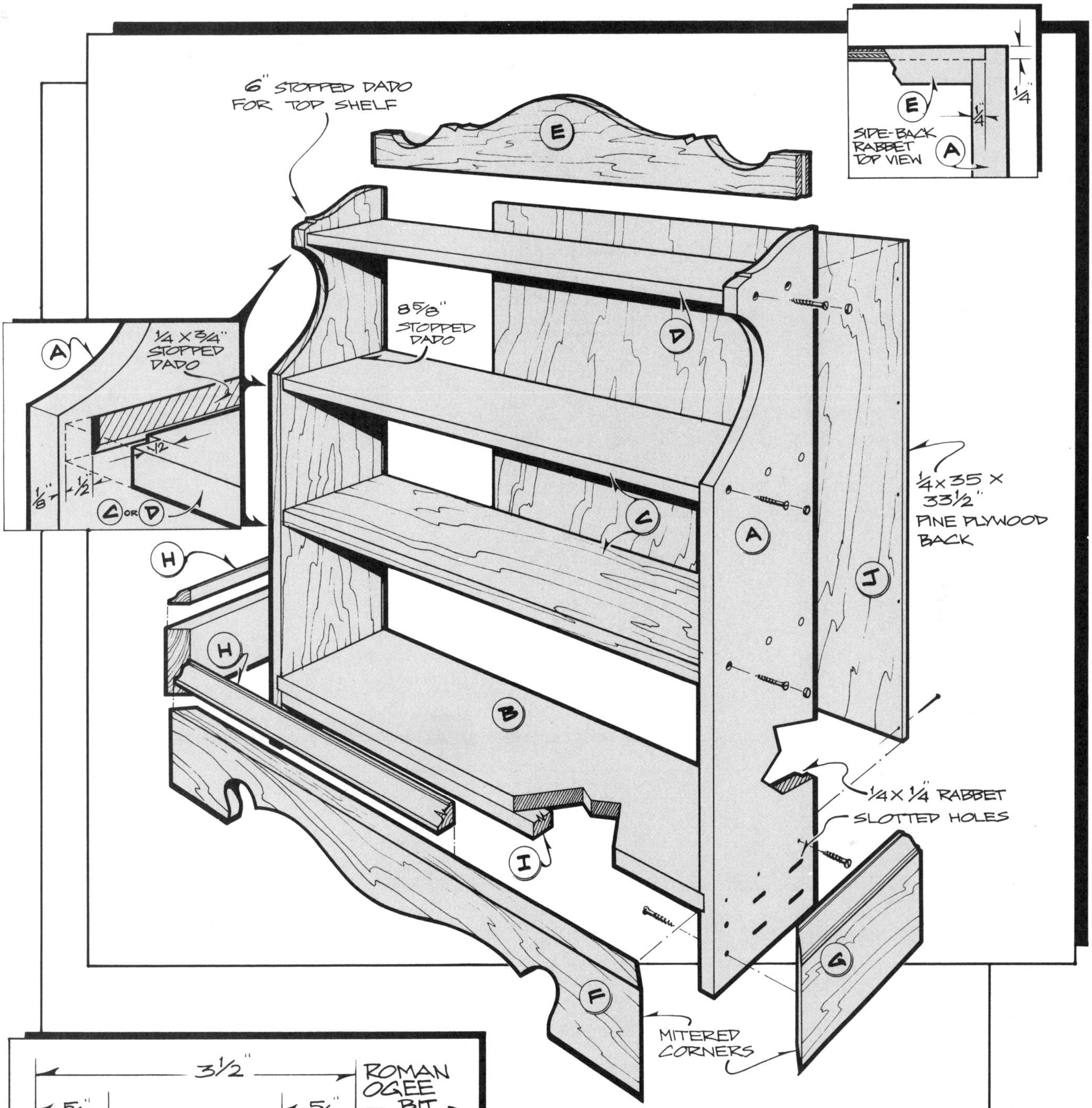
6" STOPPED DADO FOR TOP SHELF
E
1/4
1/4
SIDE-BACK RABBET TOP VIEW
A
A
1/4 X 3/4" STOPPED DADO
1/2
1/8"
1/2
C OR D
8 5/8" STOPPED DADO
D
C
A
J
1/4 x 35 x 33 1/2" PINE PLYWOOD BACK
H
H
B
I
F
G
1/4 X 1/4" RABBET
SLOTTED HOLES
MITERED CORNERS

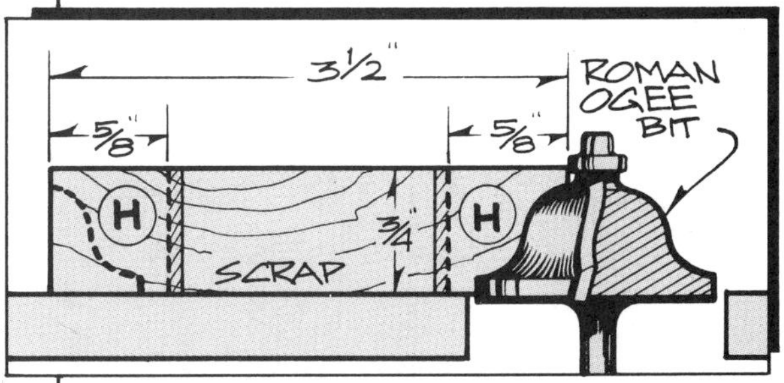
3 1/2"
5/8"
5/8"
ROMAN OGEE BIT
H
H
3/4"
SCRAP

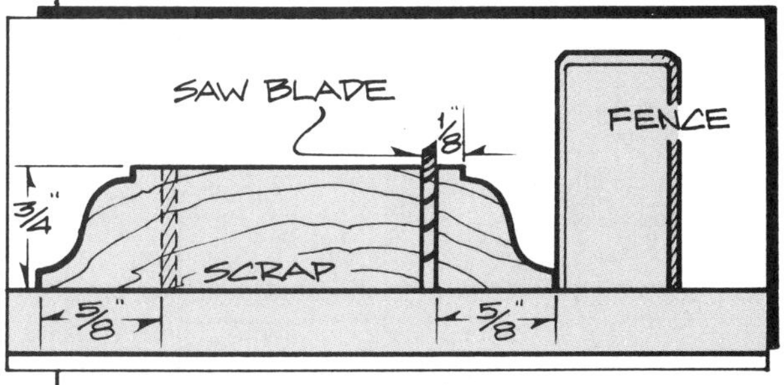
SAW BLADE
1/8"
FENCE
3/4"
SCRAP
5/8"
5/8"

Bill of Materials
(all dimensions actual)

Part	Description	Size	No. Req'd.
A	Side	3/4 × 9 1/4 × 40 3/4	2
B	Bottom Shelf	3/4 × 9 1/4 × 35	1
C	Middle Shelf	3/4 × 8 7/8 × 35	2
D	Top Shelf	3/4 × 6 1/4 × 35	1
E	Top	3/4 × 5 × 35	1
F	Base Front	3/4 × 4 1/2 × 37 1/2	1
G	Base Side	3/4 × 4 1/2 × 10	2
H	Base Molding	5/8 × 3/4 Roman Ogee	5 ft.
I	Cleat	3/4 × 1 × 34 1/2	1
J	Back	1/4 × 35 × 33 1/2	1

(continued on next page)

to accept the top (E) and back (J) are all cut *before* the side profile is laid out and cut.

We made a simple jig (see illustration) to guide the router for these stopped dadoes. The jig is made oversize so it will accomplish the dado cuts needed for this project, and so that it may also be used for any project that requires stopped dadoes up to 12 in. long. Note that the distance the fence is positioned from the dado slot will depend on the size of your router. Mark an index line to denote the end of the stopped dadoes. As noted on the exploded view, the stopped dado for the top shelf is 6 in. long, while the stopped dadoes for the middle shelves are $8\frac{5}{8}$ in. long. Both these lengths are from the back edge of the shelf, before the rabbet for the back is cut.

Notch the shelves as shown in the detail to fit the stopped side dadoes (note that shelves C and D are inset $\frac{1}{8}$ in. from the front edge of the sides). Rabbet the ends of the top, and now lay out the profiles of the top and sides as shown in the grid patterns, before cutting out with either a saber or band saw. Next, assemble parts A, B, C, D, and E. Cut the $\frac{1}{4}$ in. thick plywood

back (J) to fit, and use countersunk and plugged screws as illustrated to lock everything together. If the plywood back is cut accurately, it will serve to square up the bookcase during assembly.

Next, apply the cleat (I) which serves to back up the base front. The base front (F) and base sides (G) should be mitered and test-fitted before the base profile is laid out and cut. Note that slotted holes are drilled through the sides to allow for movement across the grain. While the base front is glued in place, the base sides are glued at the miter, but screwed through the sides as shown. The slotted holes will allow the sides to expand and contract with seasonal changes in humidity.

Cut and fit the base molding (H) before final sanding and finishing. Use glue and finishing nails to join the front section of base molding. For the two side sections, however, only use finishing nails so that the sides can expand and contract. Our favorite stains for pine are Minwax Colonial Maple and Fruitwood, both of which produce an excellent tone on pine. If you use a hardwood, use only a good penetrating oil.

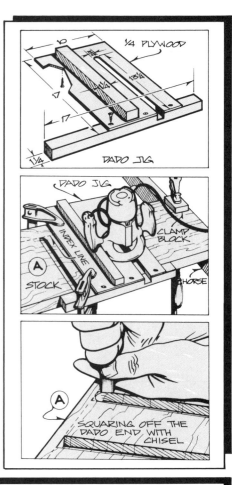

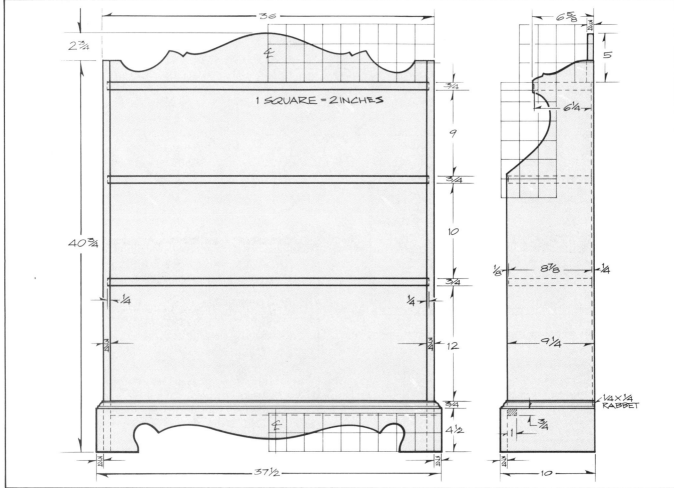

Riding Biplane

Young aviators are sure to enjoy "flying" around the house in this sturdy scaled-down version of a World War I biplane. The seat can be adjusted to any one of three positions to accommodate kids of various sizes. It's made entirely from 2 x 8 and 2 x 10 pine, which is readily available at lumberyards and home building centers. We've included a cutting diagram that shows how to obtain the stock with a minimum of waste. Keep in mind, though, that a 2 x 8 will actually measure $1\frac{1}{2}$ x $7\frac{1}{4}$, while a 2 x 10 measures $1\frac{1}{2}$ x $9\frac{1}{4}$.

The two fuselage halves (A) can be made first. Cut the 2 x 10 stock to 30 in. lengths, then transfer the grid pattern to one of the halves. Use a band or saber saw to cut out the profile, staying slightly on the waste side of the stock. Once cut out, sand the edges smooth. Use care when laying out the angled bottom edge as this establishes the angle of the lower wing (C) relative to the upper wing (B). The angles of the two drill block guides, which are used later on to drill the strut (H) holes, were calculated based on the lower

wing angled as shown. Next, using the cut-out fuselage half as a template, transfer the profile to the other half, then once again cut out and sand.

The front (D) is made by simply cross-cutting the 2 x 10 stock to $2\frac{3}{4}$. It will be trimmed later on after assembly.

To make the tail (E), cross-cut the 2 x 8 stock to a 10 in. length before transferring the grid pattern shown in the tail detail drawing. Cut out and sand smooth.

The fuselage halves can now be assembled to the front and tail. First dry assemble the three parts using clamps to hold everything together. The front edge of the front should be flush with the front edge of the fuselage halves. The top and bottom edges of the front can extend just beyond the top and bottom of the fuselages. Now orient the tail as shown in the side view, then use a pencil to scribe the fuselage profile on the tail. Once marked, the clamps can be removed and the parts disassembled.

Apply a thin coat of white or yellow glue to the mating surfaces of the three

parts (use the pencil line on the tail as a guide for the glue area), then firmly clamp each joint. Set aside to dry thoroughly.

When dry, remove the clamps and hand plane the top and bottom edges of the front (D) so that it is flush with the fuselage. Also, lay out and mark the location of the three $\frac{3}{4}$ in. diameter holes that are bored through the sides of the fuselage to accept the seat pin (I). The holes should be square, so use care when drilling. If you have one, a drill press will come in handy here. Before drilling, it's a good idea to temporarily insert a piece of scrap stock between the fuselage halves to serve as a backup block. This block will prevent tear-out at the point the drill bit breaks through the first fuselage half. Note that the holes are bored completely through both halves, so you'll also need a backup block where the drill exits the second fuselage.

To make the upper wing (B) and the lower wing (C), cut stock (see cutting diagram) to the dimensions shown in

(continued on next page)

the bill of materials.

Next, lay out and mark the center points of the strut holes (see hole layout detail) and label the reference lines "AA" and "BB" as shown. Note that the holes will be drilled on the bottom side of the upper wing and on the top side of the lower wing.

To drill the strut holes, you'll need two drill guide blocks — one angled at 16 degrees and a second angled at 21 degrees (see drawing). To make the 16-degree block, cut stock to 1¾ in. thick by 2¼ in. wide by 5 in. long. Starting at a point 1 in. from one end, scribe the 16-degree angle as shown, then band saw just outside the marked line. Use the disk sander or hand plane to smooth the cut to the line. The clamp notch can also be cut on the band saw.

At a point 1¾ in. from the top face of the block, scribe a guide line across the block's angled face. Carry this line around the remaining three faces as shown. On the bottom, scribe a center line, then carry this line around to the front and back edges.

Now flip the block so that the bottom faces up, then use a 1¼ in. diameter Forstner bit to bore a hole completely through. The intersection of the two marked lines will serve as the center point for the drill. The 21-degree drill block is made in the same manner; just make the dimensional changes shown in the drawing.

To drill the holes, locate the clamp blocks as shown in the drawing detail. The center line of the block must line up with "AA" while the wrap-around guideline must line up with "BB".

Make sure the front of the block is facing in the direction shown. Clamp the block firmly in place at two points, then use an electric hand drill with a 1¼ in. diameter Forstner bit to bore a ¾ in. deep hole. Once the holes are bored, lay out the various wing curves, then cut them out and sand smooth. A disk sander will come in handy here for smoothing the outside curves.

The lower wing can now be joined to the fuselage with glue and four 1¾ in. long by no. 10 flathead wood screws. The underside of the wing is counterbored to a depth of ¾ in. to accept the screws.

To establish the strut (H) length, temporarily clamp the upper wing in place, then use a string to measure the distance — bottom to bottom — between the holes. The two struts can be

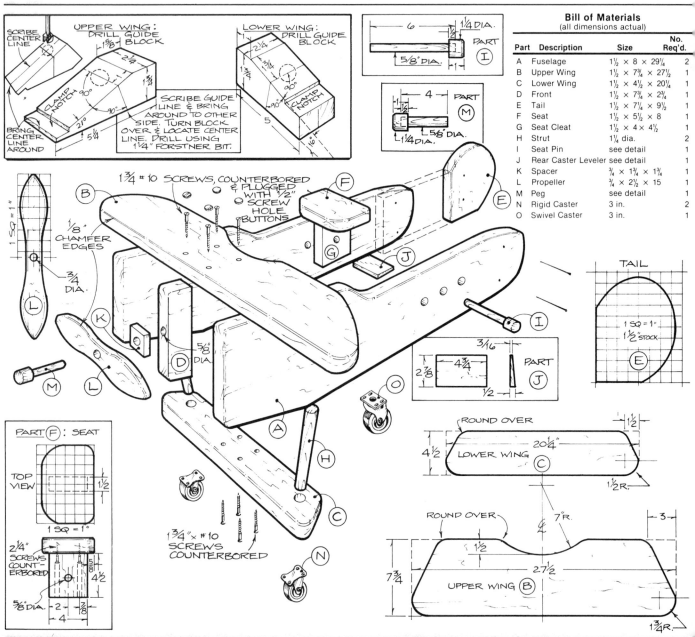

Part	Description	Size	No. Req'd.
A	Fuselage	1½ × 8 × 29¼	2
B	Upper Wing	1½ × 7¾ × 27½	1
C	Lower Wing	1½ × 4½ × 20¼	1
D	Front	1½ × 7¾ × 2¾	1
E	Tail	1½ × 7¼ × 9½	1
F	Seat	1½ × 5½ × 8	1
G	Seat Cleat	1½ × 4 × 4½	1
H	Strut	1¼ dia.	2
I	Seat Pin	see detail	1
J	Rear Caster Leveler	see detail	1
K	Spacer	¾ × 1¾ × 1¾	1
L	Propeller	¾ × 2½ × 15	1
M	Peg	see detail	1
N	Rigid Caster	3 in.	2
O	Swivel Caster	3 in.	1

cut from 1¼ in. diameter dowel stock or closet pole.

With the struts now cut to length, the upper wing can be assembled as shown. The top of the wing is counterbored to a depth of ¾ in. to accept four 1¾ in. long by no. 10 flathead wood screws. Apply glue to the ends of the struts and to their mating holes. Also add glue to the mating surfaces of the wing and fuselage, then add the screws. Four screw hole buttons will serve to cover the counterbored holes.

The seat (F) and seat cleat (G) are made next. Round the seat corners as shown in the grid pattern, then screw the seat cleat in place (see detail). Counterbore two holes to a depth of 3½ in. and use 1¾ in. long by no. 10 flathead wood screws. Once assembled, place the seat and seat cleat

assembly in position on the biplane, then use one of the already bored fuselage holes as a guide to bore a matching hole through the seat cleat. The seat pin (I) serves to lock the adjustable seat in place. It can be lathe-turned to the dimensions shown or made from ⅝ and 1¼ in. diameter dowel stock.

The spacer (K) can now be cut to size and glued to the front of parts A and D. Four finishing nails will help secure it in place. A ⅝ in. diameter by 2¾ in. deep hole can now be bored to accept the peg (M). Like the seat pin, the peg can be lathe-turned or made from two pieces of dowel stock.

Make the propeller (L) from ¾ in. thick stock. Use the grid pattern to establish the curved shape before cutting out and sanding. A ¾ in diameter

hole at the center will allow it to spin easily on the peg. Assemble the propeller to the peg, then glue the peg in the peg hole.

The rear caster leveler (J) is now cut and hand planed to the dimensions shown on the drawing. It's joined to the underside of the fuselage with glue and finishing nails.

The two rigid casters (N) and the swivel caster (O) can now be secured with roundhead wood screws. If not available locally, they can be ordered from C & H Distributors, Inc., 400 South 5th Street, Milwaukee, WI 53204. For part N, order part no. 71-191/ID; for part O, order part no. 71-188/7A.

Final sand all parts, then final finish with two coats of a good quality penetrating oil.

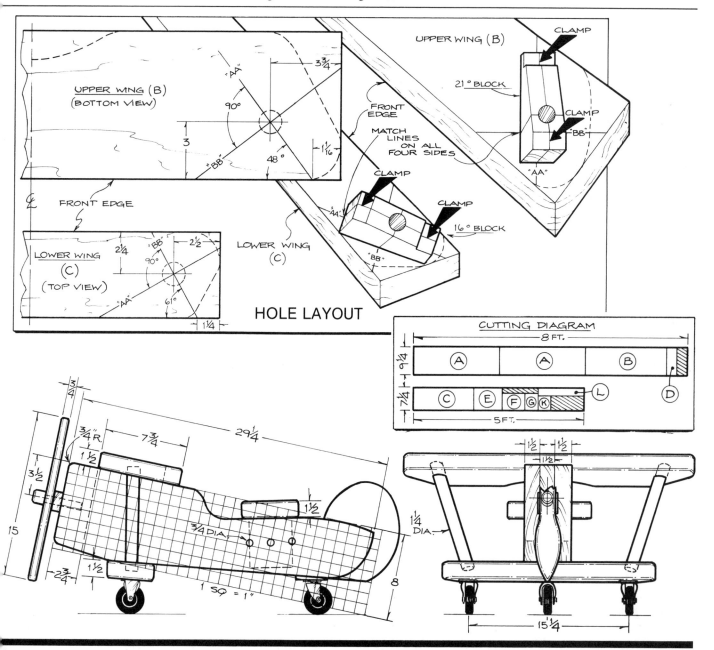

Shaker Side Table

Bill of Materials
(all dimensions actual)

Part	Description	Size	No. Req'd.
A	Long Foot	1⅝ x 6⅜ x 17½	2
B	Short Foot	1⅝ x 6⅜ x 9	2
C	Leg	1¾ x 2¾ x 23⅝	1
D	Lower Cleat	1½ x 1¼ x 11½	2
E	Upper Cleat	⅝ x 3 x 14½	2
F	Top	¾ x 21¼ x 50¾	1

This tripod side table, from the collection at Hancock Shaker Village, is an unusual and exceptionally fine piece. The table features a uniquely designed tripod which is mounted to the tapered legs with a special locking dovetail joint. Although at first glance this joint appears complicated, it is actually fairly easy to make. The rest of the table requires no special tools or skills.

In the original table, the legs and feet are maple while the top is pine. The Shakers used a single wide pine board for the top. Unless you have access to very wide stock, you will need to glue up material to achieve the necessary width. Although the Shakers preferred cherry, maple, or pine, this table would also look good in walnut or oak.

The logical place to start is the top (F). Cut, joint, glue, and clamp the stock required for the total 21¼ in. width, and set the top aside to dry. Cut the 1⅝ in. thick by 6⅜ in. wide stock for the feet (A and B) next. Lay out a one in. grid pattern as shown, and transfer the profile of the feet. As a shortcut here, make one of part B, and then use it as a template to mark the profiles of the remaining feet. After bandsawing the feet shape, round their upper edges. Then rough out the

tapered legs (C). First, cut these tapers with the band saw, and then plane them smooth.

Now fashion the special dovetail joint that locks the feet and legs together. Refer to the illustration (leg detail, bottom view) for these joint dimensions. The ¾ in. deep dovetail mortise in parts A is made by using a backsaw to establish the sides and cleaning out the waste with a large chisel. Next, cut the dovetail pin on parts B. The tricky part is making the locking tails and mortise on the lower end of each leg. A good way to approach this is to first cut a full dovetail pin on part C that will fit snugly into the dovetail mortise in part A. Then use the dovetail pin on part B to scribe for the dovetail slot in the center of the part C dovetail pin. The detail photo of the leg should help you visualize the part C locking dovetail pin. Cut the tenon on the top end of each leg, and apply a ¼ in. wide 45 degree chamfer to the leg edges as illustrated.

Now make the lower and upper cleats (D and E). Taper the ends and chamfer the edges of the lower cleats as shown, and mortise them to accept the ¾ × ⅝ × 2 in. long tenons on the leg ends. Glue and assemble the tripod feet to the legs, and glue the lower cleats in

Leg section of the locking dovetail joint.

place, locking them with ³⁄₁₆ in. diameter dowel pins. Drill four slotted holes through each upper cleat as indicated, and fasten the upper cleats to the top using round head screws and washers. The lower cleat/leg/foot assemblies are then screwed but not glued to the upper cleats and top. Counterbore and countersink these four screws.

The table will look best finished with a penetrating oil such as Watco. If you intend the table for daily use, however, use polyurethane on the top, coating both sides for stability.

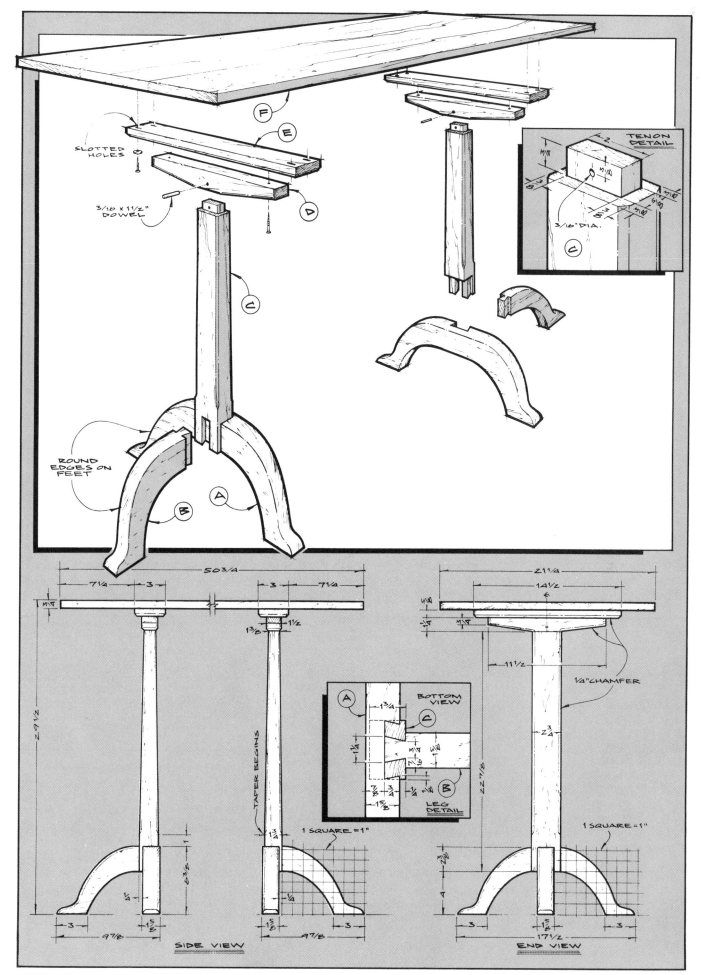

SLOTTED HOLES

F

E

3/16 x 1 1/2" DOWEL

A

TENON DETAIL

1/2

3/16

3/8

3/16 DIA.

3/16

5/16

C

C

ROUND EDGES ON FEET

B

A

503/4

7 1/4 — 3 — 3 — 7 1/4

1 3/8 — 1 1/2

29 1/2

TAPER BEGINS

1 3/4

1 3/4

6 3/4

1

1/4

3 — 1 5/8 — 9 7/8

1 5/8 — 9 7/8 — 3

SIDE VIEW

BOTTOM VIEW

A

C

1 3/4

1 1/4

3/16 1 3/4

7/8 3/4 1/4

1 5/8

B

1 SQUARE = 1"

LEG DETAIL

21 1/4

14 1/2

5/8

1/4

3/16

11 1/2

1/4"CHAMFER

2 3/4

22 7/8

2 3/8

4

3 — 1 5/8 — 3

17 1/2

1 SQUARE = 1"

END VIEW

59

Coffee Mill

Connoisseurs tell us that a really great cup of coffee starts with freshly ground beans. Our project, made from maple, is a reproduction of an antique hand-cranked coffee mill, one that doesn't just look good, but also works quite effectively.

The mill mechanism (I) is available from Woodcraft, 210 Wood County Industrial Park, P.O. Box 1686, Parkersburg, WV 26102; tel. 1-800-225-1153. Order part no. 07V41. An adjustment knob at the top allows the size of the grounds to be varied from very fine to coarse. When the coffee is ground to the right size, we found it works very nicely in all coffee makers, including the drip type that most everybody seems to have these days.

You'll need ½ in. thick stock to make the four sides (A). If you don't

have a thickness planer and can't get ½ in. thick stock locally, check with a lumberyard or millwork shop as they will often plane thicker stock for a nominal charge.

After thickness planing, cut the stock to a width of 4½ in. and a length of 5¼ in. Make sure all cuts are square. The box joints (also called finger joints) can be cut individually, either by using the dado head cutter or by making repeated passes with the regular saw blade. These joints can also be cut using a box joint jig on the table saw.

Dry assemble the four sides and check for proper fit-up of the joints. If satisfied, apply a thin coat of glue to all the mating surfaces, then assemble and clamp firmly.

When dry, remove the clamps, then

use the table saw to cut the ½ in. by 1½ in. notch on the front to accept the drawer front (D). To make the notch you'll need to make two passes, the first one with the blade set to a height

Bill of Materials
(all dimensions actual)

Part	Description	Size	No. Req'd.
A	Side	½ × 4½ × 5¼	4
B	Base	¾ × 6½ × 6½	1
C	Cover Strip	½ × ⅝ × 4¼	4
D	Drawer Front	½ × 1½ × 5¼	1
E	Drawer End	¼ × 1½ × 4	2
F	Drawer Side	¼ × 1½ × 4¼	2
G	Drawer Bottom	⅛ × 4 × 4	1
H	Drawer Knob	¾ diameter	1
I	Mill	6 × 6	1

of 1½ in., the second — at right angles to the first — with the blade set to a height of ½ in.

The base (B) can now be made. Cut ¾ in. thick stock to 6½ in. square, then use the router table with a ¼ in. Roman ogee bit to shape the molding all around (see Side View: Base). Center the four-sided box on the base then join the two members by driving four 1¼ in. long by no. 6 flathead woodscrews up through the base and into the bottom edges of the box.

You'll need to resaw thicker stock to get the ¼ in. material needed for the drawer ends (E) and sides (F). The ⅛ in. deep by ¼ in. wide rabbet on each end can be cut by setting the table saw blade to a depth of ⅛ in. and using the miter gauge to pass the stock over the blade. Two or three passes will be needed to get the ¼ in. width. To cut the ⅛ in. wide by ⅛ in. deep groove for the drawer bottom (G), locate the rip fence ⅛ in. from the sawtooth and, with the blade still set to a height of ⅛ in., pass the stock over the blade. To keep hands a safe distance from the blade, be sure to use a push stick.

After cutting the drawer bottom to size from ⅛ in. thick hardboard (Masonite), the drawer ends, sides and the drawer bottom can be assembled. Use glue and clamp firmly. When dry, remove the clamps and drill pilot holes at each rabbet joint for ½ in. long brads.

Cut the drawer front to fit the opening created by the notch that was previously cut in the front of the box, then glue and clamp it to the front drawer end.

The cover strips (C) serve to keep the coffee grounds from settling on the top edges of the box ends and sides. We've used mills that don't have them and found that when the drawer is opened, the coffee on the top edges spills all over. Cut the strips to the profile shown in the cross-section, then miter the corners and glue in place.

After final sanding, we applied two coats of Behlen's Salad Bowl Finish, a low-luster finish that contains ingredients approved by the U.S. Food and Drug Administration for use in contact with food. Woodcraft sells it (part no. 08N65).

The mill (I) is joined to the box with a pair of screws, one on each side. A porcelain knob (H) added to the drawer front completes the project.

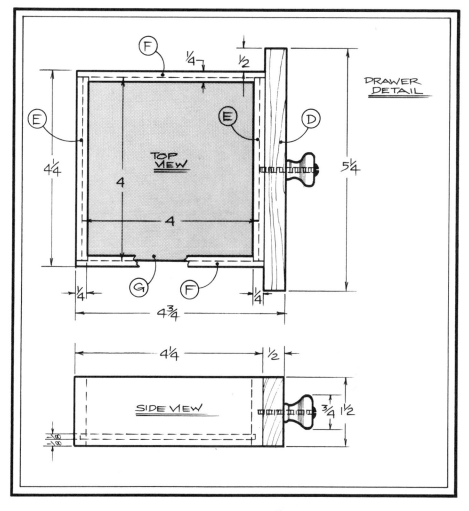

DRAWER DETAIL

TOP VIEW

SIDE VIEW

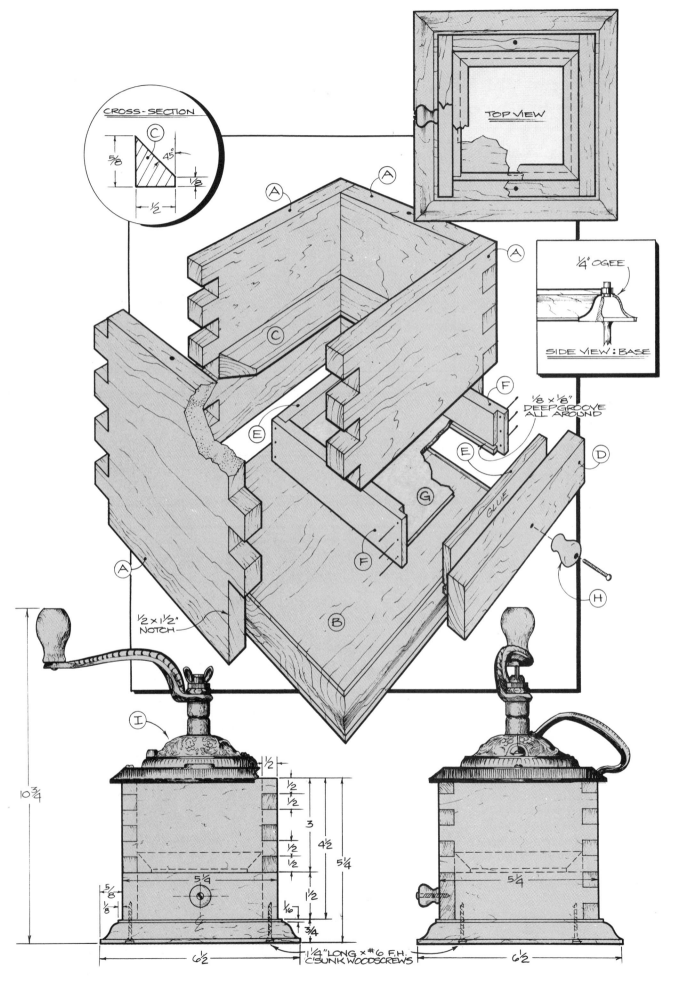

CROSS-SECTION

⑤⁄₈   45°   ¹⁄₈

¹⁄₂

Ⓒ

TOP VIEW

¹⁄₄" OGEE

SIDE VIEW: BASE

Ⓐ   Ⓐ

Ⓐ

Ⓒ

Ⓕ

¹⁄₈ x ¹⁄₈"
DEEP GROOVE
ALL AROUND

Ⓔ   Ⓔ

Ⓖ

GLUE   Ⓓ

Ⓐ   Ⓕ

Ⓗ

¹⁄₂ x 1¹⁄₂"
NOTCH

Ⓑ

Ⓘ

10³⁄₄

¹⁄₂
¹⁄₂
¹⁄₂
3
¹⁄₂
¹⁄₂
4¹⁄₂
5¹⁄₄

5¹⁄₄

1¹⁄₂

⁵⁄₈
⁵⁄₈
¹⁄₈

¹⁄₁₆

³⁄₄

6¹⁄₂   1¹⁄₄"LONG x #6 F.H.
C'SUNK WOODSCREWS

5¹⁄₄

6¹⁄₂

62

Desktop Dictionary Stand

Keep your favorite dictionary close at hand with this handsome stand. We used walnut for ours, but cherry, mahogany, or oak would also be good choices.

The front (A) and back (C) can be made first. Cut $\frac{3}{4}$ in. stock to a width of $4\frac{3}{4}$ in. and a length of about 14 in., then use the table saw to cut the $\frac{1}{8}$ in. wide by $\frac{3}{8}$ in. deep spline groove along the center of both edges. Most saw blades make a $\frac{1}{8}$ in. wide cut, so just one pass should be needed. If your saw blade makes a slightly wider or narrower cut, simply adjust the spline thickness as needed.

Once the spline grooves have been cut, set the table saw blade to make a 40 degree miter (see side view), then cut the front to an overall length of $4\frac{1}{8}$ in. The back is then cut to an $8\frac{3}{4}$ in. overall length.

To make the two sides (B), cut a piece of $\frac{3}{4}$ in. thick stock to a width of $6\frac{1}{4}$ in. and a length of about $18\frac{1}{2}$ in. With the table saw blade set to make a $\frac{3}{8}$ in. deep cut, locate the rip fence $\frac{5}{16}$ in. from the blade. One pass should be all that's needed to make each groove. As mentioned earlier, if your saw blade makes a cut that's slightly wider or narrower than $\frac{1}{8}$ in., you'll have to adjust the $\frac{5}{16}$ in. dimension accordingly.

Now that the spline grooves have been cut in both sides, crosscut the stock into two $9\frac{1}{4}$ in. lengths. Set the miter gauge to make a 40 degree cut (see side view), then cut the miter on each end. Next, set the miter gauge to make a 90 degree cut and trim the end opposite the miter to establish the $8\frac{3}{4}$ in. length.

Make the two cleats (D), boring the four screw holes as shown, then glue and screw to the front and back. The front, back, sides, and cleats can now be assembled. Rip the $\frac{1}{8}$ in. thick splines from $\frac{3}{4}$ in. thick stock. Make them a bit longer than necessary so they can be trimmed flush after assembly. Apply glue to the four splines and their respective grooves, then assemble and clamp. Check for squareness and make sure all edges are flush before setting aside to dry.

The bottom (E) is made from $\frac{1}{2}$ in. thick stock cut to $7\frac{1}{4}$ in. square. We used the router table equipped with a $\frac{1}{4}$ in. cove cutter to cut the cove as shown in the front view detail. The base (F) is made from $\frac{3}{4}$ in. thick stock that's cut $9\frac{1}{2}$ in. wide by $10\frac{1}{2}$ in. long. A $\frac{1}{4}$ in. Roman ogee bit is used to cut the molding on all four edges. The bottom and base can now be glued and clamped together as shown. Before gluing though, it's a good idea to drive a couple small brads into one of the mating surfaces, then snip the heads off so about $\frac{1}{16}$ in. protrudes. The brads will keep the two parts from sliding when clamp pressure is applied.

To make the shelf (G), cut $\frac{3}{4}$ in. stock to 13 in. wide by 19 in. long, then add the $\frac{1}{4}$ in. Roman ogee molding to all four edges. Next, cut the lip (H) to size and join it to the shelf with glue

and three $\frac{1}{8}$ in. diameter by $\frac{3}{4}$ in. dowels. Be sure to add the $\frac{3}{4}$ in. radius to each end of the lip before assembly.

All parts can now be final sanded. Take particular care to thoroughly sand the molded edges, especially the end-grain surfaces.

The shelf can now be joined to the subassembly consisting of parts A, B,

C, and D. A pair of screws driven up through the cleats and into the shelf serve to hold the shelf in place. Four flathead screws driven up through parts E and F and into the bottom ends of parts A and C will complete assembly of the project.

For a final finish we sprayed on three coats of Deft's Semi-Gloss Clear Wood Finish. One of our favorite finishes, it comes in a 13 ounce can, a convenient size for spraying small projects. Each coat takes only about 30 minutes to dry, so in $1\frac{1}{2}$ - 2 hours you'll have the three finish coats on your project. When the final coat is dry, rub down the entire project with 0000 steel wool. To complete the finish, blow or wipe off any remaining steel wool particles, then apply a very thin coat of paste (Butcher's) wax.

Bill of Materials
(all dimensions actual)

Part	Description	Size	No. Req'd.
A	Front	$\frac{3}{4} \times 4\frac{3}{4} \times 4\frac{1}{8}$	1
B	Side	$\frac{3}{4} \times 6\frac{1}{4} \times 8\frac{3}{4}$	2
C	Back	$\frac{3}{4} \times 4\frac{3}{4} \times 8\frac{3}{4}$	1
D	Cleat	$\frac{3}{4} \times 1\frac{3}{4} \times 4\frac{1}{2}$	2
E	Bottom	$\frac{1}{2} \times 7\frac{1}{4} \times 7\frac{1}{4}$	1
F	Base	$\frac{3}{4} \times 9\frac{1}{2} \times 10\frac{1}{2}$	1
G	Shelf	$\frac{3}{4} \times 13 \times 19$	1
H	Lip	$\frac{3}{8} \times \frac{3}{4} \times 14$	1

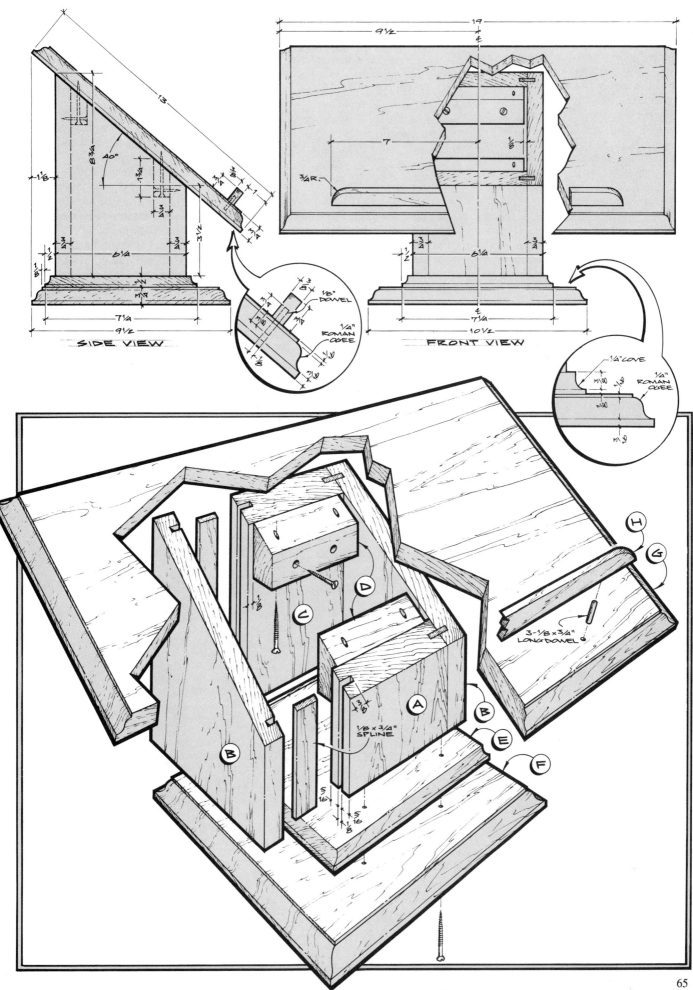

SIDE VIEW

FRONT VIEW

1/8" DOWEL

1/4" ROMAN OGEE

1/4" COVE

1/4" ROMAN OGEE

3/4 R

40°

13

9½

19

9½

7

7¼

9½

6¼

10½

6¼

7¼

3½

8¾

H

G

3-1/8 x 3/4"
LONG DOWEL

1/8 x 3/4"
SPLINE

A

B

B

C

D

E

F

ere's a weekend project that, when filled with flowers, will help brighten your yard or garden this spring. Also, we found that it can be put to use indoors as a planter or as a magazine or firewood rack.

Since we intend to use our planter out-of-doors, we chose redwood because it has good resistance to moisture and decay. Cedar is another good choice since it has similar characteristics. If your planter is to go out-of-doors, be sure to use plastic resin glue which, unlike white or yellow glue, has good water resistance. Plastic resin glue comes in the form of a brown powder that is mixed with water just before use. It's available at most hardware stores.

The front (A) is made first. Cut ¾ in. thick stock to a width of 10½ and a length of 11¾ in. Referring to the grid pattern, lay out and mark the profile of the tulip design as shown. Bore a ⅜ in. hole at the tulip center, then use a saber saw to cut out the shape. Use a file and sandpaper to smooth the cut edge. Also, at this time, lay out and mark the profile along the top edge of the front. Cut out with a band or saber saw and sand smooth.

Bill of Materials
(all dimensions actual)

Part	Description	Size	No. Req'd.
A	Front	¾ × 10½ × 11¾	1
B	Side	¾ × 10 × 20	2
C	Bottom	¾ × 10½ × 19¼	1
D	Leg	¾ × 11 × 10⅛	1
E	Handle	¾ × 2 × 40	2
F	Wheel	8¼ dia. × ¾ thick	1

The two sides (B) can be made from two pieces of ¾ in. thick stock measuring 10 in. wide by 20 in. long. Lay out the profile shown in the side view, then cut out and sand.

After cutting the bottom (C) to size, the upper box (consisting of parts A, B and C) can be assembled. Final sand all parts before joining them together with plastic resin glue and galvanized (or stainless steel) finishing nails. Set aside to dry thoroughly.

To make the wheel (F), cut ¾ in. thick stock to 10 in. square, then use a compass to scribe the 8¼ in. diameter circle. Also mark the centerpoint of the five 2 in. diameter circles as shown in the drawing. Use a hole saw or circle cutter to cut out the five circles, then

use the band or saber saw to cut the 8¼ in. diameter. Stay just outside the marked line with the band or saber saw blade. Once cut, use a disk sander to smooth the edge exactly to the line.

Next, make the leg (D) as shown, notching the upper corners to accept the handles (E). The 12-degree bevel on the front of the handle can be cut with a hand plane.

Final sand the leg, handle, and wheel before assembly. To assemble, first join the wheel to the handles by gluing the ⅝ in. diameter by 1⅜ in. long dowel into the ⅝ in. diameter by ¼ in. deep hole bored in each handle end. Now use glue and 1½ in. long galvanized finishing nails to join the handles to the leg.

The front (A), sides (B), and bottom (C) are now assembled to the handles and leg. A pair of 1¾ in. long by no. 8 flathead stainless steel wood screws are driven into the handle while two more are driven into the top edge of the leg (see top view of wheel, handle and leg). No glue is needed here.

If used outdoors, a couple of coats of spar varnish will provide a durable final finish. Indoors, two coats of a good penetrating oil will suffice.

Decorative Planter

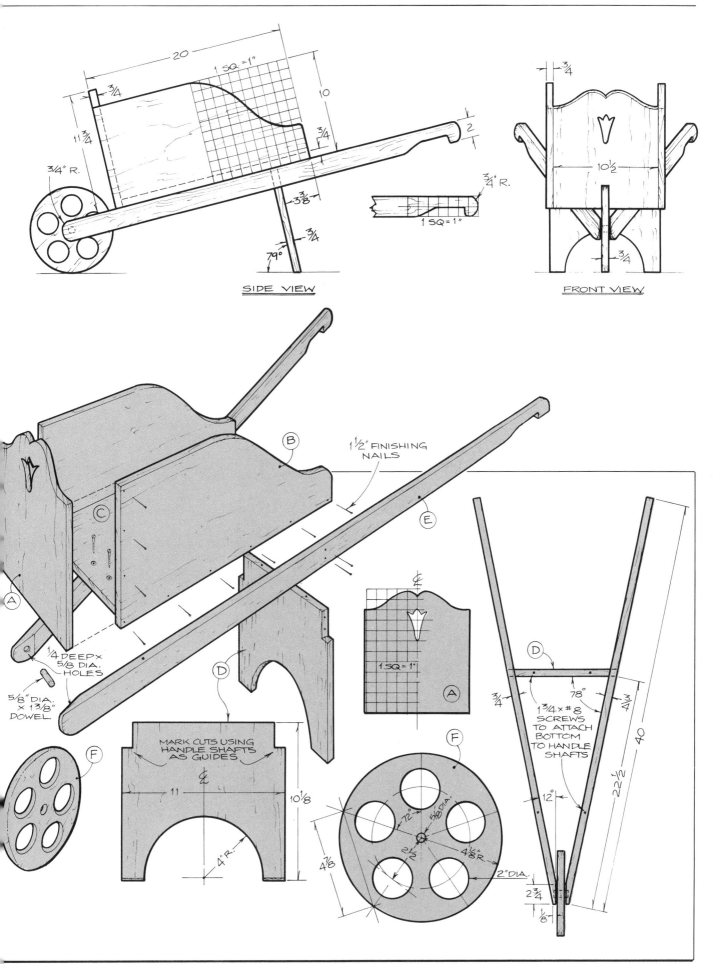

20

1 SQ = 1"

10

3/4

3/4

11 3/4

3/4" R.

2

3/4 R.

1 SQ = 1"

3 3/8

3/4

79°

SIDE VIEW

3/4

10 1/2

3/4

FRONT VIEW

B

1 1/2" FINISHING NAILS

E

C

A

1/4 DEEP x 5/8 DIA. HOLES

5/8" DIA. x 1 3/8" DOWEL

F

D

MARK CUTS USING HANDLE SHAFTS AS GUIDES

11

10 1/8

4" R.

1 SQ = 1"

A

F

72°

5/8 DIA.

2 1/2

4 1/8 R.

4 7/8

2" DIA.

D

3/4

78°

3/4

1 3/4 x #8 SCREWS TO ATTACH BOTTOM TO HANDLE SHAFTS

12°

22 1/2

40

2 3/4

1/8

Dog/Cat Bed

Given the fact that pets are such loyal and devoted friends, what better gift than a bed of their own? This bed, crafted in solid walnut, is sized to accommodate a cat or small-to-medium size dog. The bed's overall dimensions could be increased as necessary to fit a larger animal if your "best friend" tends toward Saint Bernard or Great Dane size. Of course, the bed could also be made from pine or some other hard or softwood.

Start this project by laying up stock for the bottom (C). If your stock has been edge-joined accurately, only mild pressure is required with the pipe clamps. While you are waiting for the bottom to dry, rip stock for the front and back (A) and ends (B). After mitering the ends of these pieces, use the router equipped with a wing cutter as shown to cut the stopped spline grooves. Note how parts A and B are clamped back to back with an additional guide piece for extra router support. Also note that the bearing is assembled between the router and the cutter. This permits the cutter shaft to be fully chucked in the router.

Use a chisel to square the stopped end of the spline grooves, and cut four hardwood splines with the grain running across the miter as shown. After band or jigsawing the front and back cutouts, glue and assemble the box. While the box is drying, use a bearing-guided ¼ in. Roman ogee router bit to shape the bottom perimeter. This is a good router table operation. When dry, the box perimeter is radiused as shown to establish the ¼ in. round-over.

After cutting out the four feet (D), drill and slot the base as shown to accept the six mounting screws. The slotted holes are required to allow expansion and contraction of the stock across the width of the base. Screw the bottom to the box, then glue the four feet in place.

When final sanding was complete, we finished our bed with Deft clear aerosol spray finish. This protective satin coating should wear well, and can be easily renewed when necessary.

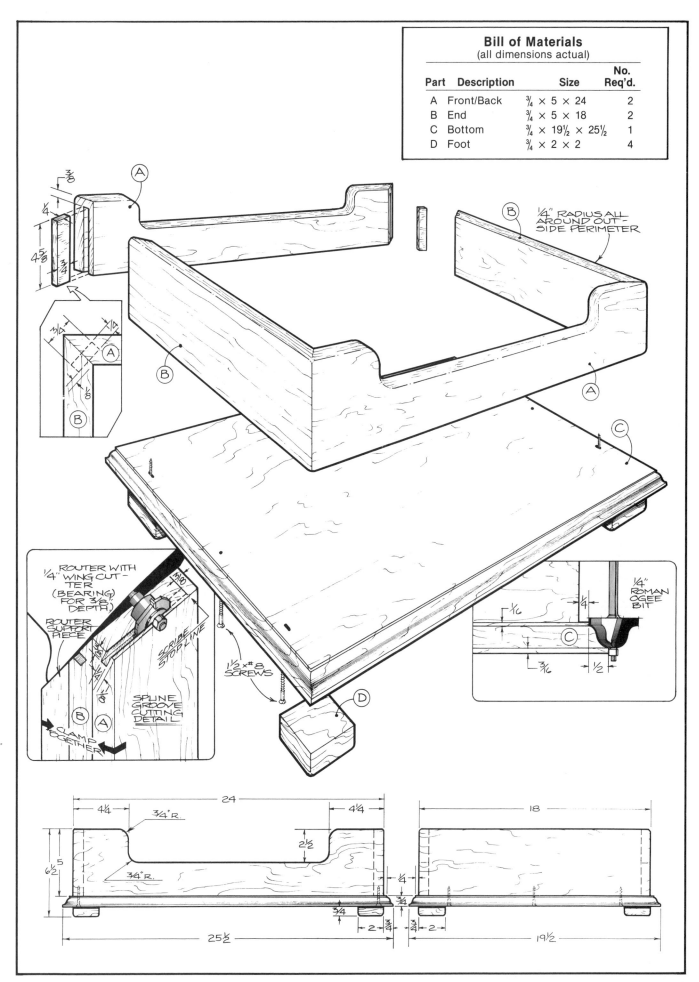

Bill of Materials
(all dimensions actual)

Part	Description	Size	No. Req'd.
A	Front/Back	$\frac{3}{4} \times 5 \times 24$	2
B	End	$\frac{3}{4} \times 5 \times 18$	2
C	Bottom	$\frac{3}{4} \times 19\frac{1}{2} \times 25\frac{1}{2}$	1
D	Foot	$\frac{3}{4} \times 2 \times 2$	4

Ⓐ

³⁄₈

¼

4⅝

³⁄₄

¾

Ⓐ

¼" RADIUS ALL AROUND OUTSIDE PERIMETER

Ⓑ

Ⓑ

Ⓐ

Ⓐ

Ⓑ

⅛

Ⓒ

ROUTER WITH ¼" WING CUTTER (BEARING) FOR ³⁄₈" DEPTH.

ROUTER SUPPORT PIECE

SCRIBE STOP LINE

1½ x #8 SCREWS

SPLINE GROOVE CUTTING DETAIL

Ⓑ Ⓐ

CLAMP TOGETHER

Ⓓ

¼" ROMAN OGEE BIT

Ⓒ

¹⁄₁₆

¼

³⁄₁₆

½

24

4¼

4¼

18

¾" R.

2½

³⁄₄" R.

5

6½

¼

³⁄₄

¾

2

³⁄₄

³⁄₄

2

25½

19½

69

Pine Woodbox

With its large upper compartment, this sturdy woodbox has room for a generous supply of firewood, while the drawer comes in handy for storing kindling wood or the pile of old newspaper that's needed to start each fire. All parts are made from pine obtained at our local lumberyard.

The two sides (A) can be made first. You probably won't be able to find 14½ in. wide stock, so it will be necessary to edge-glue two or more narrower boards in order to get the needed width.

To edge-glue, first apply a thin coat of glue to each of the mating edges, then clamp firmly with several bar or pipe clamps. No need to add dowels or splines here as this joint matches long grain-to-long grain, a joint that is as strong as the wood itself. If the edges start to slide out of alignment, though, clamp a few waxed cleats (made from stock that measures about 1 in. square by 15 in. long) across the boards every foot or so. The cleats will keep the boards flush while the wax prevents the cleats from sticking. By the way, when edge-gluing, it's a good idea to allow a little extra length and width for the stock. Later, after the clamps have been removed, it can be trimmed to final length and width on the table or radial-arm saw.

Next, on what will be the inside face of one of the sides, lay out and mark the location of the two ¼ in. deep by ¾ in. wide dadoes. Place the two sides on your workbench so that the back edges butt while the top and bottom ends are

flush (see detail: Routing the Dadoes). Clamp a fence across both pieces of stock, then use the router to cut the dadoes. If you use a ¾ in. diameter straight bit, you'll be able to cut the full dado width. However, don't make the ¼ in. deep cut in one pass. You'll get a smoother cut, with less strain on the motor, if it's done in two passes, each pass removing ⅛ in. of material. If you use a ⅜ in. diameter straight bit, you'll first need to make the two ⅛ in. deep cuts, then relocate the fence and repeat the procedure in order to widen the dado to ¾ in.

Now transfer the upper and lower grid patterns (see side view) to the stock. Mark the profile on just one of the sides, then use a band saw or jigsaw to make the cuts. Stay slightly on the waste side of the lines, then sand the edges smooth. The completed profile can now be used as a template to trace the contour on the remaining side.

The divider (B) and the bottom (C) can now be made. Edge-glue stock, then cut to the length and width shown in the bill of materials. Note that the bottom is 1⅛ in. narrower in width to allow for the thickness of the back (G).

Both the front (F) and the back (G) boards are made from ⁵⁄₄ × 6 stock, which measures 1⅛ in. thick by 5½ in. wide, and is available at just about any lumberyard or building supply center. Note that the top and bottom boards have a ½ in. × ⁹⁄₁₆ in. rabbet cut on one edge only (see detail: Back and Front Boards), while the remaining boards have the same rabbet cut on both edges. We used the table saw and dado head to make the rabbets, but a router can also be used.

Parts A, B, C, F, and G can now be final sanded. Start with 80 grit sandpaper to quickly remove the planer marks that are almost always visible on the surface of the boards. These marks are made when the board is thickness planed at the mill, and if not sanded out, they often become glaringly obvious when a stain is applied. Follow with 100, 150, and 220 grit to complete the sanding. When sanding, though, keep in mind that you will want to maintain a snug fit at the dado joint where the sides meet the divider and bottom. If too much material is removed from the ends of the divider and bottom, the fit-up will be sloppy. A sloppy joint doesn't just look bad, it won't be as strong as a joint that's tight.

Cut the front cleat (D) and the back

cleat (E) to size (see bill of materials), then glue and clamp to the sides as shown. Before gluing, though, it's a good idea to first drive a few small brads into the cleat edge that will be glued, then clip the heads off so that about 1/16 in. is exposed. The brads will keep the cleats from sliding when clamp pressure is applied. No dowels, nails, screws or other reinforcements are necessary as this is a long grain-to-long grain joint.

Next, assemble the sides to the divider and bottom with glue and 1½ in. long by number 10 flathead wood screws. Use a ½ in. diameter drill bit to counterbore ¼ in. deep holes to accept wood plugs. It's best to cut the plugs slightly long so that they protrude just above the wood. Glue in place and, when dry, sand flush.

The back boards can now be added. Each board is screwed to the back cleats with 1½ in. long by number 10 flathead wood screws. Do not use any

glue here as the back boards must be free to expand and contract with seasonal changes in humidity. Also, to allow that movement, only use two screws in each end, and space them about 1 in. either side of the board's center line. The screws do not need to be counterbored. When assembling the boards, note that (see detail: Front and Back Boards) you need to allow a ⅛ in. space between each one. Once the back is completed, the front boards can be added in the same manner.

The front apron (H) can now be cut to a length and width that will exactly fit the opening in the woodbox. Referring to the grid pattern shown on the front view, transfer the grid pattern to the stock, then cut it out with a band saw or jigsaw.

Make the front apron cleats (I) and glue them to the sides so that they are set back ¾ in. from the front edge. Once dry, assemble the front apron to the cleats by driving a pair of 1¼ in.

long by number 10 flathead wood screws through the cleats and into the front apron.

The drawer can now be made as shown. We used the table saw and dado head to cut the various rabbets and grooves, but repeated passes with a regular table saw can also do the job. Use glue and finishing nails to assemble the drawer front, back, and sides. The bottom need not be glued in place, although you may want to spot glue it in a couple of places if it tends to rattle or shift in the grooves.

Now give the entire woodbox a final sanding, taking care to round any sharp edges. Use a chisel to remove any glue that may have squeezed out of a joint. For a final finish, we applied two coats of Minwax's Colonial Maple Wood Finish. Once dry we added two coats of Watco Danish Oil. A pair of 1¼ in. diameter porcelain drawer knobs completed the project.

(continued on next page)

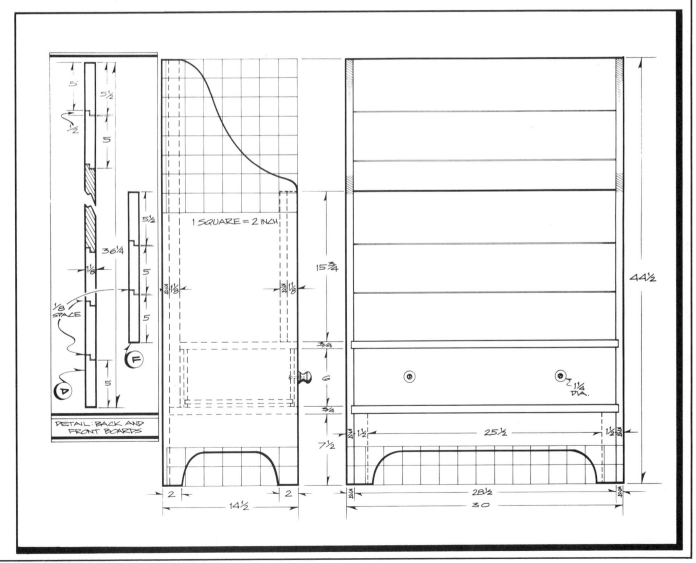

DETAIL: BACK AND FRONT BOARDS

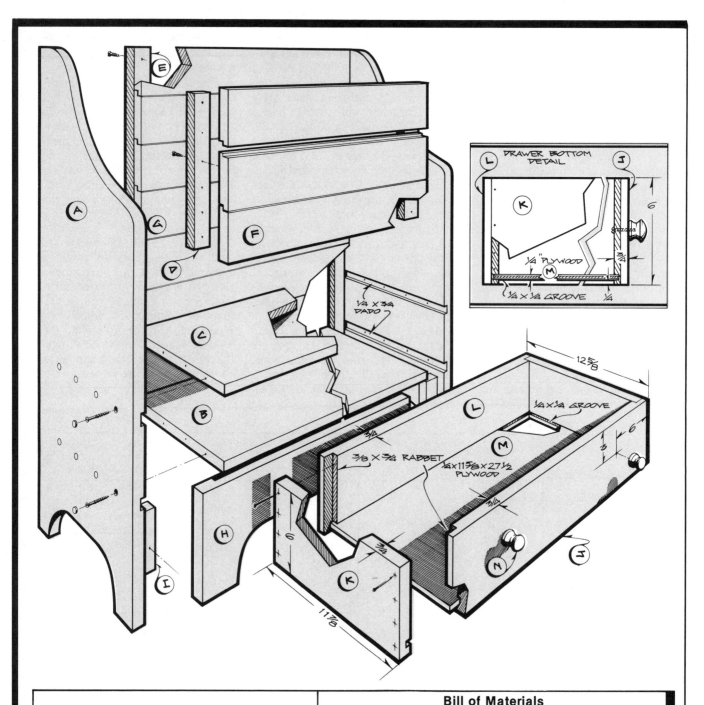

DRAWER BOTTOM DETAIL

¼ "PLYWOOD

¼ × ¼ GROOVE

¼ × ¾ GROOVE

⅜ × ¾ RABBET

¼ × 11⅝ × 27½ PLYWOOD

¼ × ¾ DADO

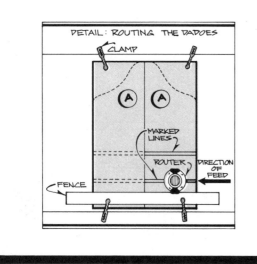

DETAIL: ROUTING THE DADOES

CLAMP

MARKED LINES

ROUTER

DIRECTION OF FEED

FENCE

Bill of Materials
(all dimensions actual)

Part	Description	Size	No. Req'd.
A	Side	¾ × 14½ × 44½	2
B	Divider	¾ × 13¾ × 29	1
C	Bottom	¾ × 12⅝ × 29	1
D	Front Cleat	¾ × 1½ × 15¾	2
E	Back Cleat	¾ × 1½ × 44½	2
F	Front	1⅛ × 5½ × 28½	3
G	Back	1⅛ × 5½ × 28½	7
H	Front Apron	¾ × 7½ × 28½	1
I	Front Apron Cleat	¾ × 1½ × 7½	2
J	Drawer Front	¾ × 6 × 28½	1
K	Drawer Side	¾ × 6 × 11⅞	2
L	Drawer Back	¾ × 6 × 28½	1
M	Drawer Bottom	¼ × 11⅝ × 27½	1
N	Porcelain Knob	1¼ diameter	2

This lovely table top vanity features a mirror that pivots out as the top is opened while a series of notches allows it to be adjusted at various angles. The mirror simply slides into the closed position when the top is shut. Inside, there are nine storage compartments.

Ours is made from oak with a walnut plywood top and bottom. This project doesn't require a lot of stock, so your materials costs should be reasonably low.

To make the box frame (consisting of parts A, B, C, E, F, and G), you'll need a piece of ⅜ in. thick stock that measures 4 in. wide and 54 in. long. Both the width and length dimensions allow a little extra stock. If you don't have a thickness planer and can't get ⅜ in. thick stock locally, check with a lumberyard or millwork shop as they will often plane thicker stock for a nominal charge. Once thickness planed, set the table saw blade to cut a 45-degree miter, then cross-cut the stock into two pieces 13½ in. long and two pieces 12 in. long. For the case to be square, the miters must be exactly 45 degrees, so it's a good idea to make some test cuts on scrap stock before starting.

Next, use the table saw and a dado-head to cut the ¼ in. wide by 3/16 in. deep groove that runs lengthwise along the top and bottom of each piece. Note that each groove is located ¼ in. from the edge.

The case bottom (D) and the lid top (H) are made from ¼ in. thick walnut plywood cut to 11½ in. wide by 13 in. long. Albert Constantine and Son, Inc., 2050 Eastchester Road, Bronx, NY 10461, sells ¼ in. walnut plywood, good two sides, in sheets measuring 12 in. wide by 48 in. long.

The box frame parts and the top and bottom can now be assembled. First dry assemble the components to make sure everything fits properly. If everything looks okay, disassemble the parts and apply glue to the miters and to the edges of the plywood. Clamp

Vanity Case

firmly to insure good pressure at the joints and check for squareness. Make any necessary adjustments before setting aside to dry.

The splined mitered construction of the box requires a simple jig (see detail) to cut the spline grooves, which are located ¼ in. apart. Set the saw blade to a height of ¼ in., then locate the rip fence ¼ in. from the blade. With the box frame in the jig, start the saw, then hold the jig against the rip fence and run it through the blade. Cut all four corners on one side, then flip the piece and do the four corners on the other side. Next, readjust the rip fence so that the saw blade is ⅝ in. from the fence and repeat the process. Three more fence adjustments, each one in ⅜ in. intervals, will complete the spline cutting operation. Note that, for greatest strength, spline grooves are not cut 1 in. down from the top edge. Later the box will be cut into two parts (the case and lid sections) at this point.

Cut the ⅛ in. thick walnut splines slightly oversized and glue in place. When dry, trim flush with a chisel and sand smooth. Note that the spline's grain direction must be perpendicular to the joint.

The table saw is used to cut the box frame into two sections: the case (parts A, B, C, and D), and the lid (parts E, F, G, and H). To do this, set the saw blade to a height of ½ in. and locate the rip fence 2⅞ in. from the blade. With the 12 in. long side facing the table, hold the box firmly against the rip fence while pushing it through the saw blade. This completes
(continued on next page)

the first cut. Make the second cut on the opposite side. Make the third cut with the 13½ in. long side facing down, then before making the fourth and final cut on the opposite side, insert a piece of ⅛ in. thick hardboard (Masonite) in the saw kerf to keep it from closing and binding on the saw blade.

To make the mirror frame (parts I and J), you'll need about 50 in. of stock measuring ½ in. thick and ¾ in. wide. Cut the stock to length, mitering the ends as shown. Apply glue to the miter joints, then clamp firmly and allow to dry. The jig is once again used to cut the spline groove on each corner, but this time the blade height is raised to ⁷⁄₁₆ in. Glue the splines in place and trim flush.

A router with a rabbeting bit is used to cut the ⅜ in. wide by ¼ in. deep rabbet all around the back of the mirror frame (see mirror frame detail). The router bit leaves rounded corners, so a sharp chisel is used to cut them square. To round the top and bottom edges, use the router and a ¼ in. rounding-

over bit. The mirror (K) is held in place with glazier's (diamond) points as shown. A pair of ⅛ in. diameter by ¾ in. long brass pins (L) are used to assemble the mirror frame to the inside of the lid.

To make the long dividers (M), rip ⅜ in. thick stock to a width of 3 in., then cut to a length of 12¾ in. Lay out and mark the location of the ½ in. diameter notches for the mirror (the hole centerline will be 2⁷⁄₁₆ in. from the bottom edge), and bore the holes with a Forstner bit. Ripping the stock to a width of 2⅜ in. will result in ³⁄₁₆ in. deep notches as shown.

Next, cut the short dividers (N) to length and width. Lay out and mark the location of the notches on both the long and short dividers, then raise the saw blade (or dado cutter) to a height of 1³⁄₁₆ in. Use the miter gauge to run the stock through the blade. You'll need to make several passes with the regular saw blade to complete each notch.

The finger grooves in the front are cut using a ¼ in. cove cutter on the

router. Use a chisel to cut the mortises for the two brass hinges (O), then give all parts a thorough final sanding. Two coats of Deft Clear Wood Finish were applied as a final finish. The addition of the two hinges completed the project.

Part	Description	Size	No. Req'd.
A	Case Front	⅜ × 2⅞ × 12	1
B	Case Back	⅜ × 2⅞ × 12	1
C	Case Side	⅜ × 2⅞ × 13½	2
D	Case Bottom	¼ × 11½ × 13	1
E	Lid Front	⅜ × 1 × 12	1
F	Lid Back	⅜ × 1 × 12	1
G	Lid Side	⅜ × 1 × 13½	2
H	Lid Top	¼ × 11½ × 13	1
I	Mirror Frame End	½ × ¾ × 11¼	2
J	Mirror Frame Side	½ × ¾ × 12¾	2
K	Mirror	⅛ × 10⅜ × 11⅞	1
L	Pin	⅛ dia. × ¾ long	2
M	Long Divider	⅜ × 2⅜ × 12¾	2
N	Short Divider	⅜ × 2⅜ × 11¼	2
O	Hinge	¾ × 1¼	2

Bill of Materials
(all dimensions actual)

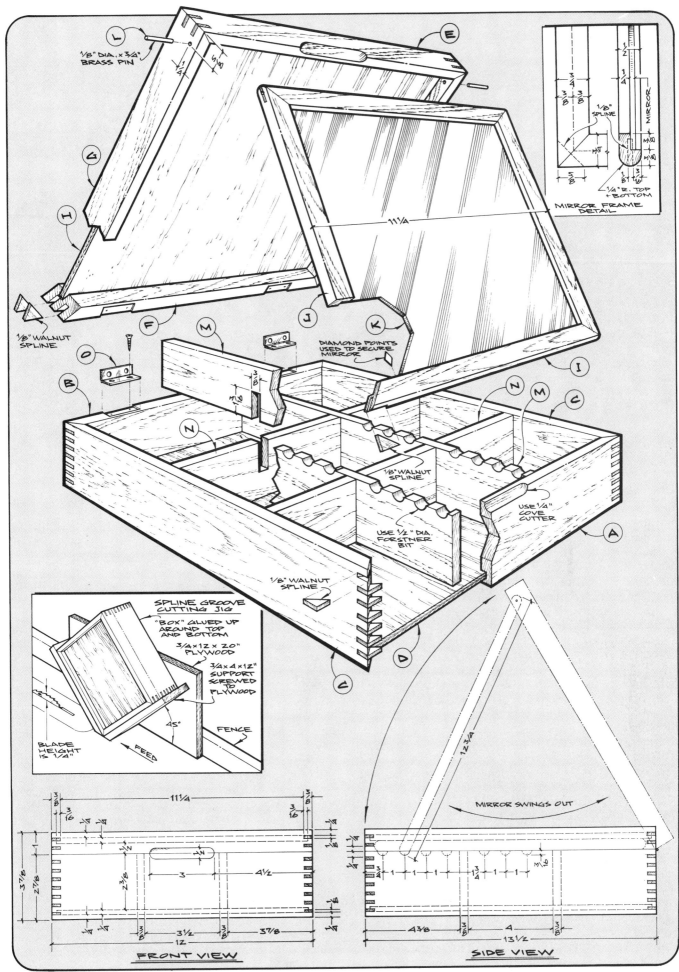

1/8" DIA. x 3/4"
BRASS PIN

L

E

G

H

MIRROR FRAME
DETAIL

1/8"
SPLINE

MIRROR

1/4" R. TOP
+ BOTTOM

11 1/4

1/8" WALNUT
SPLINE

O

F

M

J

K

DIAMOND POINTS
USED TO SECURE
MIRROR

I

B

N

N

M

C

1/8" WALNUT
SPLINE

USE 1/4"
COVE
CUTTER

USE 1/2" DIA.
FORSTNER
BIT

A

1/8" WALNUT
SPLINE

SPLINE GROOVE
CUTTING JIG

"BOX" GLUED UP
AROUND TOP
AND BOTTOM

3/4 x 12 x 20"
PLYWOOD

3/4 x 4 x 12"
SUPPORT
SCREWED
TO
PLYWOOD

BLADE
HEIGHT
IS 1/4"

45°

FENCE

FEED

D

C

12 3/4

MIRROR SWINGS OUT

11 1/4

3/8

3/16

3/8

3/16

3 7/8

2 7/8

1

2 3/8

3

4 1/2

3 1/2

3/8

3 7/8

12

FRONT VIEW

4 3/8

4

13 1/2

1

1

1

1 3/4

1

1

3/16

3/8

3/8

SIDE VIEW

75

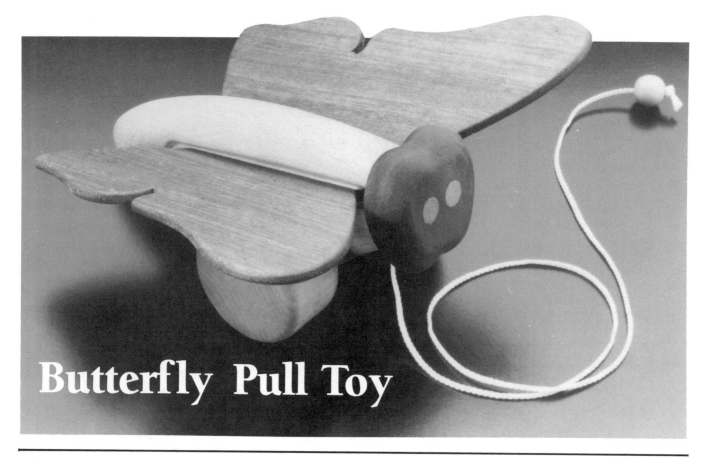

Butterfly Pull Toy

Of all the wooden pull toys we have seen, this butterfly is certainly one of the most unique. When it is constructed as shown in the photo with contrasting woods such as mahogany and maple, it is handsome enough to display.

The operation of the butterfly's wings is quite simple. The wings rest on the wheels, which are identically offset on the axle. As the butterfly is pulled along, and the offset wheels turn, the butterfly's body rises and falls while the wings "flap." The faster it is pulled along, the quicker the motion of the wings and body.

Start with the body (A). Cut a block measuring 1¼ in. by 2½ in. by 6¼ in. long, then referring to the full-size pattern, lay out the body profile and mark the centerpoint of the axle hole. Refer to the appropriate detail for the wing hole position, and mark the centerpoints of these holes. Now, drill out the axle hole, and drill the wing holes to a 5 in. depth, using the setup shown in Fig. 1. Note that the wing holes are 7/16 in. diameter, while the axle hole is 3/8 in. diameter. Next, move the body block to the router table (Fig. 2), position the fence, as shown, ¾ in. from the centerpoint of a V-groove bit, and establish the clearance that will permit the wings movement. The height of the V-groove bit is set at 3/8 in. Finally, move to the band saw (Fig. 3) and cut out the profile of the body. A rasp and sandpaper are then used to shape and final sand the rounded body edges.

Now, cut out the wings (B), wheels (C), and head (E), referring to their full-size profiles, and trace outlines (use carbon paper) directly onto the stock. Note that the wheels are cut from 1 3/16 in. thick stock, while the head is cut from ¾ in. thick stock, and the wings are 3/16 in. thick material. Round the edges of these parts to approximate their appearance in the photo. The 3/8 in. diameter by ½ in. deep offset axle hole in the wheels is also drilled at this time.

The wings are glued into a corresponding stopped slot cut into two dowel lengths, as shown in the exploded view. The best way to accomplish this is to mount a 3/16 in. diameter straight bit in the router table, set it for 3/16 in. height (depth of cut) and then use a clamp, as illustrated in Fig. 4, to hold the 3/8 in. diameter by 4½ in. long dowels (D). Note that we used a hand-screw clamp, a low fence (to clear the clamp handles), and a stopblock to insure proper length of the 4 in. long slot cut into the dowels. The distance that the fence is set from the centerpoint of the bit will be 3/16 in. plus the width of the clamp jaw. Eyeball the bit to the center of the dowel just to be certain that the fence setting is accurate.

To assemble the butterfly, first glue the wings into the dowel slots, then insert the dowels into the body. The oversize dowel holes in the body should permit the easy pivot of the wings. Insert the short eye dowels (G) into the head, then glue the head to the body. The wheels are mounted onto either end of the axle (F). Be sure that the wheels are aligned evenly on the offset axle, or neither the wheels nor the axle will turn. Finally, drill a 3/16 in. by ½ in. deep hole in the body for the pull cord, which is glued in place. A ½ in. diameter wooden ball (H) is secured to the cord with a simple knot. Given the propensity toddlers have for chewing, if you're making the butterfly as a toy, a non-toxic salad bowl finish (we use Behlen's) is best.

Notes: We suggest a dry assembly of the butterfly before final glue-up to test proper operation. When drilling the axle hole through the body, make the hole slightly oversize, so the axle will not bind. A coat of paraffin wax on the center section of the axle and on the underside of the wings where the wheels rub will serve to lubricate these potential friction and wear points.

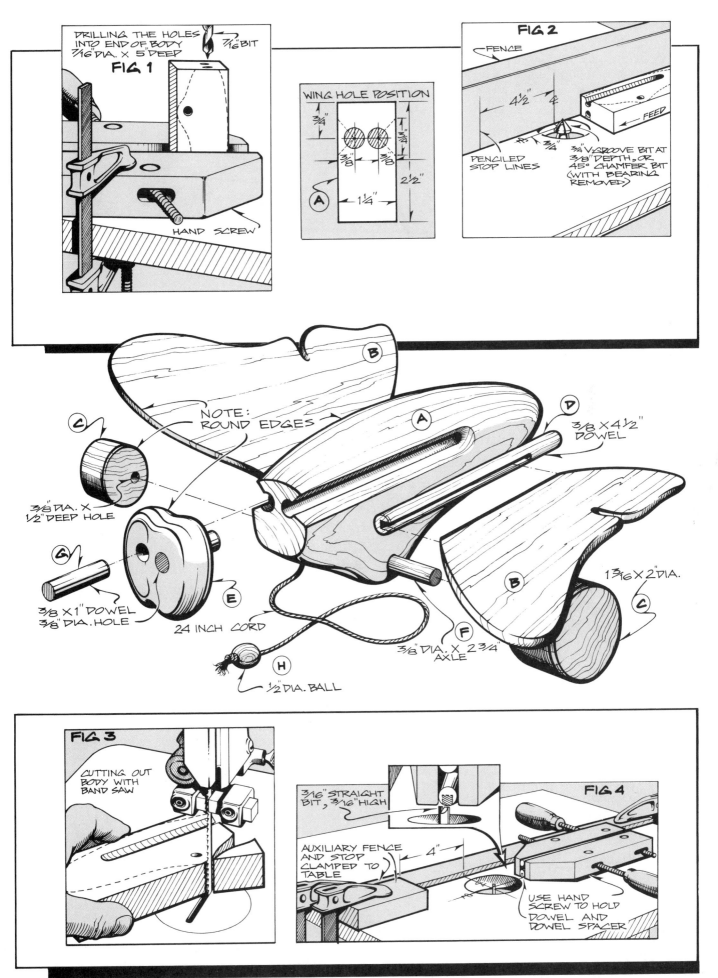

DRILLING THE HOLES
INTO END OF BODY
7/16" DIA. X 5" DEEP   7/16" BIT
FIG 1

HAND SCREW

WING HOLE POSITION
3/4"
3/4"
3/8"   3/8"
2 1/2"
1 1/4"
A

FIG 2
FENCE
4 1/2"
FEED
PENCILED
STOP LINES
3/4"
3/4" V-GROOVE BIT AT
3/8" DEPTH, OR
45° CHAMFER BIT
(WITH BEARING
REMOVED)

B

C
NOTE:
ROUND EDGES
A
D
3/8 X 4 1/2"
DOWEL

3/8" DIA. X
1/2" DEEP HOLE

G
3/8 X 1" DOWEL
3/8" DIA. HOLE
E
24 INCH CORD
B
1 3/16 X 2" DIA.
C
F
3/8" DIA. X 2 3/4"
AXLE
H
1/2" DIA. BALL

FIG 3
CUTTING OUT
BODY WITH
BAND SAW

3/16" STRAIGHT
BIT, 3/16" HIGH
FIG 4
AUXILIARY FENCE
AND STOP
CLAMPED TO
TABLE
4"
USE HAND
SCREW TO HOLD
DOWEL AND
DOWEL SPACER

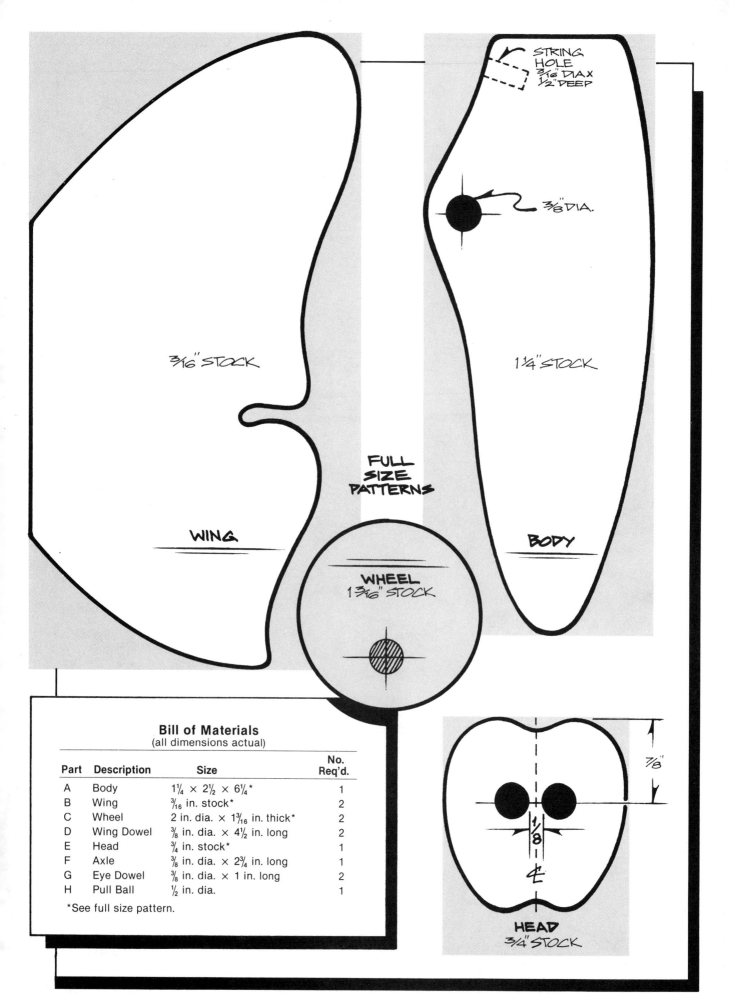

STRING HOLE ³⁄₁₆" DIA X ½" DEEP

³⁄₈" DIA.

1¼" STOCK

³⁄₁₆" STOCK

WING

FULL SIZE PATTERNS

BODY

WHEEL
1³⁄₁₆" STOCK

Bill of Materials
(all dimensions actual)

Part	Description	Size	No. Req'd.
A	Body	1¼ × 2½ × 6¼*	1
B	Wing	³⁄₁₆ in. stock*	2
C	Wheel	2 in. dia. × 1³⁄₁₆ in. thick*	2
D	Wing Dowel	³⁄₈ in. dia. × 4½ in. long	2
E	Head	¾ in. stock*	1
F	Axle	³⁄₈ in. dia. × 2¾ in. long	1
G	Eye Dowel	³⁄₈ in. dia. × 1 in. long	2
H	Pull Ball	½ in. dia.	1

*See full size pattern.

7⁄8"

1⁄8

¢

HEAD
¾" STOCK

Pineapple Napkin Holder

Many woodworkers don't always have time for large or involved projects. This easy-to-build country style napkin holder should take less than one evening in the workshop. All you need are a saw (a fretsaw, jigsaw, saber saw or band saw will all do) and one clamp with at least a 4 in. capacity.

Although we used ½ in. maple for our napkin holder, either pine or hardwood ¾ in. thick stock could be used as well. Refer to the full-size pattern for the pineapple profile, cut the two ends and the bottom and assemble as shown.

You may either paint the napkin holder green and yellow, as we have, or improvise with your own color scheme. A black felt tip pen is used to draw the diamond pattern on the pineapple and to outline the leaves. For a three-dimensional look, use a V-gouge or X-Acto knife to incise the diamond pattern before painting.

Actual Size Pattern

Three-drawer
Jewelry Chest

Editor's Note: California craftsman Tony Lydgate excels at developing functional pieces that are beautiful, yet surprisingly simple in construction. This jewelry chest is proof positive that good designs need not be complex or feature elaborate joinery.

The light chest in the photo is of birdseye maple, with edge facings of curly western maple and fronts of quilted western maple. The darker chest is of Hawaiian koa, with a spectacular curly figure featured on the edge facings.

The top (A) and the two sides (B) are cut from a single length of stock. Start with a board about 8 in. by 32 in., which should be jointed perfectly straight and smooth. If you have a thickness sander, it will produce a nice flat, smooth surface. Crosscut the board into the two sides and top in this order: side, top, side. This layout helps create a nice effect of visual continuity in the grain of the wood.

Next, rip each piece to 7¾ in. wide. I prefer using the 7¾ in. width since I have an 8 in. jointer. By crosscutting before ripping I am able to achieve greater accuracy in the final width.

Now, use the dado head blade to cut the rabbet on the top inside end of each side to make the edge that the top piece will sit on. If you do not have a dado head, this rabbet can be made on the table saw with two cuts. Make the first cut across the grain, and the second cut with the stock standing on end. Whichever method you use, make the depth of the rabbet a hair deeper than the thickness of the top, so you'll have some extra to sand off flush.

Next, rabbet the rear edges of the top and sides to accept the plywood back (C). While you can use any ¼ in. plywood or even solid stock for the back, I prefer to use a light colored hardwood plywood such as ash for the maple carcase, and a darker plywood such as walnut for the koa carcase. Because some ¼ in. thick plywoods are actually measured in millimeters, and may not be the exact equivalent of ¼ in. thick, it is important to make the depth of the rabbet equal to the actual thickness of the plywood. Remember, when assembled, the front and back edges of the sides and top must be perfectly flush to accept the facing strips that will be glued over them. Therefore, you don't want any ridges here. Don't forget to cut a ⅛ in. by ¼ in. dado in the back as shown, to accept the bottom (D).

Finally, cut the dadoes in the sides for the bottom (D) and drawer guides (E). Be careful when cutting the bottom dado, so as to not chip out the ⅛ in. remaining. This ⅛ in. thick lip is rather fragile until the bottom is in place. Next, set up the drill press and drill holes for the screws and plugs that hold the sides to the top.

I began woodworking as a boatbuilder, and later made harpsichords. In both, screws are used extensively, both for their long-lasting holding power, and because a screw-and-glue joint has the best possible clamping power. Of course, you can use finger joints or dovetails to make this side-to-top joint as well as the screw, glue and plug technique I use.

If you elect my method, first counterbore a shallow hole (about ¼ in. deep) with a ⅜ in. drill bit. Then drill a through hole of the same diameter as the shank of whatever screw you're using. I use a no. 6 by 1 in. long screw.

The plugs can be made using ⅜ and ¼ in. plug cutters which are available at most hardware stores. If you prefer you can turn a dowel on a lathe, or even start with square stock and hand-shape a dowel on your stationary sander. I take rosewood stock, then drill ¼ in. holes spaced about 1 in. apart. Then I make ¼ in. plugs of vermillion, pop them out, glue them into the holes in the rosewood and go home. It takes the glue a long time to dry — at least overnight — because no air can directly get to the glue. Fig. 1 shows the procedure for creating this plug detail.

Now you've got two sides and a top, all dadoed and rabbeted appropriately, with the plugs made and the screw holes through the sides. You also have a back and a bottom, lovingly crafted and carefully milled and fitted to fairly rigorous tolerances.

Now, assemble the carcase, using either white or yellow glue. While I use a staple gun to fasten the back into the side rabbets, small screws or brads will also work well. Whatever fasteners you use, keep them close to the edge so they will later be covered by the edge facings. I prefer to drill the pilot screw holes in the ends of part A after the carcase has been assembled, using a pilot bit about one half the diameter of the screw, and then an electric screwdriver to drive the screws home. It is particularly satisfactory to watch the little beads of glue squeeze out between the sides and top, telling you that you've got a good tight joint.

Once the carcase is together, you need to mill the edge facing strips (F). You can use the same stock (as in the koa chest) or different stock (as in the maple one) for the facing. I strongly recommend something with some figure in it. I start with standard surfaced 4/4 lumber, rip it a tad wider than the edges I'm facing, sand it to width, then cut the miters. Then I rip off the strips, about ³⁄₁₆ in. thick. I find it easier to miter the stock first, then rip it, though I suppose you could do it the other way around. I make the facing for the back about ⅞ in. wide to give me more material for covering my staple heads and glue joint.

Use masking tape or duct tape to tape the facings onto the carcase after they're glued. Put glue in the screw

countersink holes and hammer the plugs in. Leave them proud of the surface, so you can sand them flush.

Take note of the two ¼ in. by ¼ in. by ⅝ in. filler blocks (G) glued in place at the front end of the bottom dado in the sides. These are needed to fill the ends of these dadoes. The ⅛ in. space left between the filler blocks and the plywood bottom allows for any contraction that might take place across the width of the sides. The bottom should be glued in place along the back edge and along the sides for several inches starting at the back.

Now you have the carcase with the facings and plugs. At this point, mill and screw in the drawer guides (E). You can use just about any wood here; it doesn't have to be fancy. Note that I have sized these parts ⅛ in. less than the dado length, and placed a slotted

Bill of Materials (all dimensions actual)			
Part	Description	Size	No. Req'd.
A	Top	¾ × 7¾ × 15¼	1
B	Side	¾ × 7¾ × 7⅝	2
C	Back	¼ × 7⅛ × 15¼	1
D	Bottom	¼ × 6⅞ × 15¼	1
E	Drawer Guide	½ × ¾ × 7⅜	4
F	Edge Facing	³⁄₁₆ × ¾ stock* as req'd.	
G	Filler Block	¼ × ¼ × ⅝	2
H	Drawer Front	¾ × 2¼ × 14¾	3
I	Drawer Side	⅝ × 2 × 7⁷⁄₁₆	6
J	Drawer Back	⅝ × 2 × 14	3
K	Drawer Bottom	¼ × 6¹³⁄₁₆ × 14	3
L	Pull	⅜ × ⅝ × 11	3
M	Cardboard	6¼ × 13⁷⁄₁₆	3
N	Velvet	9 × 17	3
O	Divider (long)	⅜ × ¾	as req'd.
P	Divider (short)	⅛ × ⅜	as req'd.
*Edge facing at back can be ⅞ in. wide.			

screw hole at one end to allow for movement in the sides. The cutting detail (Fig. 2) shows how the drawer guides are milled. Since this is a fussy operation, be especially careful. Bring the dado-head up through a fresh table saw insert, so there will be no gaps. Use a push stick and maintain firm control at all times. The spacer is chamfered on the end so the drawer guide will not catch. If you prefer, you can use the same basic setup on the router table. The advantage with the router table is elimination of the potential for kickback. Screw the drawer guides in place with ½ in. long screws.

While you can use a shaper or router table to establish the ⅜ in. radius round-over on the top shoulders, it can

also be done by eye on a stationary belt sander. If you do intend to use the shaper or router to make this round-over, you'll need to do so prior to gluing on the facing strips, lest you risk the danger of bad chip-out.

The drawers are of a conventional construction, as you can see from the exploded and sectional views, although you might consider dovetailing rather than rabbeting the drawer cases. Take note that the bottom of the drawer front must overhang ¼ in. to conceal the butt ends of the drawer guides and the space between. Make the drawers so they just fit into the carcase. Later, when final sanded, the drawers should have the right amount of "play." Mill the drawer fronts to fit the drawer sides and back. The drawer front when unsanded should be a tad beyond flush with the carcase, so that when you're done it will be just flush. If you don't quite get it right you can always glue something to the back of the drawer to bring it out flush.

The drawer pulls (L) are Indian rosewood (as is the black in the plugs). Mill ⅝ in. by ⅜ in. thick stock, then cut a tongue on one edge as shown in the Fig. 3 detail. Be sure to use a push stick for this operation. This tongue, which fits into a corresponding groove cut into the drawer fronts, makes it a simple matter to get the pulls aligned properly for glue up, using only spring clamps. The slot in the drawer front is cut on the table saw, using a pair of stop blocks, one in front of and the other behind the blade, as shown in the Fig. 4 detail. Note that the width of the tongue should be a hair less than the depth of the slot milled to accept it.

Now, flood the carcase and the drawers with Watco oil. Thoroughly saturate the surface, but only with a single application. Then use 00 steel wool and plenty of elbow grease to work the oil into the surface, wiping off with paper towels. Let the piece dry for at least 48 hours at 70 degrees. Use 00 steel wool again to remove the Watco crust, and wax well with any good quality furniture paste wax.

Velvet is wrapped over stiff mat cardboard, and taped on the underside to create the drawer bottom liners. The drawer dividers are made as shown from ⅛ and ⅜ in. thick stock. These are optional items and could be made for only one drawer, or sized to compartmentalize the drawers for a particular type of jewelry collection.

(continued on next page)

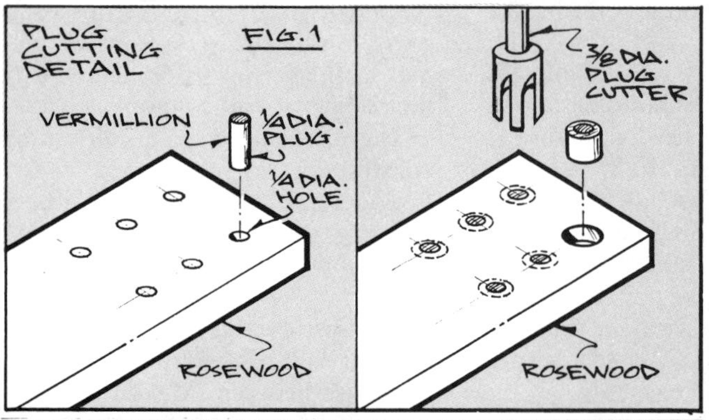
PLUG CUTTING DETAIL
FIG. 1
VERMILLION
1/4 DIA. PLUG
1/4 DIA. HOLE
ROSEWOOD
3/8 DIA. PLUG CUTTER
ROSEWOOD

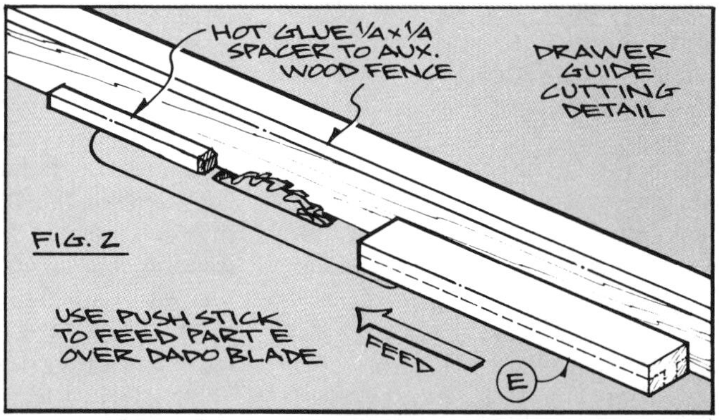
HOT GLUE 1/4 x 1/4 SPACER TO AUX. WOOD FENCE
DRAWER GUIDE CUTTING DETAIL
FIG. 2
USE PUSH STICK TO FEED PART E OVER DADO BLADE
FEED
E

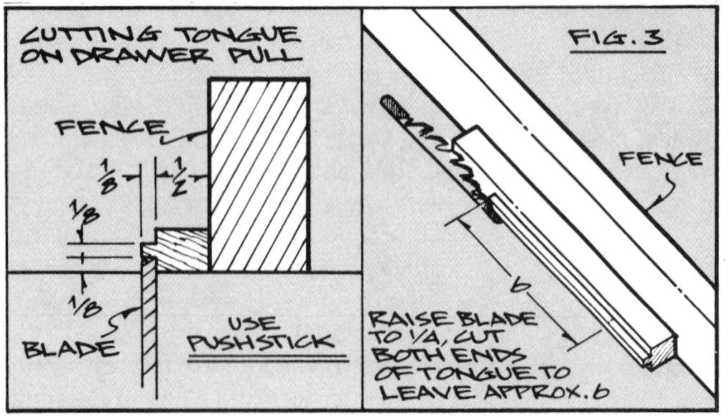
CUTTING TONGUE ON DRAWER PULL
FENCE
1/8
1/2
1/8
1/8
BLADE
USE PUSHSTICK
FIG. 3
FENCE
6
RAISE BLADE TO 1/4, CUT BOTH ENDS OF TONGUE TO LEAVE APPROX. 6

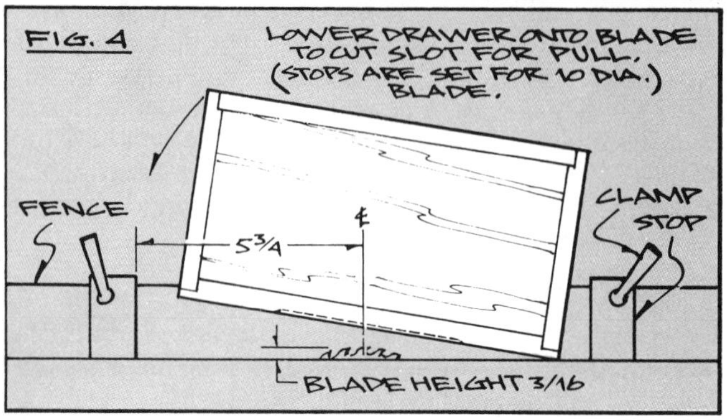
FIG. 4
LOWER DRAWER ONTO BLADE TO CUT SLOT FOR PULL. (STOPS ARE SET FOR 10 DIA.) BLADE.
FENCE
5 3/4
CLAMP STOP
BLADE HEIGHT 3/16

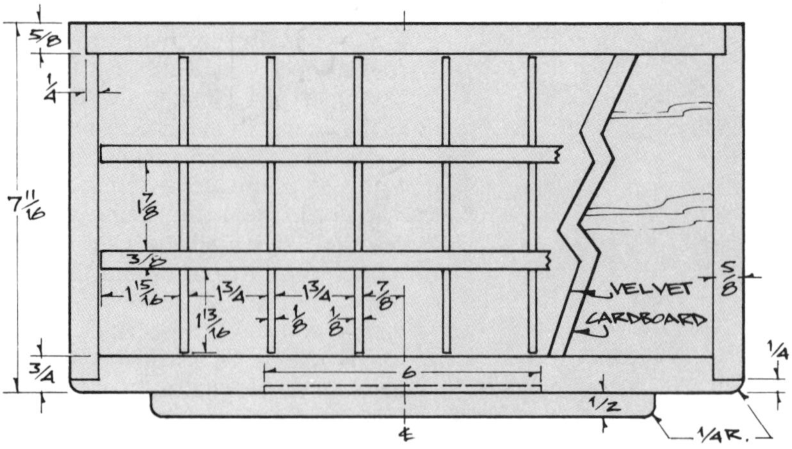
5/8
1/4
7 11/16
1 7/8
3/8
1 15/16
1 3/4
1 3/4
7/8
1 13/16
1/8
1/8
VELVET
CARDBOARD
5/8
3/4
6
1/4
1/2
1/4 R.

DRAWER TOP VIEW

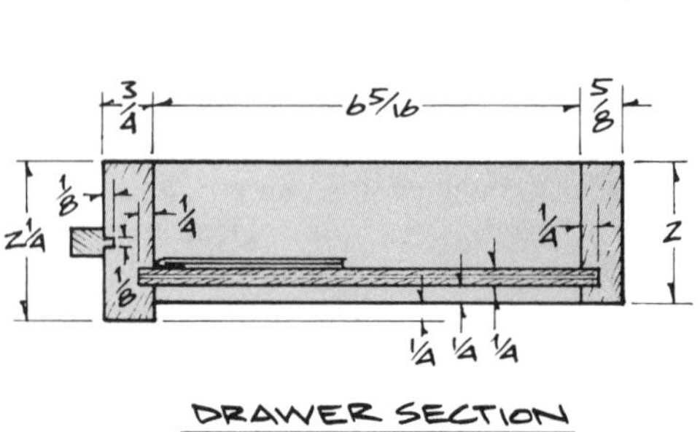
3/4
6 5/16
5/8
1/8
1/4
2 1/4
1/4
2
1/8
1/4 1/4 1/4

DRAWER SECTION

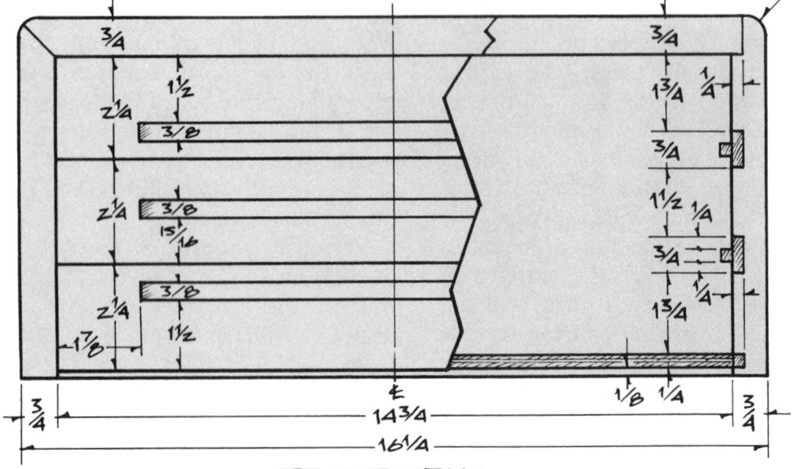
3/8 R.
3/4
3/4
1 1/2
2 1/4
3/8
1 3/4
1/4
3/4
2 1/4
3/8
15/16
1 1/2
1/4
3/4
1/4
3/8
2 1/4
1 7/8
1 1/2
1 3/4
1/8
1/4
3/4
14 3/4
3/4
16 1/4

FRONT VIEW

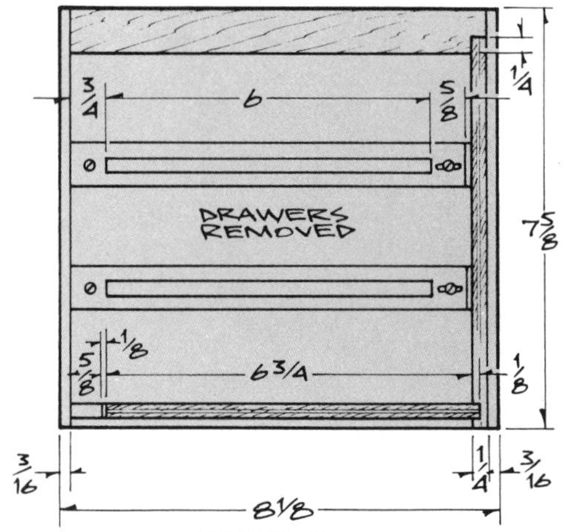
1/4
3/4
6
5/8
DRAWERS REMOVED
7 5/8
1/8
5/8
6 3/4
1/8
3/16
1/4
3/16
8 1/8

SECTION

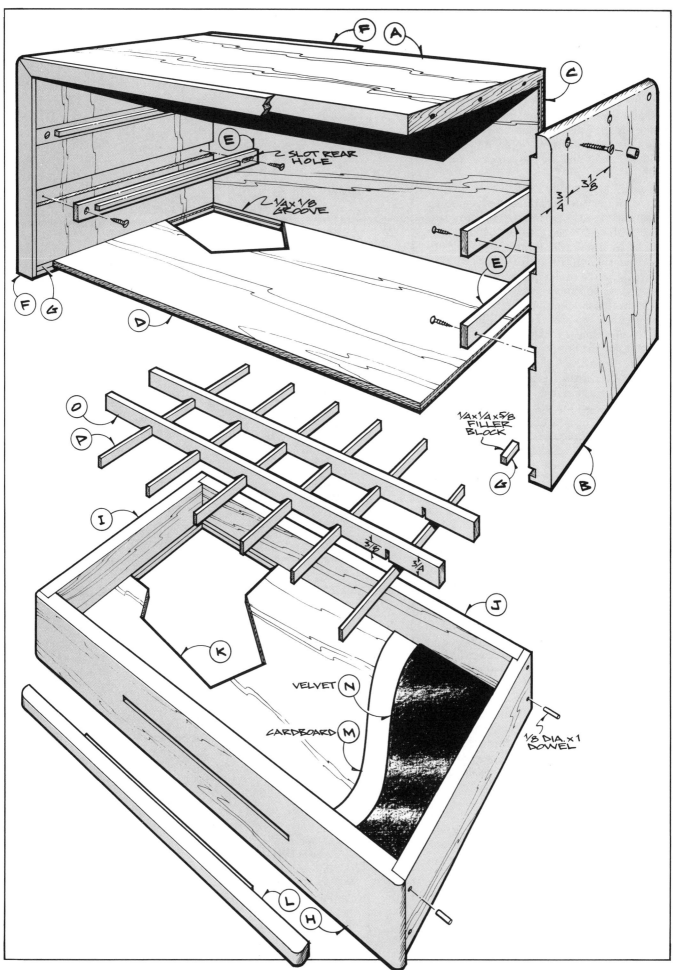

2 SLOT REAR HOLE

¼ x ⅛ GROOVE

3/8

¾

3¼/8

¾

¼ x ¼ x 5/8 FILLER BLOCK

VELVET

CARDBOARD

⅛ DIA. x 1 DOWEL

83

A pine medicine cabinet is just the right detail to complement the home featuring a country decor. This project is relatively easy to build. If you don't have a lathe, dowel stock could be substituted for the turned towel bar (G).

Start by getting out stock for the cabinet carcase. Refer to the grid patterns for the curved profiles of the sides (A) and top (E). These profiles are cut with the band saw or with the saber saw after the dadoes for the upper/lower shelves (B) and bottom (D) have been cut. Use the router equipped with a ⅜ in. rabbeting bit to rabbet the sides as shown to accept the top and the back (F). Bore the ¼ in. diameter shelf pin holes and the ¼ in. deep by ⅞ in. diameter holes for the towel bar (see side elevation for the hole location), and glue and assemble the carcase. The back should help to square up the carcase if it is mounted now. Important: The towel bar (see turning detail) must be made and in place for the assembly, since it cannot be added later.

To make the door, first construct a simple half-lapped frame consisting of the stiles (H) and rails (I). Next, use the router equipped with a bearing-guided ⅜ in. rabbeting bit, and cut a ⅜ in. by ⅜ in. rabbet around the inside of the door frame to accept the mirror (J), mirror backing (K) and retainer (L). Use a chisel to square the corners. Again using the router, but this time equipped with a ¼ in. radius round-over bit, round over both the inside and the outside perimeters of the door frame front. Then use the table saw dado head to cut the ⅜ in. deep lips as indicated around the door perimeter. Note that while this lip will be ⅜ in. wide on the door sides, it is ¾ in. wide at the top of the door, and ¼ in. wide on the bottom. Mount the mirror and the backing (a section of ³⁄₁₆ in. paneling or hardboard), and tack the retainer molding in place to secure them. This system permits future replacement of the mirror, if necessary. Cut the adjustable shelf (C) to size, and hang the door with standard ⅜ in. recessed cabinet hinges (R). The hinges, shelf pins (S), and the porcelain knobs (Q) should be available at your local hardware store.

The drawer (parts M, N, O, P) is made as shown. Round the perimeter of the drawer front with the ¼ in. radius round-over bit, and use the table saw dado head to cut the various rabbets and grooves in the drawer front, sides and back. Assemble the drawer with glue and finishing nails as shown.

After final sanding, we wiped on a light stain (take care not to darken the wood too much) and finished the cabinet with two generous coats of Watco Danish Oil.

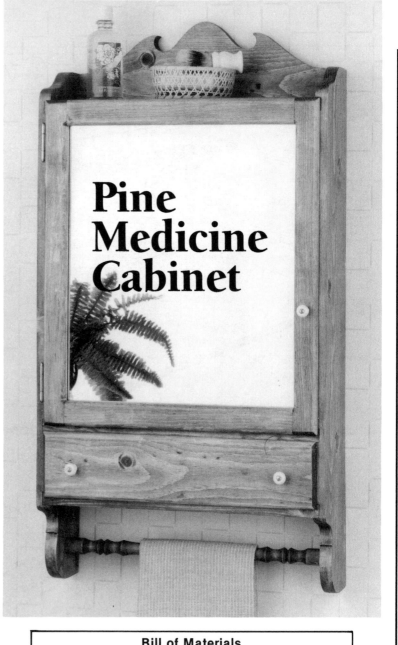

Pine Medicine Cabinet

Bill of Materials
(all dimensions actual)

Part	Description	Size	No. Req'd.
A	Side	¾ × 5½ × 31	2
B	Upper/Lower Shelf	¾ × 5¼ × 17¼	2
C	Adjustable Shelf	½ × 4¾ × 16⅜	1
D	Bottom	¾ × 5½ × 17¼	1
E	Top	¾ × 5 × 17¼	1
F	Back	¼ × 17¼ × 23⅝	1
G	Towel Bar	⅞ in. dia. × 17 in. long	1
H	Door Stile	¾ × 1½ × 19¼	2
I	Door Rail	¾ × 1½ × 17¼	2
J	Mirror	15 × 17	1
K	Mirror Backing	15 × 17	1
L	Retainer	³⁄₁₆ × ⅜ stock	65 in.
M	Drawer Front	¾ × 4 × 17¼	1
N	Drawer Side	½ × 3½ × 5¼	2
O	Drawer Back	½ × 3½ × 16	1
P	Drawer Bottom	¼ × 4⅝ × 16	1
Q	Knob	¾ in. dia. porcelain	3
R	Hinge	Offset cabinet type for ⅜ recessed doors (brass finish)	1 pair
S	Shelf Pins	For ¼ in. dia. hole	4

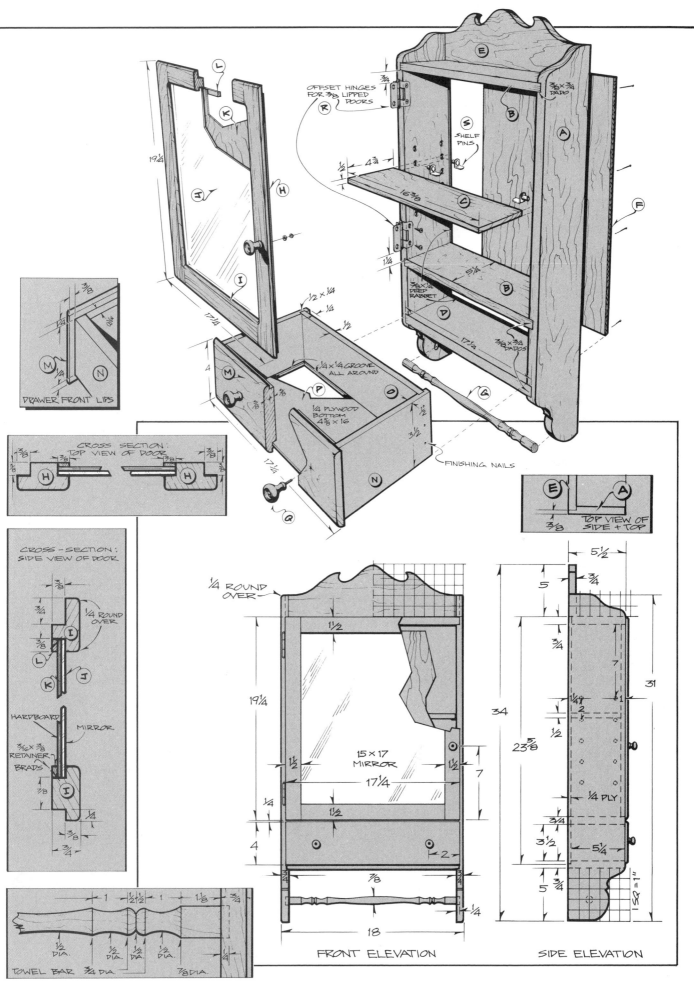

OFFSET HINGES
FOR 3/8 LIPPED
DOORS

SHELF PINS

3/4

3/8 x 3/4
DADO

4 3/4

1/2

16 3/8

5 1/4

3/16 x 1/4
DEEP
RABBET

17 1/4

3/8 x 3/4
DADOS

FINISHING NAILS

1/2 x 1/4

1/4

1/2

1/4 x 1/4 GROOVE
ALL AROUND

1/4 PLYWOOD
BOTTOM
4 3/8 x 16

1/2

3 1/2

17 1/2

19 1/4

3/8

3/4

1/4

DRAWER FRONT LIPS

CROSS SECTION:
TOP VIEW OF DOOR

3/8
3/8
3/8
3/8
3/8

CROSS - SECTION:
SIDE VIEW OF DOOR

3/8
3/4
3/8

1/4 ROUND
OVER

HARDBOARD

MIRROR

3/16 x 3/8
RETAINER
BRADS

7/8

1/4
3/8
3/4

TOP VIEW OF
SIDE + TOP

3/8

1/4 ROUND
OVER

1 1/2

15 x 17
MIRROR

19 1/4

1 1/2

1 1/2

1/4

1 1/2

4

17 1/4

7

7/8

1/4

18

FRONT ELEVATION

5 1/2

5

3/4

3/4

7

31

34

23 5/8

1/4
2

1/2

1/4 PLY

3/4

3 1/2

5 1/4

5

3/4

1 SQ = 1"

SIDE ELEVATION

TOWEL BAR 3/4 DIA.

1

1/2
2 1/2

1

1 1/8

3/4

1/2
DIA.

1/2
DIA.

1/2
DIA.

1/2
DIA.

7/8 DIA.

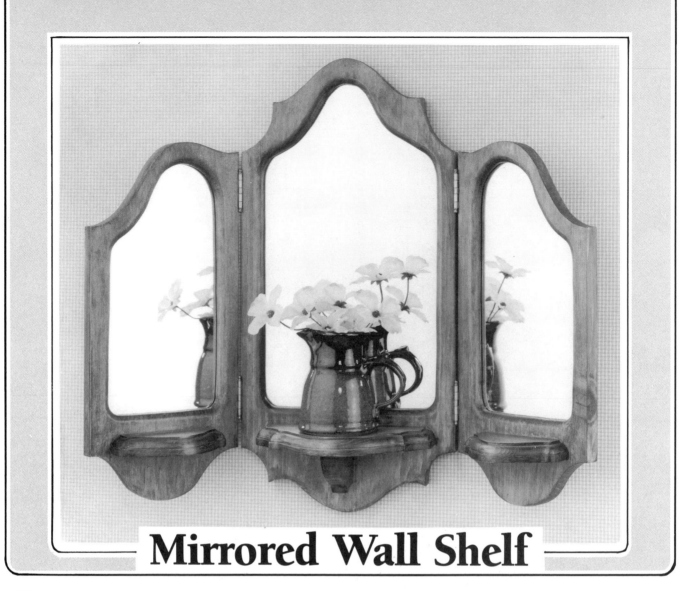

Mirrored Wall Shelf

One weekend in the shop should be all that's needed to complete this piece. The two ends, which are hinged to the center, can be pivoted to any angle up to 90 degrees. We made ours from pine and then stained it, but any wood will work well with this piece.

Begin by making the center frame (A) and the two end frames (B). Using ¾ in. thick stock, cut the three parts to overall length and width, then transfer the profile of each inner and outer curve (see front view) from the grid pattern to the stock.

The inner curve should be cut first. To establish the ½ in. radius at each lower corner, use a 1 in. diameter drill bit to bore a hole at the corners as shown. Now, with the holes bored, use a saber saw to cut out the inner curve, taking care to stay slightly on the waste side of the line. Once cut out, sand the sawn edge exactly to the line.

Note that the front of each inside curve is radiused to ¼ in. while the back has a ⅜ in. by ⅜ in. rabbet. Cut the radius first using a router and a bearing-guided ¼ in. radius bit. Don't cut the rabbet first. If you do, you won't have any stock to serve as a bearing surface for the radius bit.

To cut the rabbet use a ⅜ in. bearing-guided rabbeting bit. The bit will create rounded corners at the bottom so you'll need to cut them square with a chisel. Next, use a ruler and sharp pencil to lay out the straight lines of the mirror at the top of each frame. (These lines are shown as dotted lines in the front view). Now, use the chisel to expand the rabbet to the marked layout lines.

The saber saw can now be used to cut the previously marked outside profile. As before, cut a bit on the waste side of the line, then sand to the line. The ⅛ in. deep by ¾ in. wide by 1½ in. long hinge notches can be cut by hand with a chisel or by using the table saw dado head.

Next, cut the center and end shelves (C and D), and the support (E) to overall length and width from ¾ in. thick stock. Transfer the curved profiles shown in the top and side views to the stock, then cut out and sand smooth. Use a router and a ⅜ in. radius bearing-guided beading bit to apply the molded edge to the center and end shelves (see shelf molded edge detail).

Final sand all parts, then assemble as shown with 1½ in. long number 8 flathead wood screws. Do not use any glue as the frames need to expand and contract with seasonal changes in humidity. To permit the movement, the center frame has a pair of slotted holes, while each end frame has a single slotted hole. Once assembled, we applied two coats of Minwax's Colonial Maple Wood Finish followed by an application of their Antique Oil.

The mirror stock can be bought at just about any glass shop, and most will cut it to shape for a nominal charge. Use glazier's points to secure the glass in the rabbet, but be careful not to score the silver on the back of the glass when you install the points. If you do, it will show on the front of the mirror. The addition of a pair of brass butt hinges completes the project.

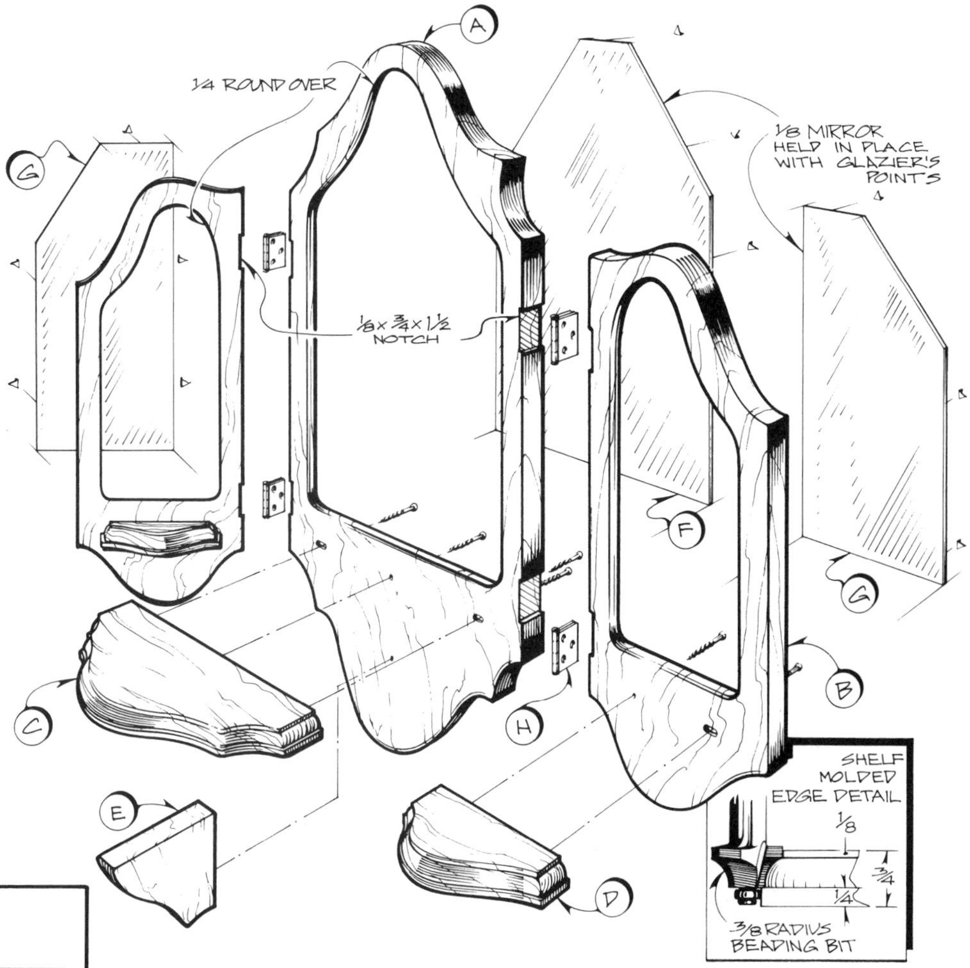
A
1/4 ROUND OVER
1/8 MIRROR HELD IN PLACE WITH GLAZIER'S POINTS
G
1/8 x 3/4 x 1 1/2 NOTCH
F
G
B
C
H
E
D
SHELF MOLDED EDGE DETAIL
1/8
3/4
1/4
3/8 RADIUS BEADING BIT

Bill of Materials
(all dimensions actual)

Part	Description	Size	No. Req'd.
A	Center Frame	3/4 × 10 × 20	1
B	End Frame	3/4 × 7 × 15 1/2	2
C	Center Shelf	3/4 × 3 3/4 × 8	1
D	End Shelf	3/4 × 2 1/2 × 5	2
E	Support	3/4 × 3 × 2	1
F	Center Mirror	1/8 × 8 3/4 × 15 1/8	1
G	End Mirror	1/8 × 5 3/4 × 11 1/2	2
H	Hinge	1 1/2 × 1 1/2	2 pair

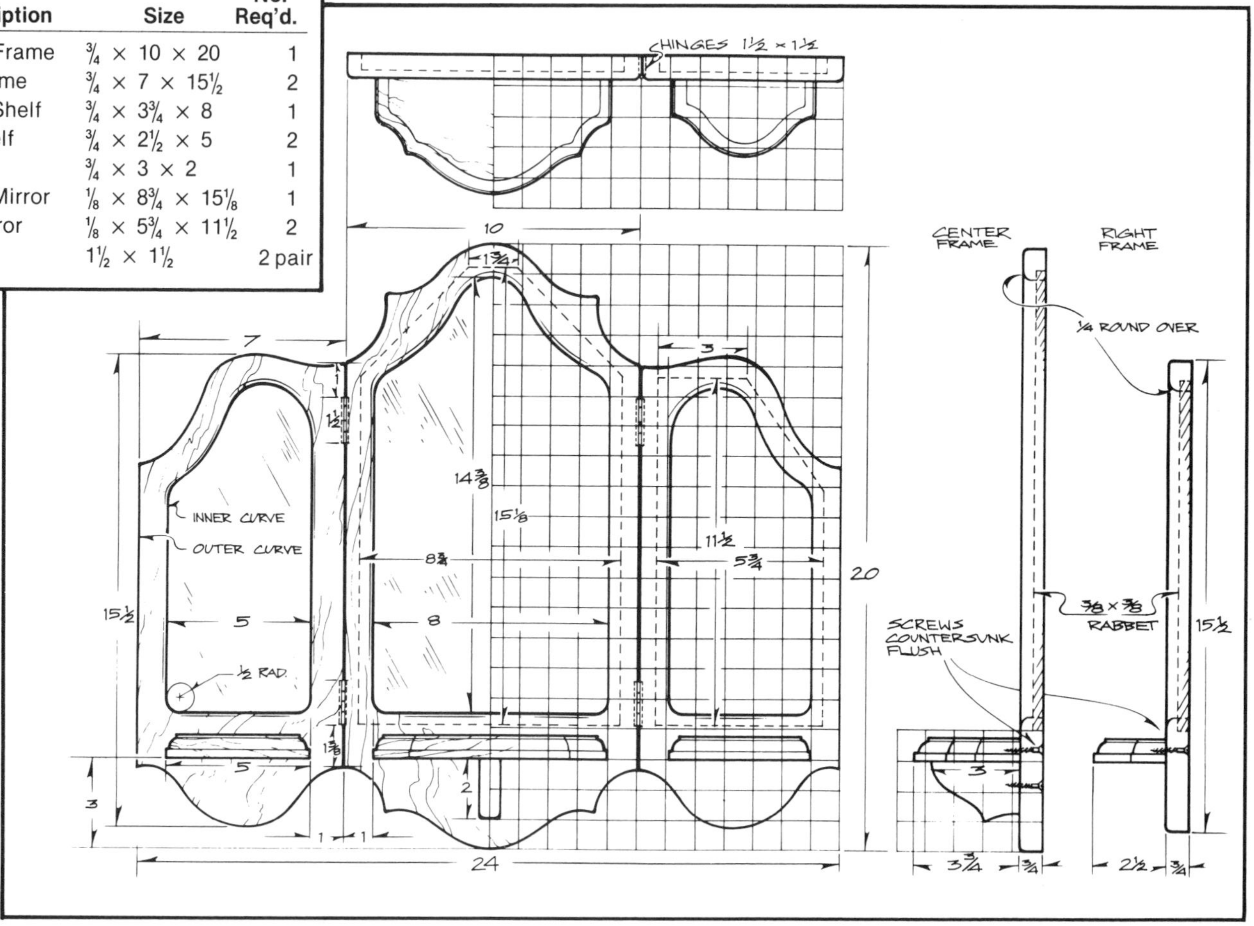
HINGES 1 1/2 x 1 1/2
10
1 3/4
7
3
1 1/2
14 3/8
15 1/8
INNER CURVE
OUTER CURVE
11 1/2
8 3/4
5 3/4
20
15 1/2
5
8
1/2 RAD.
1 3/8
5
3
2
1
1
24
CENTER FRAME
RIGHT FRAME
1/4 ROUND OVER
3/8 x 3/8 RABBET
15 1/2
SCREWS COUNTERSUNK FLUSH
3
3 3/4
3/4
2 1/2
3/4

Canada Goose Mobile

Hang this handsome bird from the ceiling, then pull the weight and stand back to watch the graceful up-and-down movement of the wings. It's a novel project, one that can make an interesting addition to a teenager's room, den, or recreation room.

The entire project is made from a 9¼ in. wide by 36 in. long piece of ¼ in. thick solid maple. If you don't have a thickness planer or can't get ¼ in. thick stock locally, you can order a ¼ in. by 9¼ in. by 36 in. piece of maple from Constantine, 2050 Eastchester Road, Bronx, NY 10461; tel. 1-800-223-8087.

Using the cutting diagram as a layout guide, transfer the wing and body profiles from the grid pattern to the stock. To get a clean cut, use a scroll saw or a narrow, fine-tooth band saw blade. A file and some sanding should be all that's needed to smooth any rough sawn edges. The wing will flex with less resistance if the end that contacts the body is rounded slightly.

Next, mark the location of the seventeen ¹⁄₁₆ in. diameter fishing line holes (six in each wing and five in the body), then bore them out. Also, at this time, cut a piece of ¼ in. dowel stock to a 9½ in. length and bore a ¹⁄₁₆ in. hole at each end.

We used clear monofilament fishing line to hang the mobile. Start with about a 40 in. length and tie an end to one of the pairs of wing holes. Run the other end of the line through one of the dowel holes so that you have about 20 in. between the wing and dowel. Tie a knot at the dowel hole, then run the end of the line down to the other pair of wing holes and add a third and final knot. Repeat the procedure for the other wing.

For the upper line, start with about a 20 in. length and tie one end to the dowel. Now loop the line around a metal key ring and tie the other end to the dowel. Keep in mind, though, that there is no hard and fast rule that dictates how long the lines must be. The bird will "fly" as long as there are at least 12 in. between the wings and the dowel.

To attach the wings, tie a loop through each pair of holes in the body, then tie the wings to the loops. When tying the wing knots, try to allow about ⅛ in. clearance between the wing and the body. This clearance will provide room for the wings to move with a minimum of interference.

The bird is now ready for balancing. A short length of 1 in. diameter dowel stock, suspended by a fishing line from the body, serves as a counterbalance. When at rest, we wanted the bird's wings to be slightly in the up position, and after a bit of experimentation, we determined that a 1 in. diameter by ¾ in. long dowel provided the proper weight. More weight (a longer dowel) will make the wings higher when the bird is at rest. Less weight (a shorter dowel) and the wings start to flatten out.

Since every bird will have some slight variation in balance, you'll no doubt have to do some of your own experimenting. Once you get the correct weight, hang the dowel from about a 10 in. length of fishing line as shown. If everything looks okay, give the weight a pull to check the goose for airworthiness.

The neck, head, and tail can now be painted with a coat of black enamel paint. Once dry, a couple of coats of penetrating oil will provide a good final finish.

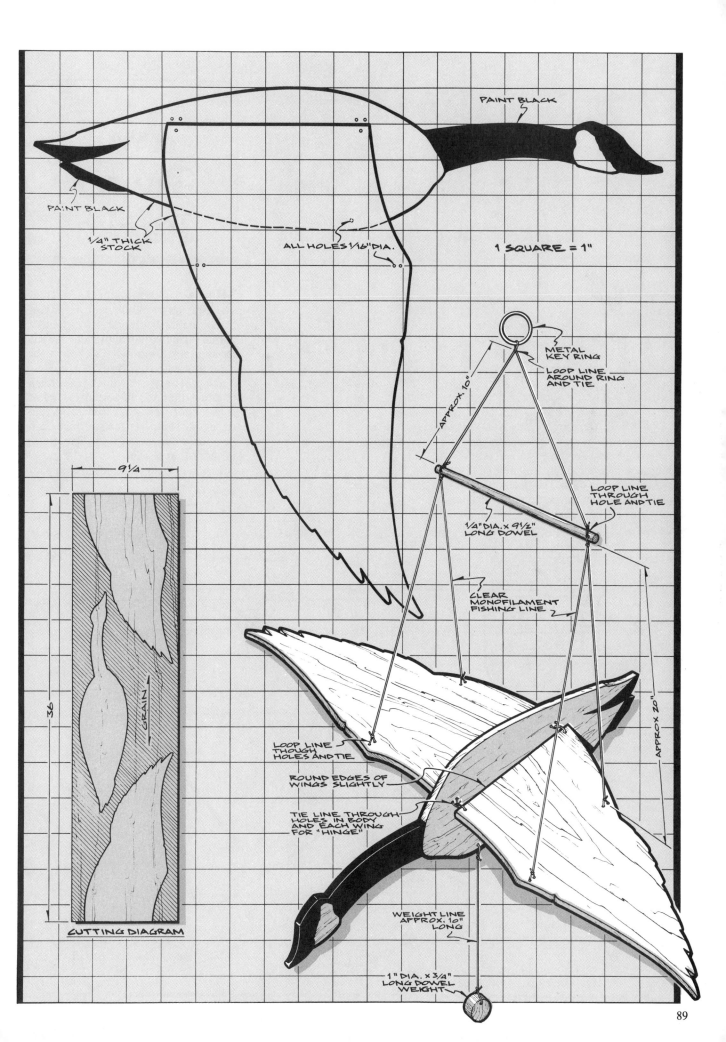

PAINT BLACK

PAINT BLACK

1/4" THICK STOCK

ALL HOLES 1/16" DIA.

1 SQUARE = 1"

METAL KEY RING

LOOP LINE AROUND RING AND TIE

APPROX. 10"

LOOP LINE THROUGH HOLE AND TIE

1/4" DIA. x 9 1/2" LONG DOWEL

CLEAR MONOFILAMENT FISHING LINE

APPROX 20"

9 1/4

GRAIN

36

CUTTING DIAGRAM

LOOP LINE THROUGH HOLES AND TIE

ROUND EDGES OF WINGS SLIGHTLY

TIE LINE THROUGH HOLES IN BODY AND EACH WING FOR "HINGE"

WEIGHT LINE APPROX. 10" LONG

1" DIA. x 3/4" LONG DOWEL WEIGHT

Two Towel Racks

These towel racks make a great gift item. While we show two traditional back designs, a heart and a gothic form (we like to think of the latter as a fanciful snowflake), you might want to create your own.

All parts are ¾ in. thick pine. Keep in mind that it's important to select clear, knot-free stock for maximum strength. The parts for two racks can be obtained from a ¾ in. by 8 in. by 38 in. board, as shown.

Begin by laying out the parts on your

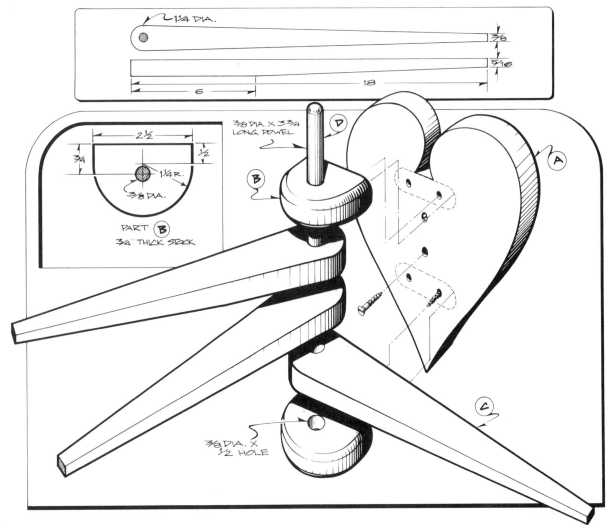

1¼ DIA.

⅜

5/16

6 18

⅜ DIA. X 3¾ LONG DOWEL

D

B

A

2½

¾

½

¼ R.

⅜ DIA.

PART B
¾" THICK STOCK

C

⅜ DIA. X ½ HOLE

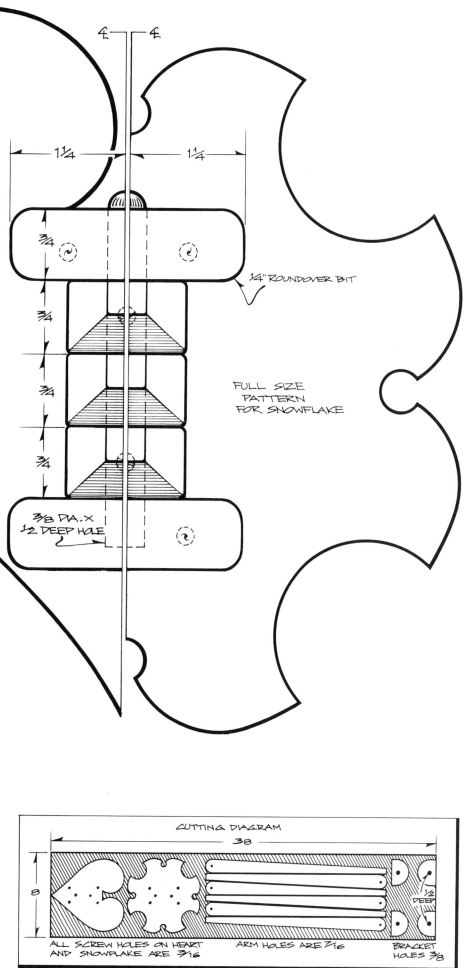

board
stock. The
full-size patterns
for the heart, snow-
flake, and mounts can
either be cut out and
taped onto the stock, or
you can use tracing paper to
first trace the pattern before
cutting out and taping in place.

Now use the drill press to drill all the
holes as indicated. Note that the arm-
holes are $\frac{1}{16}$ in. larger than the dowel
diameter, so they will pivot easily. The
hole in the bottom mount is *not* drilled
through, being only $\frac{1}{2}$ in. deep.

Next, use the band saw (or a jig or
saber saw) to cut the individual parts.
Use a hand plane to apply a 12 in. long
taper on the bottom edge of the arms,
then use the router table to radius the
edges of the mounts. Final sand all
parts and assemble the mounts to the
base with four $1\frac{1}{2}$ in. long screws
driven through the back.

Stain and finish to suit. We used
Minwax Special Walnut stain, follow-
ed by a spray coat of Zip-Guard Gloss
Polyurethane.

The arms cannot be mounted until
the base has been screwed to the wall.
Be sure to use long enough screws to
penetrate through both the back and
the sheetrock and into a stud. A $2\frac{1}{2}$ in.
long screw is recommended.

$1\frac{1}{4}$ $1\frac{1}{4}$

$\frac{3}{4}$ "STOCK

$\frac{3}{4}$

$\frac{1}{4}$" ROUNDOVER BIT

FULL SIZE
PATTERN
FOR HEART

FULL SIZE
PATTERN
FOR SNOWFLAKE

$\frac{3}{4}$

$\frac{3}{4}$

$\frac{3}{4}$

$\frac{3}{8}$ DIA. X
$\frac{1}{2}$ DEEP HOLE

CUTTING DIAGRAM

38

8

$\frac{1}{2}$ DEEP

ALL SCREW HOLES ON HEART
AND SNOWFLAKE ARE $\frac{3}{16}$

ARM HOLES ARE $\frac{7}{16}$

BRACKET
HOLES $\frac{3}{8}$

91

The ability to recognize shapes is an important part of a young child's development. This easy-to-make toy will help kids to learn several of the basic shapes — and have some fun while they learn. Five different profiles are cut into the box, one in each of the four sides and one in the top. The child is challenged to get the blocks in the box, and that can only be done if the shape of the block matches the cutout. A double ball catch keeps the hinged top shut until the youngster opens it to remove the blocks.

Ours is made from poplar, a wood that is relatively light, yet durable. Maple, which has excellent durability, is also a good choice.

A piece of stock measuring ½ in. thick by 5½ in. wide by 20 in. long will provide enough stock for the four sides (A), while a piece that's ½ in. thick by 5½ in. wide by 11 in. long will suffice for the top (C) and bottom (D). The width and length dimensions allow extra stock.

The four sides (A) are cut from the 20 in. long board. After thickness planing, set the table saw blade to 45 degrees, then raise it to a height of about ¾ in. Set the rip fence to cut the miter along one edge of the 20 in. length. When setting the fence, keep in mind that it should be located so that, after the miter is cut, the stock width is not less than 5 in. Now, with one miter cut, readjust the rip fence to establish the final stock width of 5 in., then cut the second miter.

To cut the spline groove (see spline detail), you'll need to lower the saw blade (which should still be set at 45 degrees) and relocate the rip fence. Use scrap stock to check the accuracy of your set-up. Most saw blades make a ⅛ in. wide cut, however if your blade makes a slightly wider or narrower cut, simply adjust the spline (B) thickness as needed.

Box of Shapes Toy

The stock can now be crosscut into four pieces, each piece measuring 4½ in. long. To cut the dado groove along the bottom edge of each side (see bottom detail), a ¼ in. dado head cutter is set to a depth of ¼ in. and the rip fence is located ¼ in. from the nearest tooth. Hold the stock firmly against the rip fence as it's pushed over the cutter. Be sure to use a push stick to keep hands a safe distance from the blade.

The ½ in. by 5½ in. by 11 in. board that was made earlier will serve as stock for the top and bottom. To make the bottom, cut to 4⅜ in. square, then cut the ¼ in. by ¼ in. rabbet all around. The top is 5 in. square with a ¼ in. radius cove cut on the front edge. To cut the cove, we used a router table and a ¼ in. cove bit.

Next, on the four sides and the top, lay out and mark the five shapes, then use a sharp chisel to cut out each one except the circle. To make the circle, use a Forstner bit or hole saw.

After cutting four splines, the sides and the bottom can be assembled with glue, then clamped firmly. Cut the splines a little on the long side so that after the glue dries, they can be trimmed flush with the ends of the sides. Since it must be free to expand and contract with seasonal changes in humidity, the bottom is not glued in

place. With the box assembled, the router table and ¼ in. cove bit are once again used to add a cove, this time along the top edge of the front.

The top can now be attached to the box with a pair of hinges (G). Adding the catch block (E) and the double ball catch (F) completes work on the box.

The five blocks (H, I, J, K, and L) are made as shown. The circle block (J) can be turned to the 1½ in. diameter, although closet pole (sold at most hardware stores) can also be used.

Final sand each part, taking care to round over all sharp edges and corners to a generous (about 3/16 in.) radius. Since small children have a natural inclination to chew on just about anything, we feel it's best not to apply a finish to a toy like this.

Part	Description	Size	No. Req'd.
Bill of Materials (all dimensions actual)			
A	Side	½ × 5 × 4½	4
B	Spline	⅛ × ⅜ × 4½	4
C	Top	½ × 5 × 5	1
D	Bottom	½ × 4⅜ × 4⅜	1
E	Catch Block	½ × ¾ × 2	1
F	Double Ball Catch	5/16 × 1 11/16*	1
G	Hinge	¾ × 1	2
H	Trapezoid Block	see detail	1
I	Triangle Block	see detail	1
J	Circle Block	see detail	1
K	Diamond Block	see detail	1
L	Square Block	see detail	1

*Available from Mason & Sullivan, 586 Higgins Crowell Road, West Yarmouth, MA 02673.

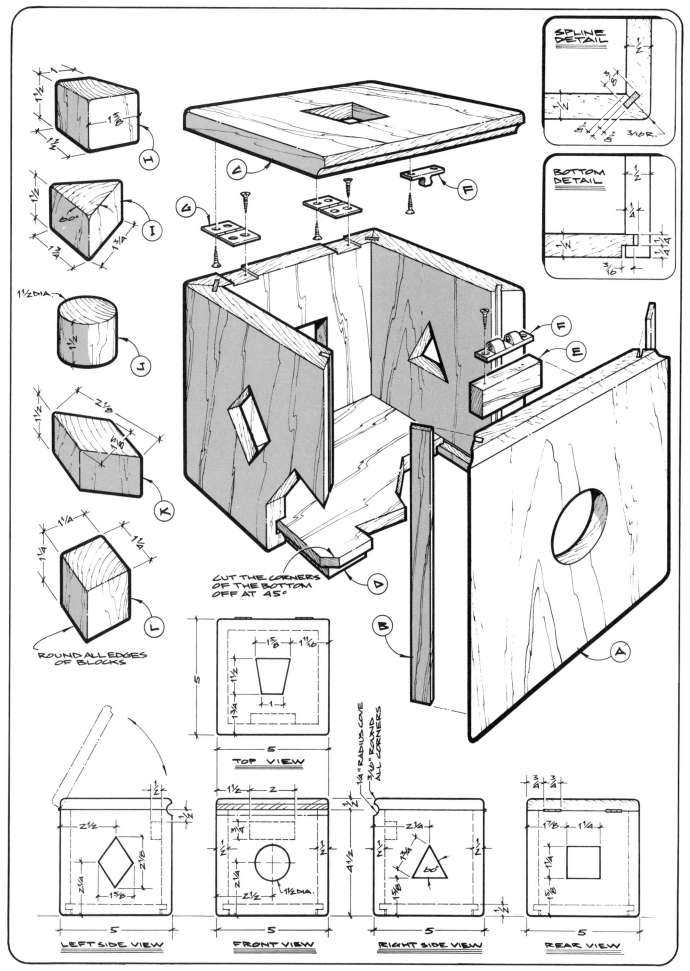

SPLINE DETAIL

BOTTOM DETAIL

1½ DIA.

CUT THE CORNERS OF THE BOTTOM OFF AT 45°

ROUND ALL EDGES OF BLOCKS

¼" RADIUS COVE
3/16" ROUND ALL CORNERS

TOP VIEW

LEFT SIDE VIEW

FRONT VIEW

RIGHT SIDE VIEW

REAR VIEW

Here's a somewhat scaled-down version of a basket commonly used by early New England clam-diggers. This one is rather unusual in that the handle is not centered. Instead, it runs diagonally, presumably to improve balance. If there are no clam beds in your area, it will still serve nicely as a magazine rack or as a means to display your favorite floral arrangement.

Make the two sides (A) first. Cut ¾ in. thick pine to a width of 10 in. and a length of 12 in., then use the table saw to cut the 45 degree corners as shown. Note that each corner measures 4⅛ in. Next, use a compass to scribe the 4⅛ in. radius before cutting it out with the band or saber saw.

The 15 slats (B) are made from five-quarter pine stock (which measures 1⅛ in. thick) ripped to ½ in. widths. It's best to cut them slightly longer than necessary so that after assembly they can be trimmed and sanded flush to the sides. Use glue and 1¼ by no. 8 flathead wood screws to join the slats to the sides. The end view shows the proper slat spacing. Note that each screwhead is countersunk slightly below the surface.

To make the handle (C) you'll need a piece of ¾ in. thick stock measuring 4½ in. wide and 22 in. long. Lay out the handle shape as shown in the top view before cutting it out with a band or saber saw. Trim the ends for a snug fit between the sides, then assemble

with a pair of 1½ by no. 8 flathead woodscrews on each end. Once again, apply a slight countersink to each of the screwheads.

Final sand all surfaces, taking particular care to smooth the upper curve on each side. Start with 80 grit, then follow with 120, 150, and finally 220. Slightly round over all sharp corners and edges.

Final finish is a matter of personal taste. We chose to leave ours natural and simply add a couple of coats of Watco Danish Oil. We found a brush helped to apply the finish between the slats. Once the second coat was thoroughly dry, it was rubbed down with a clean cloth to complete the project.

Clamdigger's
Basket

Bill of Materials
(all dimensions actual)

Part	Description	Size	No. Req'd.
A	Side	¾ × 10 × 12	2
B	Slat	½ × 1⅛ × 20	15
C	Handle	¾ × 4½ × 22*	1

*Length and width dimensions allow extra stock.

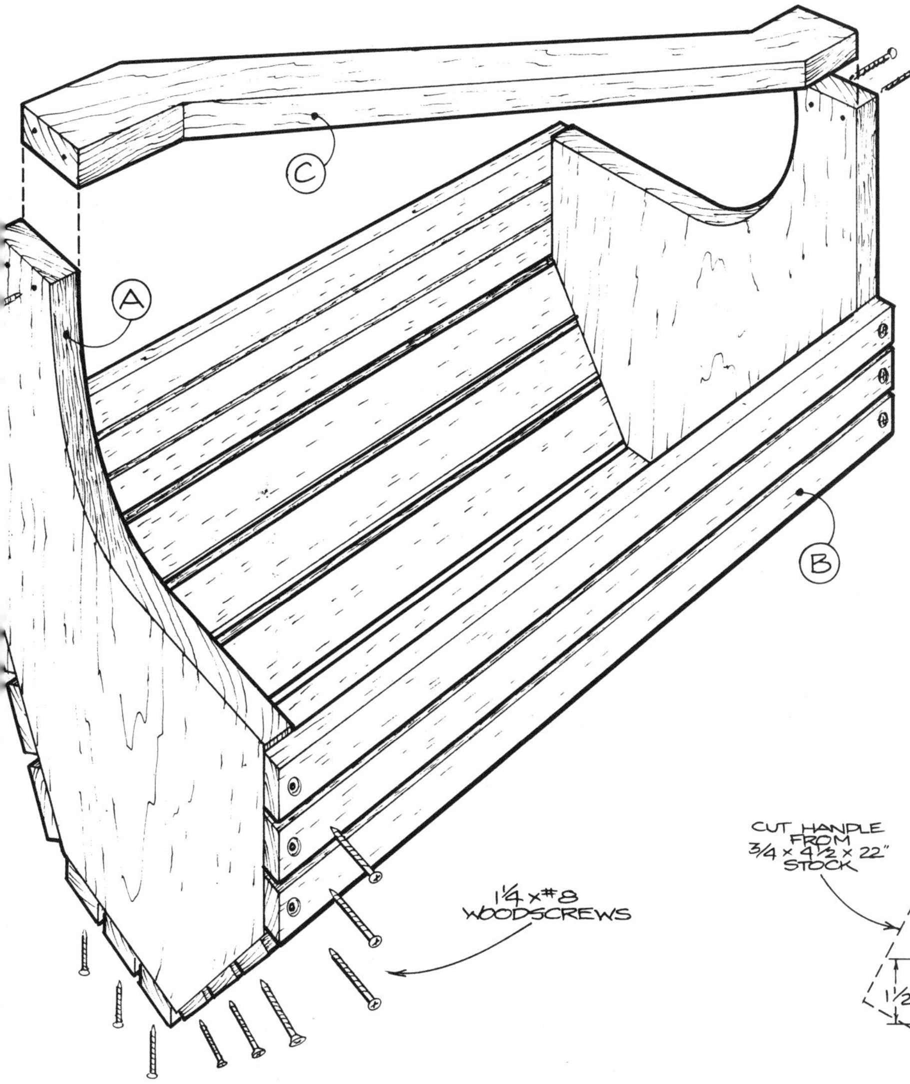

C
A
B
1¼ x #8 WOODSCREWS

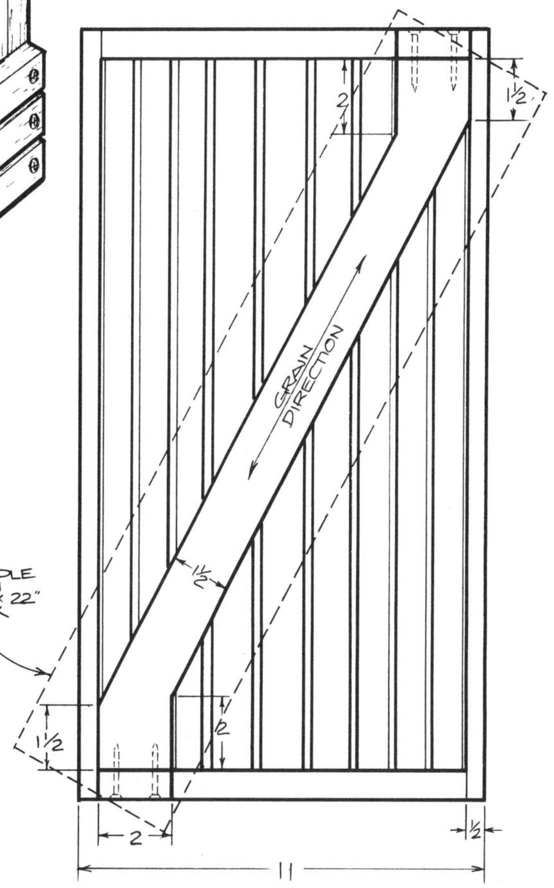

CUT HANDLE FROM 3/4 x 4½ x 22" STOCK
GRAIN DIRECTION
2
1½
½
2
1½
2
½
11

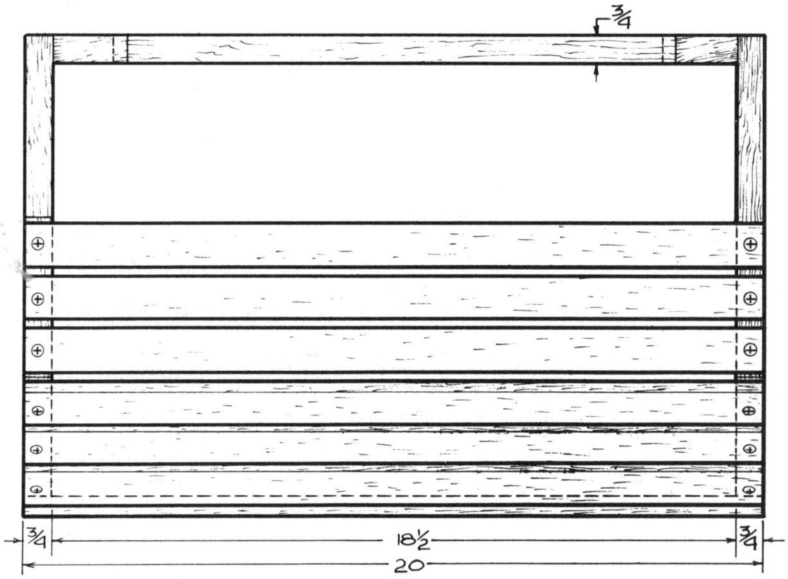

¾
¾
18½
¾
20

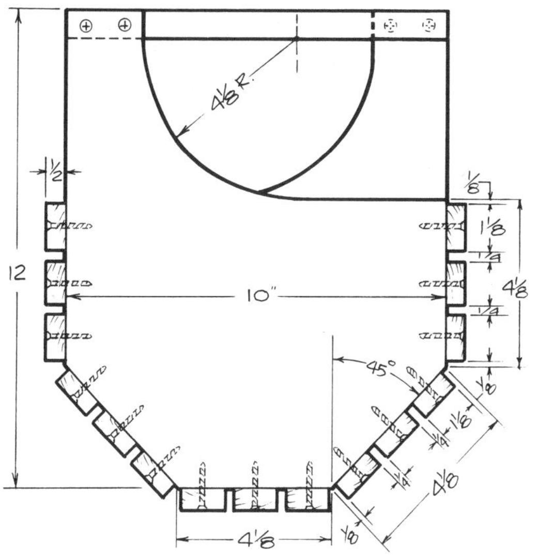

4⅛ R.
½
12
10"
45°
⅛
1⅛
¼
4⅛
4⅛

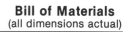

Latticework Planter

As a well chosen picture frame compliments a painting, an attractive planter can effectively display a favorite houseplant. Ours is a low-cost, easy-to-make design that looks as good in the living room as it does outside in the garden. The planter measures 12 in. square by 12 in. high, dimensions we found suitable for a fairly wide range of plant pots, but it can be made somewhat larger or smaller, if necessary. Check the dimensions of your pot before starting.

Since our pot is rather tall (about 9 in.), it simply rests on the bottom lattice. Shorter pots, however, will need a plywood shelf (see Detail: Optional Shelf) in order to be raised to an acceptable height.

The lattice is made up of ¼ in. thick by 1½ in. wide crisscrossed strips spaced 2¾ in. apart. Although you can make your own, we found it much easier to purchase the commercially made lattice sold at many lumberyards and building supply centers. It's sold in 4 ft. by 8 ft. and 2 ft. by 8 ft. sheets, with the lattice strips stapled and glued together. It's generally available in pine or cedar, either planed smooth or roughsawn. If you plan to keep it outside, cedar would be your best choice.

Five-quarter stock (which measures 1⅛ in. thick) can be ripped to 1⅛ in. widths to get the square stock needed for the four upper frames (A), four legs (B), and four lower frames (C). The ½ in. wide by ¼ in. deep groove can be cut with a dado head or by making repeated passes with the regular saw blade. Note that the upper frames have a single groove while the legs and lower frames have a pair of grooves. Before cutting the grooves, it's a good idea to measure the actual lattice thickness and, if necessary, adjust the groove width as needed.

Once the grooves are cut, the 12 in. long upper and lower frames can be mitered on each end. The legs, which have square cut ends, can then be cut to a length of 9¾ in.

Next, using the table saw, cut the lattice (D) to 10¼ in. square. Keep in mind, however, that most of the commercial lattice is assembled with a staple at the point the lattice crisscrosses. This means you'll have to make sure you don't hit one with the saw blade when making the cut.

Assemble the parts as shown using glue and clamps. If you intend to use the planter outdoors, be sure to use plastic resin glue. Available at most hardware stores, this brown powder is mixed with water to create a glue with excellent moisture resistance. White or yellow glue will not stand up to water for any length of time. Once dry, a pair of finishing nails are driven at each mitered corner.

If a shelf is needed (see Detail: Optional Shelf) a notch must be cut at each corner as shown. The plywood shelf is cut to fit in the notches, then a few ½ in. diameter holes are drilled to allow water to drain off.

If your planter will be used indoors, a couple of coats of a good penetrating oil are all that's needed for a good final finish. For outdoor use, where rain or exposure to water is a problem, Cuprinol brand wood preservative is a good choice.

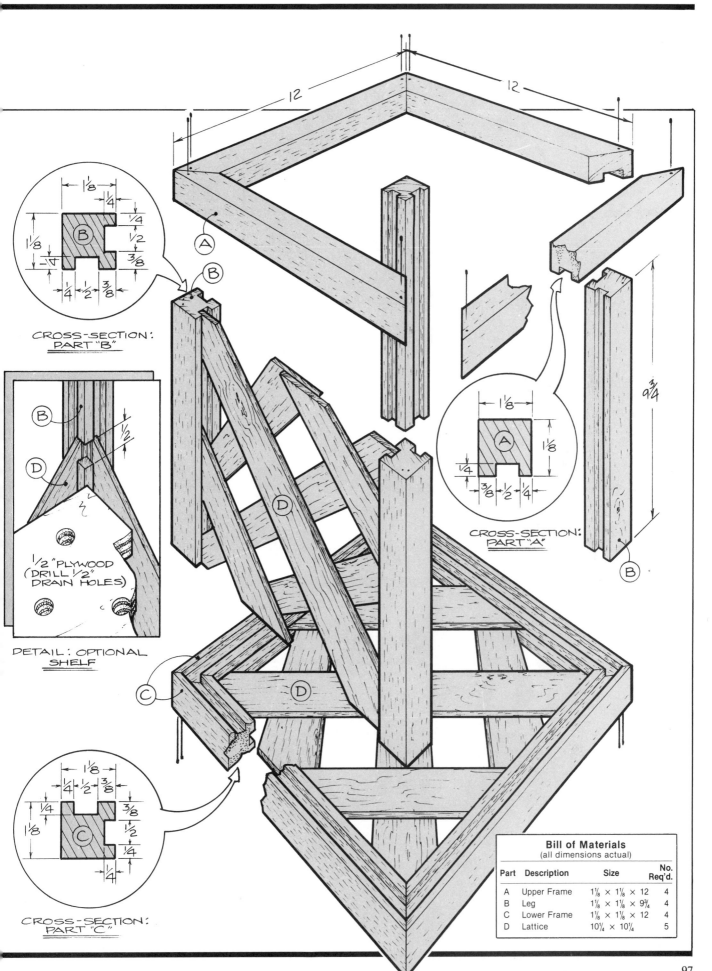

CROSS-SECTION:
PART "B"

CROSS-SECTION:
PART "A"

1/2" PLYWOOD
(DRILL 1/2"
DRAIN HOLES)

DETAIL: OPTIONAL
SHELF

CROSS-SECTION:
PART "C"

12

12

9¾

A

B

B

C

D

D

D

B

A

Bill of Materials			
(all dimensions actual)			
Part	Description	Size	No. Req'd.
A	Upper Frame	1⅛ × 1⅛ × 12	4
B	Leg	1⅛ × 1⅛ × 9¾	4
C	Lower Frame	1⅛ × 1⅛ × 12	4
D	Lattice	10¼ × 10¼	5

Old-Time Sled
Wall Shelf

Made to look like an old-fashioned sled, this easy-to-make project will be a charming addition to any room in the house. The sides and shelves are made from pine solid stock while the back is knotty pine plywood.

To make the sides (A), start by cutting ½ in. thick stock to a width of 2¼ in. and a length of 24 in. Lay out and mark the location of the ½ in. wide by ³⁄₁₆ in. deep dado grooves, then use the table saw and dado head to cut them out. Next, the ³⁄₁₆ in. wide by ¼ in. deep by 18¾ in. long rabbet is cut with an edge-guided router and ⅜ in. diameter bit. Note that the rabbet is stopped 3¾ in. from the top and 1½ in. from the bottom. Because the router bit leaves rounded corners, you'll need to square them with a sharp chisel.

Referring to the side view, transfer the upper and lower profiles to the stock. Use the band saw to cut out, then sand smooth. To complete work on the sides, bore a ¾ in. diameter hole at the top of each one as shown.

After cutting the three shelves (B) to length and width, glue and clamp the sides and shelves, making sure the corners are square. When dry, remove the clamps and drive a pair of finishing nails in the end of each shelf. Countersink each nail about ⅛ in. before filling with wood filler.

Cut the back (C) to overall length and width before laying out the curved profiles of the top and bottom. Cut out on the band saw and sand smooth. The cutout (see detail) is best cut with a saber saw after first boring a ⅜ in. diameter starter hole.

Apply glue to the rabbet on the back edge of the sides and to the back edges of the shelves, then assemble and clamp the back to the sides and shelves. When dry, remove the clamps and add finishing nails through the back and into the rabbet and the back edge of the shelves.

Final sand all parts before applying a final finish. Stain to suit your personal taste, then add two coats of a good penetrating oil. When dry, buff thoroughly with a soft cloth.

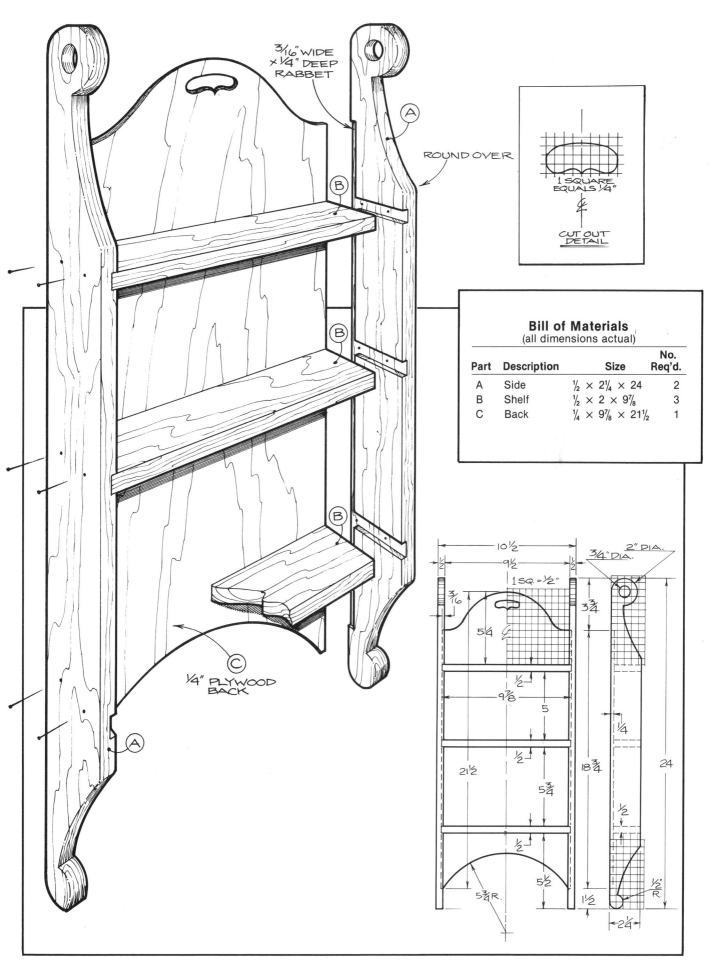

3/16" WIDE × 1/4" DEEP RABBET

ROUND OVER

1 SQUARE EQUALS 1/4"

⊄

CUT OUT DETAIL

Bill of Materials
(all dimensions actual)

Part	Description	Size	No. Req'd.
A	Side	$\frac{1}{2} \times 2\frac{1}{4} \times 24$	2
B	Shelf	$\frac{1}{2} \times 2 \times 9\frac{7}{8}$	3
C	Back	$\frac{1}{4} \times 9\frac{7}{8} \times 21\frac{1}{2}$	1

1/4" PLYWOOD BACK

10 1/2
9 1/2
1/2
1/2
3/16
1 SQ. = 1/2"
5 1/4
⊄
9 7/8
5
21 1/2
5 3/4
5 1/2
5 3/4 R.

2" DIA.
3/4" DIA.
3 3/4
1/4
1/2
1/2 R.
18 3/4
24
1 1/2
2 1/4

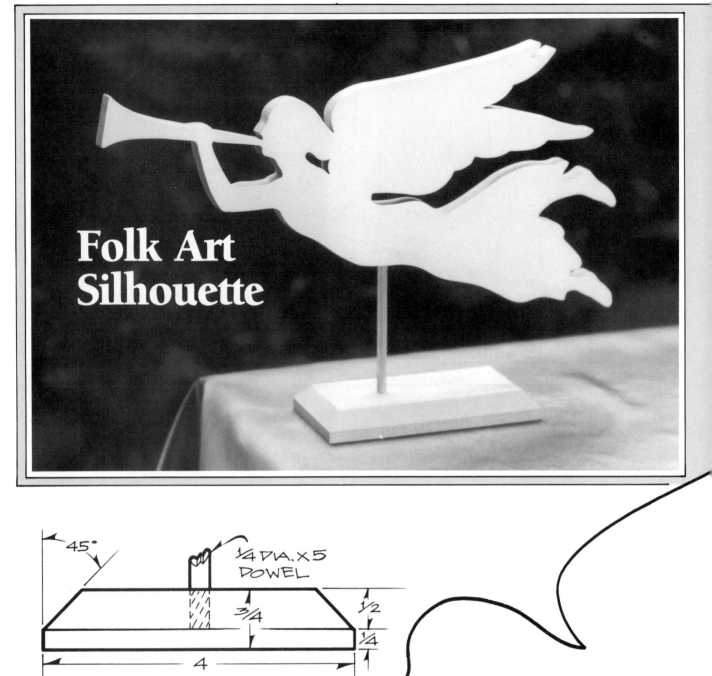

Folk Art Silhouette

45°

¼ DIA. X 5
DOWEL

3/4

½

¼

4

FULL SIZE PATTERN

Seventeenth and eighteenth century weathervanes were made in a wide variety of shapes and styles. Many of the folk-art silhouettes that have been enjoying considerable popularity of late owe their origins to those old-time weathervane designs. This one, the angel Gabriel, dates from that early period and it is one of our favorites.

Gabriel, an angel of Christian, Jewish, and Muslim tradition, is identified in some stories as one of the seven unnamed angels that trumpet to announce judgments on the world. And, according to the Old Testament, it is Gabriel who announces the birth of Jesus to Mary.

Begin by cutting a piece of 1 × 8 pine (which will actually measure ¾ in. thick by 7¼ in. wide) to a length of 16 in. A sharp smooth plane will reduce the ¾ in. stock to a thickness of ½ in. in short order. Try to avoid using a board with knots though, as they tend to reduce strength and to make planing difficult. Also, unless the knots are treated with a wash coat of shellac, their resin often bleeds into a painted surface.

Once the stock has been planed, transfer the full-sized pattern as shown. The entire outside profile can be cut out using a band saw with a narrow blade or a scroll saw. When cutting, stay just slightly on the waste side of the marked line, then sand the edge exactly to the line. To make the two inside profiles, first drill a small hole within each one before using a scroll or jigsaw to cut out. If you have them, a few small files (half-round, rattail, and triangular) will help to smooth the edges here.

The base is made from ¾ in. thick pine stock cut to 4 in. wide and 6 in. long. The table saw, with the blade set at 45 degrees, can be used to cut the bevel on all four edges. At a point 2 in. from one end, lay out and mark the location of the ¼ in. diameter dowel hole. Bore the ½ in. deep hole in the base and also in the bottom edge of the silhouette.

Final sand all parts, then cut the ¼ in. diameter dowel pin to a length of 5 in. and glue it in place as shown. The project can be painted any color that suits your fancy. We chose to paint the base, dowel, and edges an antique blue, while the back and front face surfaces were done in an off-white. The job will be easier if you paint the edges before doing the face surfaces. We used two coats to provide complete coverage.

¼ DIA. X ½ DEEP

Toy Wagon

This sturdy wagon provides room for a sizable supply of blocks, stuffed animals, books, or any other valued possession that a toddler might enjoy hauling around the house. Except for the birch dowel pins and the plywood bottom, all parts are made from maple, a wood that's both hard and durable.

Make the sides (A) and ends (B) first. Cut ¾ in. thick stock to a width of 4 in. and a length of about 54 in. The length dimension allows for some extra stock. Use the dado cutter to cut a ¼ in. by ⅜ in. rabbet all along one edge, then use the regular saw blade to crosscut the stock into four pieces: two pieces 16 in. long (for the sides) and two pieces 9¼ in. long (for the ends). Following this, the dado head is once again used, this time to cut the ⅜ in. by ¾ in. rabbet on each end of the sides.

Now, cut the bottom (C) from ¼ in. thick birch plywood, making sure the cuts are square. After giving each part a thorough sanding, the sides, ends, and bottom can be assembled. Apply glue to all mating surfaces, then apply pressure with bar or pipe clamps. Check for squareness before setting aside to dry overnight.

You'll need 1½ in. thick stock to make the back axle (D) and the front axle (E). Rip the back axle to a width of 2¾ in. and the front axle to a width of 2

in., then cut both parts to a length of 7½ in. At a point ¾ in. from the bottom edge of each axle (see side view) bore a ½ in. diameter hole to a depth of 1 in. on each end. On the front axle, use a dado cutter to cut the two ¾ in. by ¾ in. dadoes at a point 2⅛ in. from each end (see front view). At the centerpoint of the top edge (see cross section, front axle assembly) bore a ⅜ in. diameter hole through the front axle. Then, on the top edge counterbore the hole to ⅞ in. diameter by ½ in. deep; on the bot-

tom edge counterbore the hole to 1⅛ in. diameter by ¾ in. deep.

To make the spacer (F), cut ¾ in. thick stock to 3½ in. square. With a compass scribe a 3 in. diameter circle, then use a band or saber saw to cut it out. Stay just outside the marked line, and after the cut is complete, sand the rough edge exactly to the line. Bore a ⅜ in. diameter hole at the centerpoint, then counterbore the hole to ⅞ in. diameter by ¼ in. deep. Assemble a ⅜ in. diameter by 2½ in. long carriage bolt to the spacer (see exploded view), then add a 1¼ in. diameter washer and nut to hold it in place. The spacer can now be glued to the underside of the bottom. For maximum glue strength, be sure the grain direction of the spacer runs parallel to the grain direction of the bottom. Clamp firmly to insure a good glue bond.

Cut the two yokes (G) to length and width from ¾ in. thick stock before rounding over the front end with a band or saber saw. Sand smooth before gluing and clamping to the front axle as shown. When dry, bore pilot holes and assemble two 1¾ in. by no. 8 flathead wood screws in the end of each yoke.

Make and assemble the handle shaft (H) and the handle (I) as shown. The base of the handle shaft is joined to the yoke with a pair of 1¼ in. by no. 8 flathead wood screws. Fully tighten the screws then back off about one turn to allow the handle shaft to pivot freely.

Glue and clamp the back axle to the underside of the bottom. When dry, the front axle is assembled to the carriage bolt with a 1 in. diameter washer and a locking nut (most hardware stores carry them).

To make the axle pin (J), cut ½ in. diameter birch dowel stock into four pieces, each piece 2 in. long. Glue into the axle holes as shown.

The four wheels (K) can be turned on the lathe or cut out on the band or saber saw. The cap (L) can be made in the same manner before boring a ½ in. diameter by ³⁄₁₆ in. deep hole in each one. Assemble a washer to each axle pin, then add the wheel. The cap is then glued in place. Avoid any glue squeeze out which could cause the cap to stick to the wheel.

Round over all sharp edges before final sanding. No final finish is necessary.

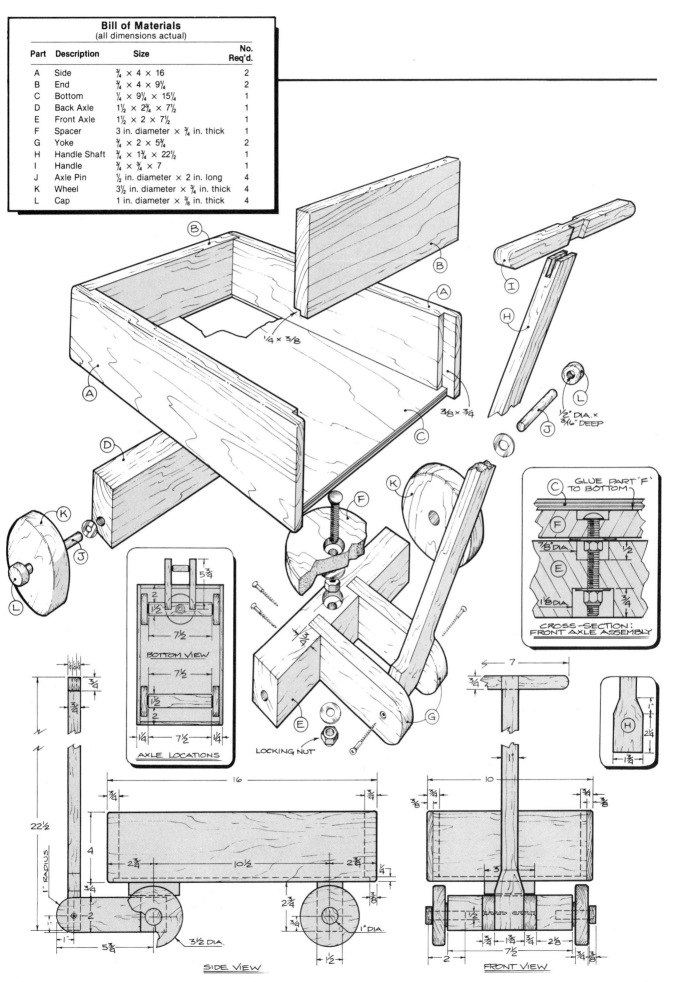

Bill of Materials
(all dimensions actual)

Part	Description	Size	No. Req'd.
A	Side	¾ × 4 × 16	2
B	End	¾ × 4 × 9¼	2
C	Bottom	¼ × 9¼ × 15¼	1
D	Back Axle	1½ × 2¾ × 7½	1
E	Front Axle	1½ × 2 × 7½	1
F	Spacer	3 in. diameter × ¾ in. thick	1
G	Yoke	¾ × 2 × 5¾	2
H	Handle Shaft	¾ × 1¾ × 22½	1
I	Handle	¾ × ¾ × 7	1
J	Axle Pin	½ in. diameter × 2 in. long	4
K	Wheel	3½ in. diameter × ¾ in. thick	4
L	Cap	1 in. diameter × ⅜ in. thick	4

¼ × ⅜

⅜ × ¾

½" DIA. × 3/16" DEEP

GLUE PART "F" TO BOTTOM

⅞"DIA.

1⅛ DIA.

CROSS-SECTION: FRONT AXLE ASSEMBLY

5¾

7½

BOTTOM VIEW

7½

¼   7½   ¼

AXLE LOCATIONS

LOCKING NUT

7

3¾

16

¾   10½   ¾

22½

1" RADIUS

4

2¾   10½   2¾

¾

1"

1"   5¾

3½ DIA.

2¾   ¾   1" DIA.

½

SIDE VIEW

10

¾   ¾   ⅜

3

½

¾   1¾   ¾   2⅛

7½

2   ¾   ⅜

FRONT VIEW

Early American Wall Box

Since most early American homes were small, space was hard to come by, which perhaps explains why wall boxes were so popular during the period. They could be found in all shapes and sizes, sometimes with one or two drawers, but often without. Once a convenient location was found, the box was hung on a peg or cut nail and used to store candles, spices, salt and other small items.

Ours is a reproduction of a pine wall box made during the 18th century. The maker probably sized it to accept candles, but we were delighted to find that it's just the right size for 20th-century letter-sized envelopes.

Like the original, ours is made from pine. A piece like this usually looks best if clear pine is used, although a few small knots are acceptable. The sides and back are made from ¾ in. thick stock while the fronts and bottoms are ⅜ in. thick.

Most lumberyards don't carry ⅜ in. material, so you'll need to start with thicker stock and reduce it. Some lumberyards have thickness planers and they are willing to plane stock to any thickness for a nominal charge. If your lumberyard doesn't do this, check some local millwork shops as they often offer this service.

A band saw, if you have one, can also be used to get thinner stock. Select a piece of ¾ in. thick stock that measures 4 in. wide by about 48 in. long, then use a marking gauge to scribe the ⅜ in. thickness. With this as a guideline, the band saw is used to cut the stock just slightly on the outside of the guideline. Now use a hand plane to smooth the band saw marks, then rip the stock to width on the table saw.

Of course, there's still another way to reduce the thickness of a board. A sharp hand plane and a little hard work will produce a thinner board in short order.

The two sides (A) can be made first. Rip ¾ in. thick stock to a width of 3⅝ in. and a length of 11 in. Lay out and mark the location of the curved profiles and also the 7½-degree angled front. Now, using a band saw with a narrow (¼ in.) blade, cut out both the curves and the angled front.

The back (D) can be made from edge-glued stock or from a piece of 1 x 12 stock (which measures 11¼ in. wide) ripped to 10¼ in. Bore the 1 in. diameter hanger hole, then lay out and mark the curved profile at the top. Cut out with the band saw, staying slightly on the waste side of the line, then sand smooth.

Cut the two fronts (B) to size, and rip the front edge of the two bottoms (C) to 7½ degrees. Assemble as shown using both glue and countersunk finishing nails. Use wood putty to fill the countersunk holes.

The original box was assembled with cut nails to reinforce the glue joints. If you want to add this authentic look, cut nails can be ordered from the Tremont Nail Co., P.O. Box 111, Wareham, MA 02571. We suggest using their fine cut headless brads (part number N-13). The 1½ in. length is

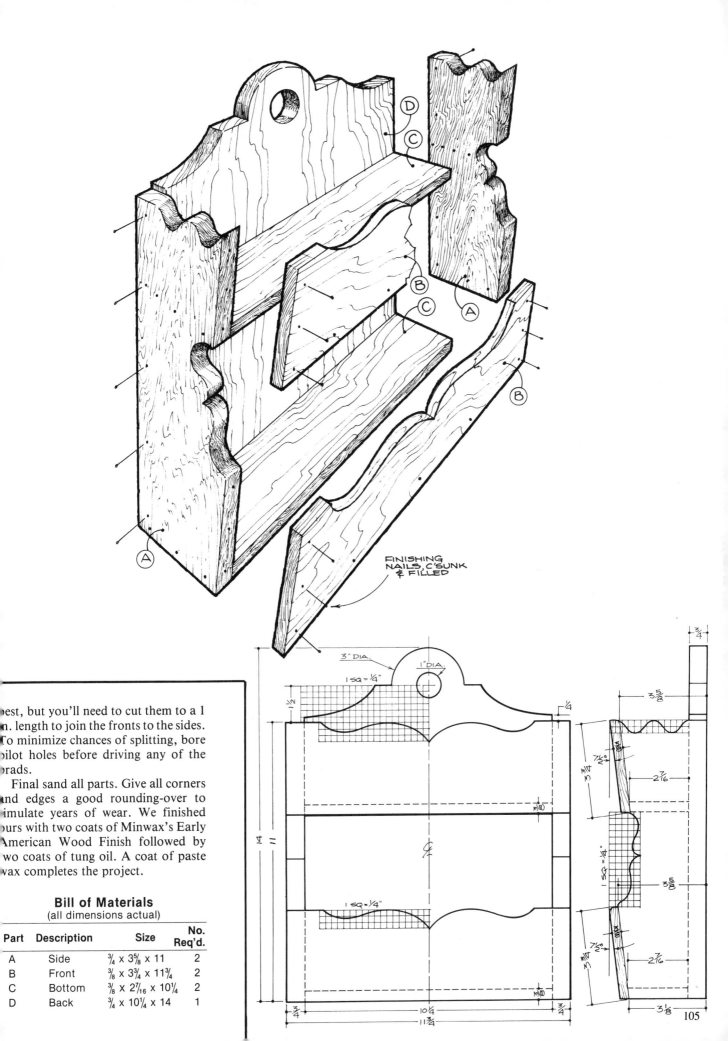

FINISHING
NAILS, C'SUNK
& FILLED

est, but you'll need to cut them to a 1
n. length to join the fronts to the sides.
To minimize chances of splitting, bore
pilot holes before driving any of the
brads.

Final sand all parts. Give all corners
and edges a good rounding-over to
simulate years of wear. We finished
ours with two coats of Minwax's Early
American Wood Finish followed by
two coats of tung oil. A coat of paste
wax completes the project.

Bill of Materials
(all dimensions actual)

Part	Description	Size	No. Req'd.
A	Side	¾ x 3⅝ x 11	2
B	Front	⅜ x 3¾ x 11¾	2
C	Bottom	⅜ x 2⁷⁄₁₆ x 10¼	2
D	Back	¾ x 10¼ x 14	1

105

A stool provides handy extra seating anywhere. In spite of its fine lines, light weight, and delicate appearance, this small stool is surprisingly sturdy.

Begin by laying up stock for the top. We chose to lay up a butcher block of 1 in. by 1 in. by 11 in. maple, but other hardwoods could be used as well. The butcher block construction provides the top with considerably more strength than if we had turned it from a single width of stock. Once the top is dry, scribe a 10½ in. diameter, and rough cut round using a saber saw or band saw.

Now attach the seat to the lathe faceplate and turn to the profile shown in the cross-sectional view of part A. It is important that you establish the flat 8-degree taper on the seat bottom, since this flat area aids in the next step, drilling the holes to accept the four leg tenons. Lay out as shown in the top view for these holes, then drill each of the holes with a 1 in. diameter Forstner bit by clamping the top on the 8-degree flat to the drill press table. You will need a backing block under the seat, since the holes are drilled through.

Next, cut 1¾ in. by 1¾ in. by 28 in. long leg turning blanks from oak, mount in the lathe, and turn to a 1½ in. diameter. Index the stock ends and locate for the rung tenon holes 8 in. from what will be the bottom ends of the legs. As shown in the rung mortise drilling illustration, these tenon holes must be positioned 98 degrees apart to accommodate the 8-degree splay of the legs. Construct a simple V-block to hold the leg stock. The leg and V-block are clamped to the drill press table. Note that the V-block must be inclined at 5 degrees to the drill press table. Now, using a ½ in. diameter Forstner bit, drill the ½ in. deep holes that will accept the rungs (C).

Turn the legs to establish the tapers as illustrated, and turn the 1 in. diameter tenon on the top end of each leg. Also turn the rungs, which taper gradually from ⅝ in. at the center to ½ in. at the ends.

After trimming the legs and rungs to final length, cut a cross-grain kerf 1 in. deep into the ends of the leg tenons. Assemble the stool using glue throughout, and wedge the leg tenons to lock them. These wedges (D) can be made from a contrasting wood that will provide the stool top with an attractive detail. A band clamp will help in clamping up the legs and rungs.

After trimming the leg tenons flush with the seat top, final sand and finish the stool with two coats of Watco Danish Oil.

Stool

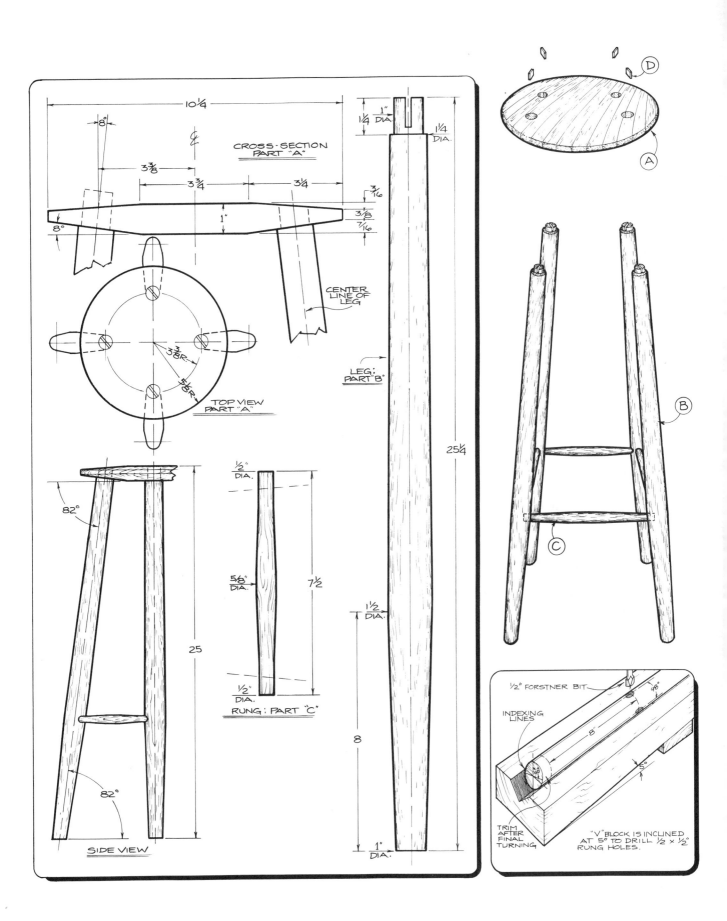

CROSS-SECTION
PART "A"

10¼

8°

3⅜

3¾

3¼

1"

8°

CENTER
LINE OF
LEG

1¼

1"
DIA.

1¼
DIA.

3/16

3/8
7/16

TOP VIEW
PART "A"

3/8 R.

5/8 R.

82°

82°

25

SIDE VIEW

½"
DIA.

5/8"
DIA.

½"
DIA.

7½

RUNG: PART "C"

LEG:
PART "B"

25¼

1½
DIA.

8

1"
DIA.

A

D

B

C

½" FORSTNER BIT

INDEXING
LINES

8"

5°

TRIM
AFTER
FINAL
TURNING

"V" BLOCK IS INCLINED
AT 5° TO DRILL ½ x ½"
RUNG HOLES.

Small benches like this, made of pine, were found in many Early American homes, probably because they were lightweight and could be moved from the supper table to an out of the way wall with a minimum of effort. In the winter, it might be found next to the hearth, arranged so that it was perpendicular to the wall. Here, a couple could sit facing the warm fire while the backboards shielded them from the chilling drafts that regularly meandered through those old houses.

We used clear pine for ours, although a few small sound knots are acceptable.

To make the two sides (A) you'll need to edge-glue two or three $1\frac{1}{8}$ in. thick (five-quarter stock) pine boards. It's best to cut the boards so that the glued-up stock will be slightly wider and longer than necessary. Use two or three waxed alignment cleats to keep the boards aligned as clamp pressure is applied. When dry, remove the clamps and trim the stock to 16 in. wide and $34\frac{1}{2}$ in. long.

The $\frac{3}{4}$ in. by $\frac{3}{4}$ in. rabbet along the back edge is best cut using the table saw equipped with a dado head cutter, although it can also be made by making repeated passes with the regular saw blade.

To cut the $1\frac{1}{8}$ in. wide by $\frac{3}{8}$ in. deep stopped dado we used a router equipped with a $\frac{3}{8}$ in. diameter straight bit. As a guide for the router, a fence is clamped to the side. A straight piece of $\frac{3}{4}$ in. thick by $1\frac{1}{2}$ in. wide pine serves well as a fence. Locate the fence so that the first cut will establish the lower edge of the dado at a point $15\frac{3}{8}$ in. from the bottom. Make the first pass with the router bit set to make a $\frac{1}{8}$ in. deep cut, starting the cut from the back of part A and stopping it at a point $\frac{3}{4}$ in. from the front edge. To complete the cut, make two more passes, the second with the bit set to a $\frac{1}{4}$ in. depth and the third with the bit set to a $\frac{3}{8}$ in. depth. Next, move the fence and repeat the process to widen the groove to $\frac{3}{4}$ in. Finally, make one more fence adjustment and one more series of $\frac{1}{8}$ in. deep cuts to complete the $1\frac{1}{8}$ in. wide dado. Use a chisel to square the corners at the point the dado is stopped.

Referring to the side view, transfer the grid pattern profile to the side, then cut out with a band or saber saw. Also lay out, mark, and cut out the 4 in. radius at the bottom as shown. Sand the edges, finishing with 220 grit.

Next, cut the stretcher (B) to overall length and width, then lay out and mark the dovetails on each end. Use a fine-tooth backsaw or a dovetail saw to cut out. Now, using the stretcher dovetails as templates, trace the profile on the front edge of the sides. Note that the top edge of the stretcher is located $15\frac{3}{8}$ in. from the bottom of the side. Cut out with a back or dovetail saw and a sharp chisel.

You'll need to edge-glue $1\frac{1}{8}$ in. thick stock to get enough width for the seat (C). Trim to length and width before cutting the $\frac{3}{8}$ in. deep by $1\frac{1}{8}$ in. long notch on each front corner.

The four backboards (D) are made from 1 by 12 stock (which measures $\frac{3}{4}$ in. thick by $11\frac{1}{4}$ in. wide) ripped to $10\frac{1}{4}$ in. wide. We used a router table to cut the tongue and groove on each board, although this joint can also be cut using the dado head on the table saw. Also, at this time, cut the dado groove to accept the seat. Note that this groove is cut only on the second board from the bottom.

Transfer the grid pattern profile (shown in the front view) to the upper backboard, and cut out with a saber or band saw. Lay out the $1\frac{1}{2}$ in. radius on the bottom backboard and cut out in the same manner.

Sand all parts, then assemble the sides, stretcher, and seat. Use glue on all joints. As shown, use countersunk flathead wood screws with plugs to join the sides to the seat. Three or four clamps will provide adequate pressure at the glue joint between the seat and the stretcher.

Next, the grooved backboard is glued and screwed (use four or five screws) to the seat. The remaining backboards can now be added, each one joined to the rabbeted back edge of the sides with a single screw at the centerpoint (measured across the width). As shown in the edge view, allow $\frac{1}{4}$ in. between each board. The single screw in each board allows for expansion and contraction with changes in humidity.

Final sand all parts, then stain. We used two coats of Minwax's Early American Wood Finish. When dry, two coats of their Antique Oil Finish were added to complete the project.

Early American Bench

Part	Description	Size	No. Req'd.
A	Side	$1\frac{1}{8} \times 16 \times 34\frac{1}{2}$	2
B	Stretcher	$\frac{3}{4} \times 3 \times 48$	1
C	Seat	$1\frac{1}{8} \times 16 \times 46\frac{1}{2}$	1
D	Backboard	$\frac{3}{4} \times 10\frac{1}{4} \times 47\frac{1}{4}$	4

Bill of Materials
(all dimensions actual)

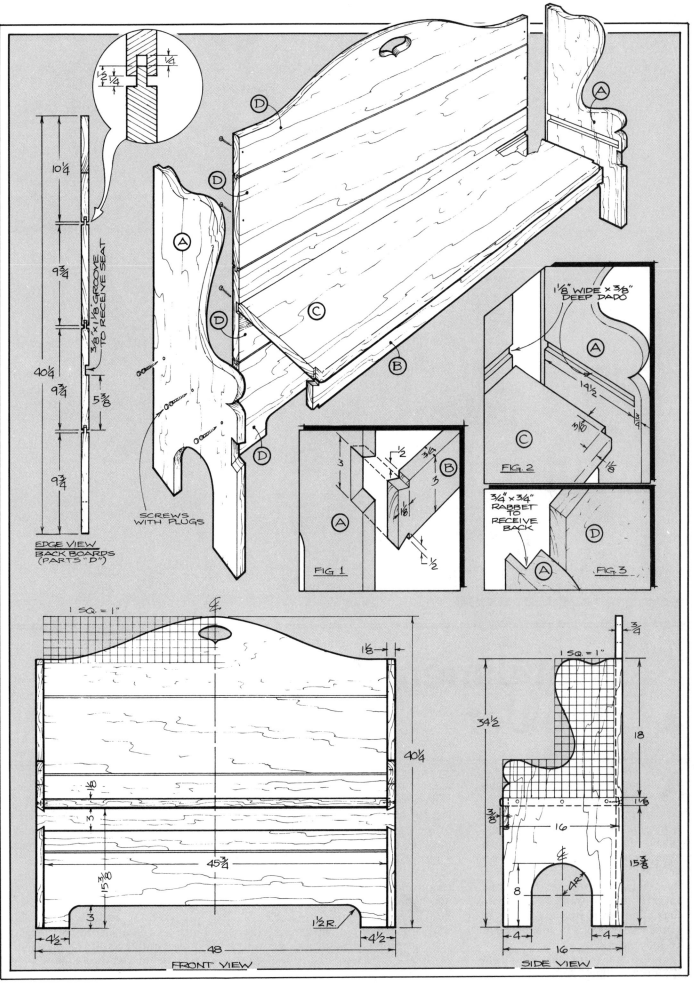

1/4

1 1/4

10 1/4

9 3/4

40 1/4

9 3/4

3/8" × 1 1/8" GROOVE
TO RECEIVE SEAT

5 3/8

9 3/4

9 3/4

SCREWS
WITH PLUGS

EDGE VIEW
BACK BOARDS
(PARTS "D")

D

D

D

A

C

B

D

A

1 1/8" WIDE × 3/8"
DEEP DADO

A

14 1/2

3/8

3/4

1/8

C

FIG. 2

3
1/2
3/4
3
1 1/8
1/2

A

B

FIG 1

3/4" × 3/4"
RABBET
TO
RECEIVE
BACK

A

D

FIG. 3

1 SQ. = 1"

1 1/8

40 1/4

1/8

3

45 3/4

15 3/8

3

1 1/2 R.

4 1/2

4 1/2

48

FRONT VIEW

3/4

1 SQ. = 1"

34 1/2

18

1 1/8

3/8

16

15 3/4

8

4 R.

4

16

4

SIDE VIEW

109

Condiment Holder

Although we designed this condiment holder with outdoor barbecues in mind, it can be handy on the kitchen table as well. The holder conveniently has a place for catsup and mustard squeeze bottles, salt and pepper shakers, and napkins. We have dimensioned the squeeze bottle and shaker holes for standard size containers, however you may wish to customize these holes to your own bottles and shakers.

All the stock for the condiment holder is ⅜ in. thick. Although we used mahogany, any wood, including pine, will serve as well. Start by cutting the legs (A) and braces (B). Both the ends of the legs and the ends of the braces must be cut off at 70 degrees, as shown. Next, cut parts C, D, E, and F to size. After cutting the top (G) to length and width, use hole saws to cut out the shaker and bottle holes.

Glue and assemble the table as shown. Take care when applying the glue since any glue squeeze-out will cause the effected area to appear lighter after a stain or finish is applied.

This is because glue prevents the stain or finish from being absorbed by the wood. Spring type clamps, available at most hardware stores, are especially handy for the kind of small clamping work required in this project.

The napkin holder (H) is simply a section of wire coat hanger, bent as indicated. Drill two holes for the wire, and epoxy the ends in place. Our holder was final sanded and finished with penetrating oil. If you use a light-colored wood, redwood stain will give the piece an outdoorsy look.

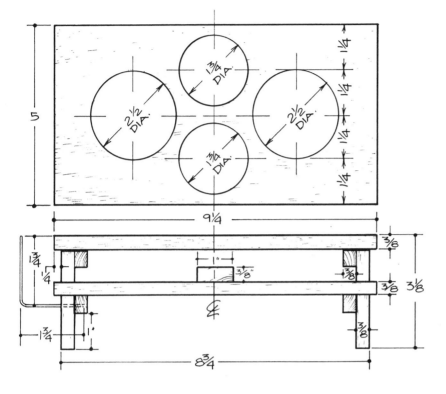

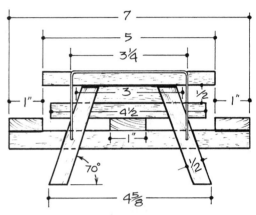

Bill of Materials
(all dimensions actual)

Part	Description	Size	No. Req'd.
A	Leg	$\frac{3}{8} \times \frac{1}{2} \times 3$	4
B	Brace	$\frac{3}{8} \times \frac{1}{2} \times 3$	2
C	Rail	$\frac{3}{8} \times \frac{1}{2} \times 7$	2
D	Seat	$\frac{3}{8} \times 1 \times 9\frac{1}{4}$	2
E	Stretcher	$\frac{3}{8} \times 1 \times 8$	1
F	Shaker Support	$\frac{3}{8} \times 1 \times 4\frac{1}{2}$	1
G	Top	$\frac{3}{8} \times 5 \times 9\frac{1}{4}$	1
H	Napkin Holder	coat hanger wire	1

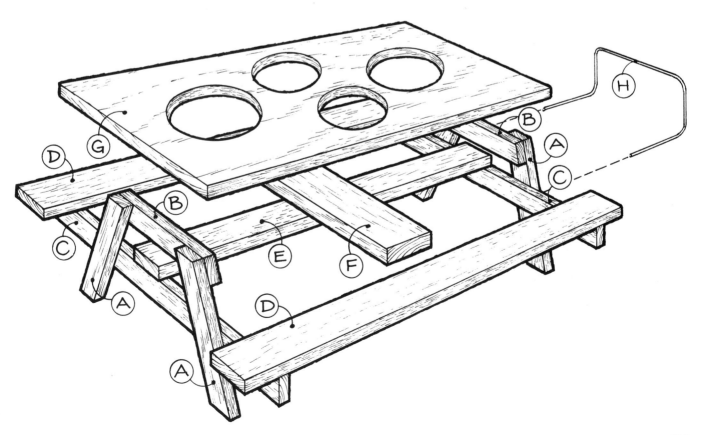

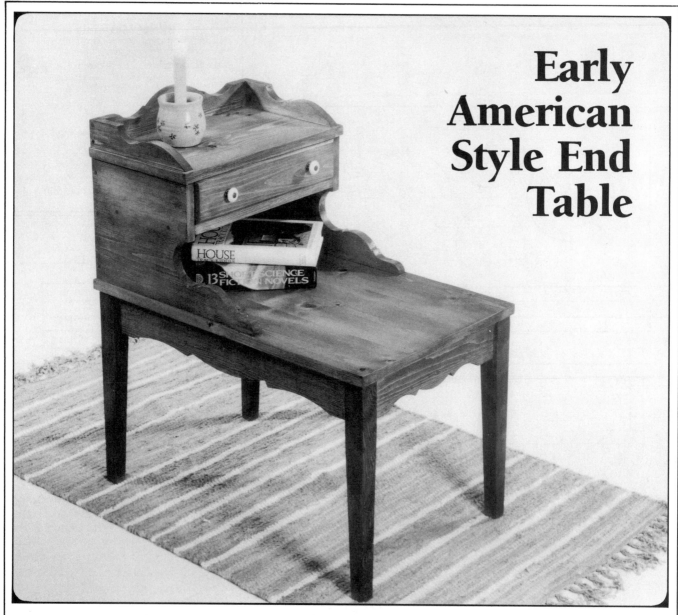

Early American Style End Table

This attractive Early American style table makes a useful side piece to your favorite chair. The upper shelf is at a convenient height for a reading lamp, with a considerable amount of additional space for books, magazines, and other odds and ends. Except for the plywood drawer bottom, all parts are made from solid pine stock.

The four legs (A) can be made first. Rip 2 in. stock (which measures 1¾ in. thick) to 1½ in. square, then cut to 15¼ in. lengths. Referring to the side and front views, note that the legs are tapered only on the two inside edges, and that the taper starts 3½ in. from the top end and narrows to 1 in. square at the bottom. If you have one, a table saw tapering jig will come in handy here. If not, lay out and mark the tapers on each leg, then hand plane the stock to the marked line.

Next, lay out and mark the location of the ⅜ in. wide by 2½ in. long by ¹⁵⁄₁₆ in. deep apron mortises at the top of each leg (see apron tenon detail). They can be chopped out by hand using a sharp chisel or, if you prefer, they can be cut on the router table using a ⅜ in. diameter straight bit. If you use the router though, you won't be able to cut the full ¹⁵⁄₁₆ in. depth in one pass. You'll get a smoother cut with less strain on the motor if you make several cuts, each one removing no more than ³⁄₁₆ in. of material. Once cut, use a chisel to square the corners.

To make the two end aprons (B) and two side aprons (C), cut ¾ in. thick stock to the length and width shown in the bill of materials. The tenons on each end are best cut using the table saw equipped with a dado head cutter, although repeated passes with a regular saw blade will also work (see tenon and cleat detail). Carefully lay out and

mark each tenon, then raise the dado head cutter or saw blade to a height of ³⁄₁₆ in. Next, using the miter gauge, pass the stock over the cutter to establish the ⅞ in. tenon length. A second pass with the dado head will clean up the remaining material; several more passes will be needed if a regular saw blade is used.

Now flip the stock over and repeat the procedure on the opposite side. Once both sides are cut, raise the dado head or saw blade to a height of ½ in. and repeat the process on the bottom edge. Finally, to complete work on the tenon, use the table saw to bevel the end of the tenon to 45 degrees.

Keep in mind that the tenon thickness is regulated by the height of the cutter or saw blade. Before starting it's always a good idea to make some trial cuts in scrap stock to get the tenon thickness just right.

| **Bill of Materials** | | | |
| (all dimensions actual) | | | |
Part	Description	Size	No. Req'd.
A	Leg	$1\frac{1}{2} \times 1\frac{1}{2} \times 15\frac{1}{4}$	4
B	End Apron	$\frac{3}{4} \times 3 \times 15\frac{1}{4}$*	2
C	Side Apron	$\frac{3}{4} \times 3 \times 24\frac{3}{4}$*	2
D	Cleat	$\frac{3}{4} \times \frac{3}{4} \times 14\frac{1}{4}$	2
E	Top	$\frac{3}{4} \times 17 \times 26\frac{1}{2}$	1
F	Side	$\frac{3}{4} \times 9\frac{1}{4} \times 16\frac{1}{2}$	2
G	Back	$\frac{3}{4} \times 9\frac{1}{4} \times 15$	1
H	Lower Shelf	$\frac{3}{4} \times 9\frac{1}{4} \times 15\frac{1}{2}$	1
I	Upper Shelf	$\frac{3}{4} \times 10\frac{1}{4} \times 17$	1
J	Side Gallery	$\frac{3}{4} \times 2 \times 10$	2
K	Back Gallery	$\frac{3}{4} \times 3 \times 15$	1
L	Drawer Front	$\frac{3}{4} \times 3 \times 15$	1
M	Drawer Side	$\frac{1}{2} \times 3 \times 9\frac{1}{4}$	2
N	Drawer Back	$\frac{1}{2} \times 3 \times 14\frac{1}{2}$	1
O	Drawer Bottom	$\frac{1}{4} \times 14\frac{1}{2} \times 8\frac{3}{4}$	1
P	Drawer Knob	$\frac{3}{4}$ diameter	2

*Length includes tenons.

Referring to the side and front views, transfer the apron grid patterns to the stock before cutting out with a jig or saber saw. When cutting, stay just outside the marked line, then use a rasp and sandpaper to smooth the edge exactly to the line.

The legs and aprons can now be assembled. Final sand thoroughly, then add a thin coat of glue to the tenons and mortises. Assemble as shown using bar or pipe clamps to apply light pressure to the joints. Check for squareness and, if all looks okay, set aside to dry thoroughly.

The two cleats (D) can now be made. Note that $\frac{3}{4}$ in. square stock is cut to fit between the side aprons, then notched on each end (see tenon and cleat detail) to fit around the legs. Three holes are bored in each cleat: a center hole and a pair of slotted holes located about $1\frac{1}{4}$ in. from each end. Later, when the top (E) is attached to the base (parts A, B, and C), the slotted holes will allow the top to expand and contract with seasonal changes in humidity.

To make the top (E) you'll need to edge-glue two or three $\frac{3}{4}$ in. thick boards. It's best to cut the boards so that the glued-up stock will be slightly wider and longer than necessary. Use at least three pipe clamps to apply pressure to the joint. When dry, remove the clamps and trim the stock to 17 in. wide by $26\frac{1}{2}$ in. long.

Each side (F) is made from a piece of 1 by 10 stock (which actually measures $\frac{3}{4}$ in. thick by $9\frac{1}{4}$ in. wide) cut to a length of $16\frac{1}{2}$ in. Once cut to overall length and width, refer to the side view and transfer the curved profile from the grid pattern to the stock. Also, at this time, lay out and mark the location of the $\frac{3}{4}$ in. wide by $\frac{1}{4}$ in. deep groove that is cut to accept the lower shelf. Use a router with an edge guide to cut the groove, stopping it $\frac{3}{4}$ in. short of the front and back as shown. Use a chisel to square the corners. Next, use a band or saber saw to cut out the grid pattern profile. Sand the edges smooth.

Cut the back (G) and the lower shelf (H) to length and width from $\frac{3}{4}$ in. thick stock. Since there is a stopped groove in each side, you'll need to cut a $\frac{1}{4}$ in. by $\frac{7}{8}$ in. notch in the front corners of the lower shelf. The notch is cut $\frac{7}{8}$ in. long, rather than $\frac{3}{4}$ in., to allow the shelf to expand and contract in width.

After final sanding, the back, lower shelf, and sides can be assembled. Since the lower shelf must be free to move in the side grooves, no glue is applied to the shelf ends. Also, since end grain glue joints have little strength, we did not bother to add glue to the ends of the back.

Assemble the back to the sides with $1\frac{1}{2}$ in. long by number 8 flathead wood screws. Counterbore the holes about $\frac{3}{16}$ in. to accept wood plugs. It's best to

cut the plugs slightly long so that they protrude just above the surface of the wood. Glue in place and, when dry, sand flush. The lower shelf is added in the same manner except the two end screw holes in the side are made slightly oversized to allow for movement of the shelf.

The upper shelf can now be cut to overall length and width from $\frac{3}{4}$ in. thick stock. Since this part must also be free to expand and contract with seasonal changes in humidity, three slotted holes are cut on each end.

To make the side gallery (J) cut $\frac{3}{4}$ in. thick stock to 2 in. wide by 10 in. long, then transfer the grid pattern shown in the side view. Cut out with the band or saber saw and sand smooth.

The back gallery (K), which is made from $\frac{3}{4}$ in. thick stock that measures 3 in. wide, can be made next. Refer to the front view for the grid pattern profile. After final sanding, the side and back galleries can be assembled as shown.

Next, assemble the upper shelf and galleries. Note that the shelf is not glued in place. Instead it is secured between parts F and G and parts J and K. To do this, place part I in its proper position on parts G and F, then mark the centerpoint of the slotted hole. At each centerpoint bore a $\frac{1}{4}$ in. diameter by $\frac{3}{8}$ in. deep hole. At the same time, lay out, mark and drill identical holes in parts J.

Now, with part I properly located, glue $\frac{1}{4}$ in. diameter by $1\frac{1}{2}$ in. long dowels in part F as shown. Avoid getting glue on part I as it must be free to move. Add glue to the dowel holes in parts J and to the end of the dowel pins, then mount the gallery assembly. Use clamps to provide pressure. Keep glue to a minimum to avoid squeeze-out.

After cutting the six slotted holes in part E, attach the upper part of the table by screwing up through part E and into part F. Part E can now be attached to the base by screwing through parts D and into part E.

The drawer is made next. Refer to the exploded view and the drawer top view, and make the drawer as shown. As mentioned earlier, we used $\frac{1}{4}$ in. thick plywood for the bottom (O). Two porcelain knobs (P) are used for drawer pulls.

Final sand all parts and stain to suit. We used two coats of Minwax's Maple Wood Finish. Once dry, two coats of Minwax's Antique Oil were added as a final finish.

(continued on next page)

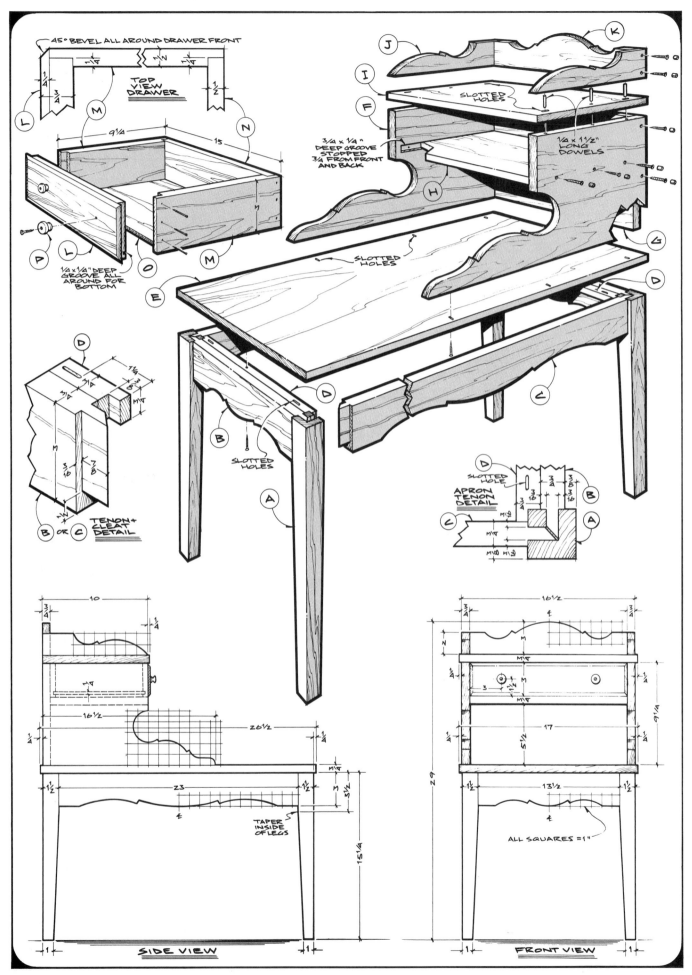

45° BEVEL ALL AROUND DRAWER FRONT

TOP VIEW DRAWER

$1\frac{1}{4}$ W $1\frac{1}{4}$

$\frac{1}{4}$ $\frac{3}{4}$ $\frac{1}{2}$

L   M   N

9¼   15

L   P   O   E   M

1/4 × 1/4" DEEP GROOVE ALL AROUND FOR BOTTOM

J   K

I   F   SLOTTED HOLES

3/4 × 1/4" DEEP GROOVE STOPPED 3/4 FROM FRONT AND BACK

H   1/4 × 1½" LONG DOWELS

G   SLOTTED HOLES

D   D

C

D   D   B   SLOTTED HOLES   A

TENON + CLEAT DETAIL   B OR C

$\frac{1}{4}$ $\frac{1}{4}$ $\frac{3}{4}$ M   T

M $\frac{3}{16}$ $\frac{7}{8}$ W

APRON TENON DETAIL

D   SLOTTED HOLE $\frac{3}{8}$ $\frac{3}{8}$ B

$\frac{3}{8}$ $\frac{3}{16}$

C   M $\frac{1}{2}$ A

M $\frac{1}{4}$ T

M $\frac{3}{8}$ M $\frac{1}{2}$

10   $\frac{3}{4}$ $\frac{1}{4}$

$\frac{1}{4}$ T

16½

26½ $\frac{1}{4}$

$\frac{1}{4}$ $\frac{1}{4}$

M $\frac{1}{4}$ T   M

$1\frac{1}{2}$ 23 $1\frac{1}{2}$ M $3\frac{1}{2}$

4

TAPER INSIDE OF LEGS

15¼

1   SIDE VIEW   1

16½ $\frac{3}{4}$ 4 $\frac{3}{4}$

2

$\frac{1}{4}$

M $\frac{1}{4}$ T

2   M $\frac{1}{4}$ 9¼

3   $1\frac{1}{2}$

M $\frac{1}{4}$ T

29   17   5½

$1\frac{1}{2}$ 13½ $1\frac{1}{2}$

4

ALL SQUARES = 1"

1   FRONT VIEW   1

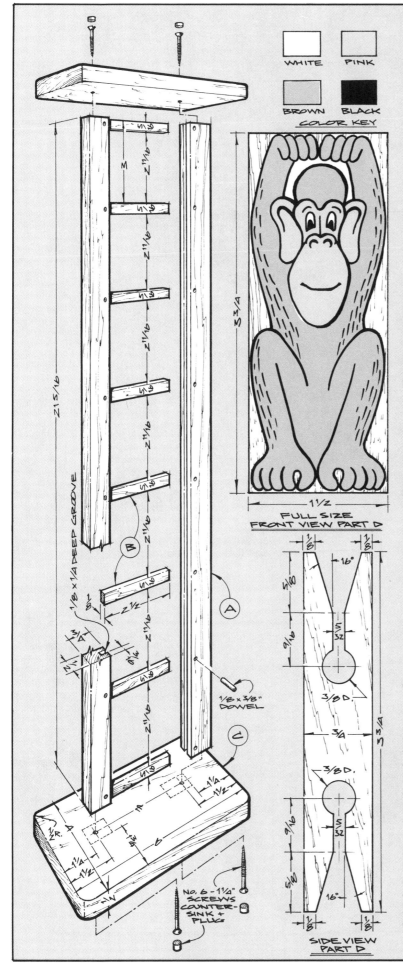

WHITE   PINK

BROWN   BLACK

COLOR KEY

FULL SIZE
FRONT VIEW PART D

1/8 × 1/4 DEEP GROVE

1/8 × 3/8"
DOWEL

NO. 6 - 1 1/4"
SCREWS
COUNTER-
SINK +
PLUG

SIDE VIEW
PART D

Tumbling Monkey Toy

This "executive toy" is sure to amuse young and old alike.

Begin by making the ladder section parts (A, B, and C), as shown. Cut the stock for part D, and drill the two ⅜ in. diameter holes as indicated. Then use the tenoning jig on the table saw to first cut the 5⁄32 in. wide slots, and next establish the 16 degree sides of the V-shaped slot approach. Transfer the monkey profile to both sides and color it, following the key.

When making and assembling this toy, all measurements must be followed exactly if the monkey is to tumble as intended. The ladder is assembled with the monkey in place, since he cannot be removed. The ⅛ × ⅜ in. dowel pins help to locate and anchor the rails. Flip the ladder end-over-end and watch the monkey go!

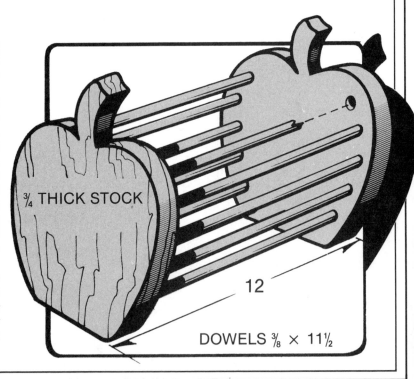

Country Basket

A small basket like this is ideal for serving bread, rolls, or fresh fruit. It's also useful when you want to display a favorite flower arrangement.

To make the apple ends, you'll need an 18 in. length of 1×8 common pine (which actually will measure $\frac{3}{4}$ in. thick by $7\frac{1}{4}$ in. wide). Transfer the full-size apple profile to the stock and mark the center points of the $\frac{3}{8}$ in. diameter dowel holes. Use a band saw or saber saw to cut out the profile, then sand the entire edge smooth. Now, using this cutout as a template, trace the second apple profile. Once again, mark the center points of the dowel holes before cutting out the profile and sanding the edges smooth.

Next, bore the $\frac{3}{8}$ in. diameter by $\frac{1}{2}$ in. deep dowel holes in each end, then cut the dowels to length and glue in place. When dry, paint the entire basket with red enamel, as we did, or you could paint the apple red and the stem green.

$\frac{3}{4}$ THICK STOCK

12

DOWELS $\frac{3}{8} \times 11\frac{1}{2}$

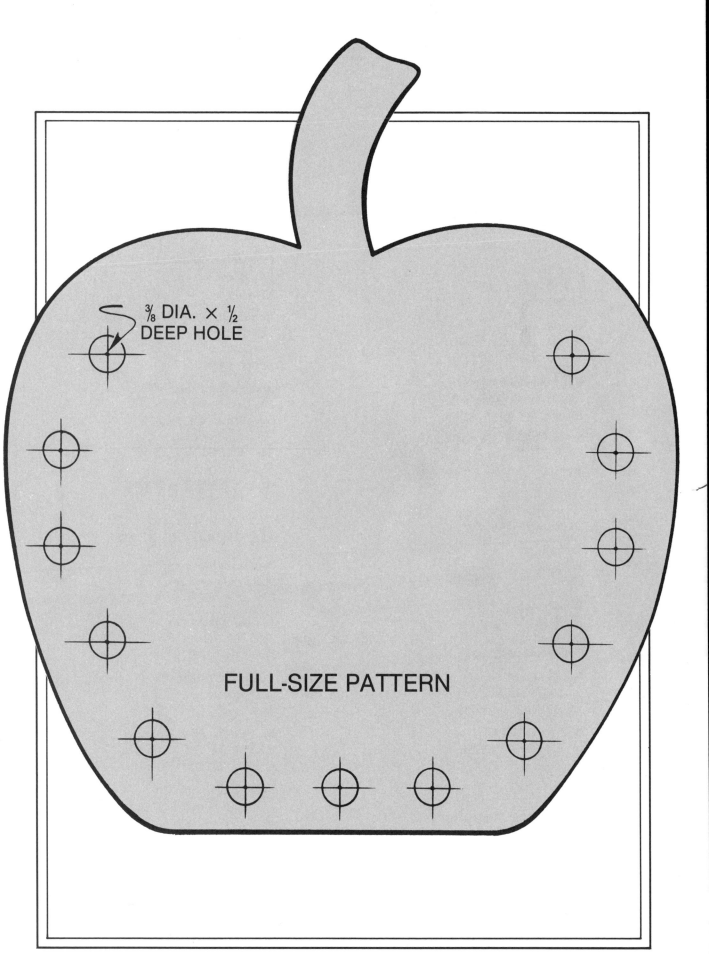

⅜ DIA. × ½
DEEP HOLE

FULL-SIZE PATTERN

Sources *of* Supply

The following pages list companies that specialize in mail order sales of woodworking supplies

United States

General Woodworking Suppliers

Constantine's
2050 Eastchester Rd.
Bronx, NY 10461

Craftsman Wood Service
1735 West Cortland Ct.
Addison, IL 60101

Frog Tool Co.
700 W. Jackson Blvd.
Chicago, IL 60606

Garrett Wade
161 Avenue of the Americas
New York, NY 10013

Highland Hardware
1045 N. Highland Ave., N.E.
Atlanta, GA 30306

Seven Corners Ace Hardware
216 West 7th Street
St. Paul, MN 55102

Shopsmith, Inc.
3931 Image Drive
Dayton, OH 45414-2591

Trend-Lines
375 Beacham St.
Chelsea, MA 02150-0999

Woodcraft Supply Corp.
210 Wood County Industrial Park
P.O. Box 1686
Parkersburg, WV 26102

Woodworker's Supply
5604 Alameda, N.E.
Albuquerque, NM 87113

W.S. Jenks and Son
1933 Montana Ave., N.E.
Washington, DC 20002

Hardware Suppliers

Anglo-American Brass Co.
Box 9487
San Jose, CA 95157-0792

Ball and Ball
463 West Lincoln Highway
Exton, PA 19341

Horton Brasses
Nooks Hill Rd.
P.O. Box 120
Cromwell, CT 06416

Imported European Hardware
4320 W. Bell Dr.
Las Vegas, NV 89118

Meisel Hardware Specialties
P.O. Box 70
Mound, MN 55364-0070

Paxton Hardware, Ltd.
P.O. Box 256
Upper Falls, MD 21156

Period Furniture Hardware Co.
123 Charles St.
Box 314, Charles Street Station
Boston, MA 02114

Stanley Hardware
195 Lake Street
New Britain, CT 06050

The Wise Co.
6503 St. Claude
Arabi, LA 70032

Hardwood Suppliers

American Woodcrafters
905 S. Roosevelt Ave.
Piqua, OH 45356

Arroyo Hardwoods
2585 Nina Street
Pasadena, CA 91107

Austin Hardwoods
2119 Goodrich
Austin, TX 78704

Bergers Hardwoods
Route 4, Box 195
Bedford, VA 24523

Berea Hardwoods Co.
125 Jacqueline Dr.
Berea, OH 44017

Maurice L. Condon
250 Ferris Ave.
White Plains, NY 10603

Craftwoods
10921-L York Rd.
Hunt Valley, MD 21030

Croy-Marietta Hardwoods, Inc.
121 Pike St., Box 643
Marietta, OH 45750

Dimension Hardwoods, Inc.
113 Canal Street
Shelton, CT 06484

Educational Lumber Co.
P.O. Box 5373
Asheville, NC 28813

General Woodcraft
531 Broad St.
New London, CT 06320

Hardwoods of Memphis
P.O. Box 12449
Memphis, TN 38182-0449

Henegan's Wood Shed
7760 Southern Blvd.
West Palm Beach, FL 33411

Kaymar Wood Products
4603 35th S.W.
Seattle, WA 98126

Kountry Kraft Hardwoods
R.R. No. 1
Lake City, IA 51449

Leonard Lumber Co.
P.O. Box 2396
Branford, CT 06405

McFeely's Hardwoods & Lumber
P.O. Box 3
712 12th St.
Lynchburg, VA 24505

Native American Hardwoods
Route 1
West Valley, NY 14171

Sterling Hardwoods, Inc.
412 Pine St.
Burlington, VT 05401

Talarico Hardwoods
RD 3, Box 3268
Mohnton, PA 19540-9339

Woodcrafter's Supply
7703 Perry Highway (Rt. 19)
Pittsburgh, PA 15237

Wood World
1719 Chestnut
Glenview, IL 60025

Woodworker's Dream
P.O. Box 329
Nazareth, PA 18064

Wood Finishing Suppliers

Finishing Products and Supply Co.
4611 Macklind Ave.
St. Louis, MO 63109

Industrial Finishing Products
465 Logan St.
Brooklyn, NY 11208

The Wise Co.
6503 St. Claude
Arabie, LA 70032

Wood Finishing Supply Co.
100 Throop St.
Palmyra, NY 14522

WoodFinishing Enterprises
1729 N. 68th St.
Wauwatosa, WI 53212

Watco-Dennis Corp.
1433 Santa Monica Blvd.
Santa Monica, CA 90401

Clock Parts Suppliers

The American Clockmaker
P.O. Box 326
Clintonville, WI 54929

Armor Products
P.O. Box 445
East Northport, NY 11731

Klockit, Inc.
P.O. Box 542
Lake Geneva, WI 53147

Kuempel Chime
21195 Minnetonka Blvd.
Excelisor, MN 55331

S. LaRose
234 Commerce Place
Greensboro, NC 27420

Mason & Sullivan Co.
586 Higgins Crowell Rd.
West Yarmouth, MA 02673

Newport Enterprises
2313 West Burbank Blvd.
Burbank, CA 91506

Miscellaneous

Byrom International
(Router Bits)
P.O. Box 246
Chardon, OH 44024

Brown Wood Products
(Balls, Knobs, Shaker Pegs)
P.O. Box 8246
Northfield, IL 60093

Country Accents
(Pierced Tin)
P.O. Box 437
Montoursville, PA 17754

DML. Inc.
(Router Bits)
1350 S. 15th St.
Louisville, KY 40210

Floral Glass & Mirror
(Beveled Glass)
895 Motor Parkway
Hauppauge, NY 11788

Formica Corporation
(Plastic Laminate)
1 Stanford Rd.
Piscataway, NJ 08854

Freud
(Saw Blades)
218 Feld Ave.
High Point, NC 27264

Midwest Dowel Works
(Dowels, Plugs, Pegs)
4631 Hutchinson Road
Cincinnati, OH 45248

Homecraft Veneer
(Veneer)
901 West Way
Latrobe, PA 15650

MLCS
(Router Bits)
P.O. Box 4053
Rydal, PA 19046

The Old Fashioned Milk Paint Co.
(Milk Paint)
P.O. Box 222
Groton, MA 01450

Sears, Roebuck and Co.
(Misc. Tools & Supplies)
925 S. Homan Ave.
Chicago, IL 60607

Wilson Art
(Plastic Laminate)
600 General Bruce Drive
Temple, TX 76501

Canada

General Woodworking Suppliers

House of Tools Ltd.
131-12th Ave. S.E.
Calgary, Alberta T2G 0Z9

J. Philip Humfrey International
3241 Kennedy Rd., Unit 7
Scarborough, Ontario M1V 2J9

Lee Valley Tools
1080 Morrison Dr.
Ottawa, Ontario K2H 8K7

Nautilus Arts & Crafts
6075 Kingston Road
West Hill, Ontario M1C 1K5

Stockade Woodworker's Supply
291 Woodlawn Rd. West, Unit 3C
Guelph, Ontario N1H 7L6

Tool Trend Ltd.
420 Millway Ave.
Concord, Ontario L4K 3V8

Treen Heritage Ltd.
P.O. Box 280
Merrickville, Ontario K0G 1N0

Hardware Suppliers

Home Workshop Supplies
RR 2
Arthur, Ontario N0G 1A0

Lee Valley Tools
1080 Morrison Dr.
Ottawa, Ontario K2H 8K7

Pacific Brass Hardware
1414 Monterey Ave.
Victoria, British Columbia V8S 4W1

Steve's Shop, Woodworking & Supplies
RR 3
Woodstock, Ontario M9V 5C3

Hardwood Suppliers

A & C Hutt Enterprises Ltd.
15861 32nd Ave.
Surrey, British Columbia V4B 4Z5

Farrell Lumber Co.
1229 Advance Rd., Unit 3B
Burlington, Ontario L7M 1G7

Hurst Associates, Ltd.
74 Dynamic Drive, Unit 11
Scarborough, Ontario M1V 3X6

Longstock Lumber & Veneer
440 Phillip St., Unit 21
Waterloo, Ontario N2L 5R9

MacVeigh Hardwoods
339 Olivewood Rd.
Toronto, Ontario M8Z 2Z6

Unicorn Universal Woods Ltd.
4190 Steeles Ave. West, Unit 4
Woodbridge, Ontario L4L 3S8

Woodcraft Forest Products
1625 Sismet Road, Unit 25
Mississauga, Ontario L4W 1V6

Clock Parts Suppliers

Hurst Associates
405 Britannia Rd. E., Unit 10
Mississauga, Ontario L4Z 3E6

Kidder Klock
39 Glen Cameron Rd., Unit 3
Thornhill, Ontario L3T 1P1

Murray Clock Craft Ltd.
510 McNicoll Ave.
Willowdale, Ontario M2H 2E1

Miscellaneous

Freud
(Saw Blades)
100 Westmore Dr., Unit 10
Rexdale, Ontario M9V 5C3

EAU CLAIRE DISTRICT LIBRARY

Also From Madrigal Publishing

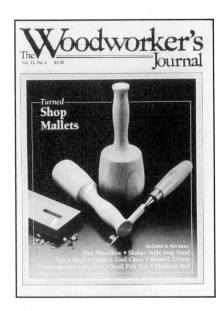

the magazine for woodworkers by woodworkers

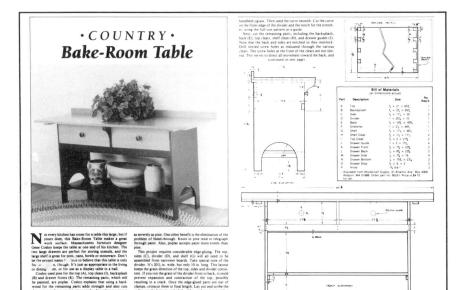

Over 50 great project plans each year!

Furniture ● Shop-Built Tool
Toys ● Easy Weekend Projec
Clocks ● Gifts

In-Depth Woodworking Articles!

- *Woodworking Basics* — fundamental skills for those just starting out
- *Special Techniques* — more advanced procedures
- *In The Shop* — safe use and care of tools
- *Finishing* — what you need to know about all kinds of finishes
- *Shop Tips* — quick ideas to save you time and trouble

The Practical Projects Magazine

It's like having a master woodworker at your side to
help you plan, design, build and enjoy every project.

Subscribe Now!

$17.95 — One Year (6 issues)
$31.90 — Two Years (12 issues)

Madrigal Publishing Company
P.O. Box 1629, 517 Litchfield Road, New Milford, CT 06776